Tribune of the People
The Minnesota Legislature
and Its Leadership

The research for this book was conducted at the Hubert H. Humphrey Institute of Public Affairs of the University of Minnesota as part of the Future of the State Legislature Project.

The research was funded by contributions from the following organizations and individuals:

Elmer L. and Eleanor J. Andersen
  Foundation
Apache Foundation
Bemis Company Foundation
Blandin Paper Company
Blandin Foundation
Blue Cross and Blue Shield of Minnesota
Cargill, Inc.
CENEX
John and Sage Cowles
Cowles Media Company
Kenneth H. Dahlberg
Dayton-Hudson Foundation
Kenneth N. Dayton
Mark B. Dayton
Deluxe Check Printers, Inc.
Donaldson Company
Dorsey and Whitney
Economics Laboratory, Inc.
Faegre and Benson
First Bank System Foundation
H. B. Fuller Company
General Mills Foundation
Honeywell Foundation

Lutheran Brotherhood
Magnetic Controls Company
Medtronic
The Minnesota Legislature
Minnesota Mining and Manufacturing
  Foundation
Minnesota Power
Northwestern Bell
Northwestern National Life Insurance
  Company
Norwest Foundation
Owatonna Tool Company
George S. Pillsbury
The Pillsbury Company
Piper, Jaffray, and Hopwood, Inc.
Kathleen and Robert Blair Ridder
The St. Paul Companies
St. Paul Pioneer Press and Dispatch
Robert L. Searles
Super Valu Stores
Touche Ross & Company
Valspar Foundation
Irene Hixon Whitney Family
  Founder-Advisor Fund

Tribune of the
PEOPLE

*The Minnesota Legislature
and Its Leadership*

Royce Hanson

with the assistance of
Charles Backstrom
Patrick McCormack
and
The Future of the State Legislature Study Team

Charles Finn
Philip Frickey
Craig Grau
Virginia Gray
James Jernberg
Arthur Naftalin
Dale Olsen
Earl Shaw
Ben Somerville

University of Minnesota Press, Minneapolis

Published by the University of Minnesota Press
2037 University Avenue Southeast, Minneapolis MN 55414.
Printed in the United States of America.

Library of Congress Cataloging-in-Publication Data

Hanson, Royce.
     Tribune of the people : the Minnesota Legislature and its leadership / Royce Hanson ; with the assistance of Charles Backstrom, Patrick McCormack, and the Future of the State Legislature Study Team.
        p.   cm.
     Bibliography: p.
     Includes index.
     ISBN 0-8166-1790-2
     1. Minnesota. Legislature.   2. Minnesota. Legislature—Leadership.   I. Title.   II. Title: Minnesota Legislature and its leadership.
JK6171.H36   1989
328.776—dc20   89-5147
                                                                  CIP

Contents

Preface

Soon after I arrived in Minnesota, in 1983, to become associate dean of the Hubert H. Humphrey Institute of Public Affairs, I received a visit from Jerome Hughes, the president of the Minnesota Senate. Senator Hughes said that he and others felt that Minnesota's Legislature was "pretty good" (like the grocery store in Garrison Keillor's mythical Lake Wobegon), but that it probably could be better. He had managed to obtain a small amount of funding through the Committee on Elections and Ethics, which he chaired, for a study of the Legislature. He thought that Speaker Harry Sieben, of the Minnesota House of Representatives, might be willing to match the Senate contribution if the institute could be interested in conducting the study. While the combined funding of the House and Senate would not be enough for a full study, it would show that the Legislature would take seriously any recommendations of the institute, and Hughes thought it might be possible to raise additional funds from the private sector.

I was intrigued with Senator Hughes's proposal, especially by the apparent openness of the leadership of the Minnesota Legislature to thinking about improvements in its capacity to deal with the problems of the state. I knew that several suggestions had been made to reduce the size of the Legislature, and that the Citizens League (a nonpartisan, privately funded public policy research group) planned a study of the Legislature. I wanted assurance that if the institute were to undertake a study, it would not be used primarily as a way of diffusing interest in reform proposals. I emphasized that any study we conducted must be entirely independent, and that we would have the right to publish results and conclusions, even if they were not to the liking of the legislators who helped provide the financing. Senator Hughes asked only one thing: that as we produced reports they be released first to his committee, at a public hearing where members could ask questions of those who did the studies and make any comments they wished. I could think of no more desirable condition, since one of the greatest problems of scholars in public affairs is gaining the attention of the officials who decide whether or how to act on policy recommendations.

With this agreement, Senator Hughes arranged for me to speak before the House Rules Committee to request a House match of the Senate contribution.

This appearance was an instructive introduction to legislative politics, Minnesota style. My presentation was postponed to permit the committee, chaired by the majority leader, Willis Eken, to hear a room full of Libertarians from rural Minnesota urge the committee to report favorably a joint resolution calling for the abolition of the Federal Reserve System. The committee listened courteously, then engaged in a rather sharp debate on the resolution. The opposition to it was led by my University colleague, John Brandl, who was at pains to try to explain some fine points of monetary theory to an audience quite unreceptive to ideas other than their own.

After disposing of the resolution, Chairman Eken called on me. The mention of the Humphrey Institute was more coals on the heads of the audience. Their hoots were taken up by the more conservative members of the committee, whose memories of the devastation wrought upon the conservative cause in Minnesota by Hubert Humphrey made them unreceptive to suggestions for state funding of anything associated with the late senator's name. As many of the Democratic-Farmer-Labor (DFL) members of the committee had left after the vote on the Federal Reserve resolution, Eken was without the votes to approve the few thousand dollars requested. He stepped down from the chair, left the room and returned in a short while. Other committee members filtered into the room. Shortly, a member moved reconsideration of the institute's request, and, over the objections of the conservative members, funding was approved.

The legislative support of $16,000 was a good start (about one-fifth) on the total amount that I figured would be needed to do the job properly. George Pillsbury took on the considerable task of raising the additional money to finance the study. Pillsbury had recently retired from the Senate after serving four terms as an Independent-Republican (IR). He had decided that one of his major avocations would be legislative reform, and he eagerly volunteered to help find support for the project, making a generous contribution himself. At his suggestion, we decided to fund the project through a large number of relatively small contributions from foundations, corporations, organizations, and individuals. In this way, we could both broaden interest in the study and reduce the danger of it being perceived as too heavily influenced by any donor. Ultimately, we found over 40 sponsors who contributed from $500 to $5,000, for a total of about $80,000 over the three-year period of the study. Without the dedication, encouragement, goading, and flat-out cheerleading provided by George Pillsbury, this study never would have gotten off the ground, much less been finished.

Conducting research in which the object of the study is in a real sense also a client poses some particular problems. As I was determined to maintain the intellectual credibility of the enterprise, it was necessary to design the study and the publication process in a way that would ensure the academic quality of the work. But it was also necessary, if we were to retain the support and interest of the Legislature, to design the project in a way that would produce information relevant to issues of institutional concern to the Legislature itself.

The first step was to organize a strong team of scholars to guide and participate in the study. Nine University of Minnesota faculty members — seven from the Humphrey Institute, the Law School, and the Political Science Department on the Twin Cities campus, and two from the Political Science Department on the Duluth campus — and three graduate students formed the study team. Others participated from time to time. James Jernberg and I organized graduate seminars in legislative decision making and budgeting as a means of engaging a number of graduate students in the study.

This study team of faculty developed a research strategy that balanced investigation of issues of some political urgency to the Legislature — the question of whether to change the size of the Legislature, for example — with a longer-term exploration of problems we regarded as central to understanding the legislative process and providing a foundation for rethinking basic institutional arrangements and processes.

I had secured an understanding with Senator Hughes and other legislative leaders that the study should be done incrementally over at least three years. This was important for two reasons. First, it allowed us to produce results from specific parts of the overall study as they were completed, and give legislators and other interested publics time to absorb the findings. Second, it allowed the study itself to benefit from reactions to the working papers by members and others who were knowledgeable about the Legislature. This gave us the opportunity to refine the study as it proceeded and to test some of the original premises with which we started. As the study progressed, and as we increased our dialogue with members and with others interested in the future of the Legislature, we became convinced that we should address some of the basic philosophical issues that impinge on the role of legislatures in American governance. I have tried to do that, to discuss theory without being too theoretical, and to relate notions of what a legislature in a democratic society should do to the realities of legislative practice in Minnesota.

It is customary for authors to say that their work could not have been done but for the labor and help of others. In this case, not only is this true, but it is essential to point out that much of what appears here is the product of a long collaboration with my colleagues in the study team and more than two dozen graduate students in the Humphrey Institute and the Department of Political Science at the University of Minnesota, not to mention the current and former members of the Legislature, who, along with dozens of other legislative mavens in Minnesota, shared their experience, insights, and frustrations. Some require special thanks and attention.

Charles Backstrom designed, conducted, and analyzed a survey of current and former members of the Legislature and wrote chapter 9. I have drawn on the find-

ings of the survey in several other chapters of the book. Backstrom was, moreover, a valued critic of drafts of other parts of the book, and generously shared his
insights from several decades of observation of the Legislature as a scholar and a
citizen of Minnesota.

Chapter 6 is based on Patrick McCormack's working paper on conference
committees. I have reworked and added material and analysis, but the essential
research was done by McCormack. His paper generated considerable public and
legislative reaction, the latter occurring over the ensuing two or three years since
publication. It is not immodest to say that McCormack's "The Third House:
Conference Committees in the Minnesota Legislature" (1986) contributed to efforts in the Legislature to restrain the insertion of nongermane material into conference reports. That this paper would not fully turn the tide was fully predictable. The study also was one of the few detailed assessments of the conference
process in a state legislature.

In Chapter 6, McCormack is responsible for the facts, I for any misinterpre-
tation of them. We shared in developing the ideas concerning options to past
practices of conference committees. Along with several other graduate students,
whose work is acknowledged below, McCormack assisted in the development of
information for the chapter on legislative budgeting (chapter 8) and, with Charles
Finn and Ben Somerville, who succeeded him as my graduate assistants, he was
instrumental in arranging and contributing to the many interviews on which
much of the book is based. Somerville undertook the arduous task of analyzing
the interviews and grouping responses into common categories of information on
a great number of historical, institutional, and policy issues about which we
asked questions. Finn was indispensible in organizing both the seminars and for
his ability to apply computer skills to the analyses of membership data and to the
information produced by the seminars.

I owe a particular debt to Earl Shaw, whose careful review of an early draft of
chapter 2 and his suggestions regarding the treatment of theoretical issues concerning the functions of legislatures contributed greatly to my thinking and, to
the extent that I have been successful, to the clear exposition of those issues. My
University of Texas at Dallas colleague, Edward Harpham, also read an earlier
draft of this chapter and made a number of useful suggestions. Both gave good
advice. The reader must hold me responsible for whether I used it wisely.

My other colleagues on the study team, Virginia Gray, Dale Olsen, Craig
Grau, Philip Frickey, James Jernberg, and Arthur Naftalin, played important
roles in the study and development of this book. Gray, Frickey, and Grau and
Olsen prepared working papers that illuminated issues of legislative reform.

The public clamor about the size of the Legislature could not be ignored. So
we decided that a careful study of the size issue had to be made. But we were
determined to take a thorough look at the issue, and to treat it in a way that was
unlikely to duplicate the discussion of it by the Legislature itself (where there was

little support for reducing the size of either chamber), the press (which seemed to see it as a "neatness" issue), or the Citizens League (which seemed likely to look at the matter as a question of governmental efficiency). Virginia Gray took on the size issue. Her study examined the size of each of the 99 legislative chambers in the 50 states, both individually and in bicameral combinations. In the first working paper published by the project, "Does Legislative Size Make a Difference?" (1985), she attempted to find statistical correlations between the size of chambers or of the whole legislature of a state and varied measures of legislative activity, such as bills introduced and enacted, size of legislative staff, cost of the legislature, length of sessions, total cost of state government, etc. She reviewed the findings of this statistical examination against the arguments advanced in the literature concerning the size of legislatures. No strong relationship was found between size, as such, and any particular set of alleged advantages or disadvantages. The principal effects of size were on the costs of election and public accessibility to the legislators. The costs of campaigning for office were greater in larger districts. One could also infer that access to legislatures was marginally harder for citizens in smaller legislatures, where each member represented more people. Gray's research effectively laid the size issue to rest as a panacea for the problems of the Minnesota Legislature and also established the credibility of the project with both the Legislature and the media.

I have not drawn material from the Size study here, and raise the issue only in the concluding chapter, where my conclusion about the future size of the Minnesota Legislature may be at odds with aspects of Gray's study. Her participation in the study is not an endorsement of my conclusion, which is based on a consideration that she did not address. Her work made it possible for me to avoid attributing wondrous powers to a change in the size of the Legislature and to treat the issue in, I hope, a more useful way, as one element in an overall set of proposed reforms.

Grau and Olsen's study (1986) of the unicameral option for Minnesota was valuable in dealing dispassionately with the issue, and it had a considerable influence on my thinking, as is clearly reflected in the concluding chapter. While I have recommended that Minnesota adopt a unicameral legislature, this conclusion is not shared by all members of the study group—particularly by Gray and Frickey. While I felt constrained, after three years of study and thinking about the Legislature, to reveal my own predilections, I have also tried to avoid the conceit that mine is the only sensible solution to the problems that are discussed. I alone take responsibility for all of the recommendations. I am grateful for the debate and thinking of my colleagues who helped me reach the conclusions I did, and for any support they now give. But that they helped me decide does not mean they should share the blame. Had I listened better, I might have written more wisely.

Rod Searle, who was speaker of the House in the traumatic 1979 session, when control was evenly divided between the parties, was one of the first people to read the nearly complete draft of this book in 1987. His help in catching errors of historical fact and his encouragement were invaluable. Similarly, my Humphrey Institute colleague John Brandl, who served in both the House and Senate, made many comments that helped me to improve on earlier drafts. Both did their best to save me from embarrassments that I could not avoid even through geographic distance.

Arthur Naftalin took a continuous interest in the study, and served me often as a sounding board for ideas. As observer and participant in the political history of Minnesota, he was a penetrating questioner in the seminars and a fertile source of state political lore. Tapes of interviews he conducted for his public affairs television program, *Minnesota Issues*, helped fill gaps in our own interviews. His programs with the late Nicholas Coleman, Senate majority leader during the late 1970s, were especially valuable, providing a better feel for that lively and able leader than could be gained from secondhand accounts of those who had served with him.

James Jernberg conducted a seminar on the budget process in the Minnesota Legislature and, together with his graduate students, Patrick McCormack, Kevin Kajer, and Sarah Hackett, provided much of the raw material, and some of the refined ideas, for chapter 8. I drew substantially on his extensive knowledge of the state budgetary process in developing the chapter on the legislative budget system.

My seminar on legislative decision making produced the case studies discussed in chapter 7 and a mound of other information, examples, ideas, and anecdotes, some of which are used in other places. Jim Roche, Debra Dailey, RaDene Hatfield, Amy Sandburg, and Arnie Anderson conducted research for the specific case studies I used in the chapter.

Other graduate students who participated in the study at various times, compiling and analyzing data, preparing briefing papers for faculty, and joining in the seminars with legislative leaders were: Brownie Lewis, Patrick Mendis, Franc Fennessey, Paula Schnepp, Craig Cheney, Dave Haugen, Dawna Tierney, Janna Wallin, and Gloria Christopher.

My secretary at the institute, Judy Leahy, lived the study with us. She was, in every sense, a key member of the study team, helping prepare the memorandums and documents; encouraging the graduate students and helping prepare their drafts and working papers; sharing editing chores; and handling the mailing of the survey, the maintenance of research records, and the distribution of newsletters and requests for publications. She was, and has remained, the glue that kept the research team together, organized, and cheerful.

My daughter, Juliette Hanson, assisted me in the final push, in the summer of 1987, to complete the book. She analyzed data on the membership of the Legislature, compiled tables and prepared computer graphics, and assisted in the editing of the manuscript.

A special word of thanks is due the Minnesota Legislature and its leaders. In over 30 years as a student of government, I have rarely encountered a group of public officials more open to ideas and receptive to what might charitably be described as constructive criticism. The study period spanned two Legislatures, during which control of the House changed twice. DFL and IR leaders in both houses were supportive of the study and, even when they did not especially like the findings or recommendations, they were willing to have them considered on their merits. At no time did they try to influence the findings or dismiss them as academic piffle. While this book is at times critical of current practices and often recommends changes, it is written with a deep appreciation of the fact that the Minnesota Legislature is, indeed, above average, and that it has, perhaps more than almost any other legislature in the country, the capacity and the luck of being in the kind of state where more can be not only expected, but achieved.

In many respects, the three years devoted to this study have only scratched the surface of the rich lode of information and ideas about legislatures. The experience has enriched my appreciation of the institution and of the need for a better public understanding of its centrality in democratic governance. Legislatures embody the best hopes and some of the most serious shortcomings of representative government. Yet, for all of its problems, the legislature remains the manifestation of the vision of self-government and, more than any other institution deserves nurture.

R. H.

Tribune of the People
The Minnesota Legislature
and Its Leadership

1

Introduction

It is conceivable that a state government could operate without a separate executive branch, or even an independent judiciary. It is inconceivable that a state could be governed without a legislature. Legislatures are important because they decide public questions and allocate public resources. The jibe that "no person is secure in one's life or property while the legislature sits" carries the warning that every citizen has a stake in what legislatures do, and in the way they do it.

Within the states, legislatures are the principal forums for the discussion and enactment of state policy. They regulate the formation and powers of local and regional governments and agencies. They raise taxes and spend public monies. State legislatures have, with few exceptions, surrendered less power to the executive branch of government than has occurred at the national level.

In spite of their importance to everyday governance, legislatures are more cursed than understood. In his insightful study of *Democracy in America*, Alexis de Tocqueville (1835) recognized the importance of state legislatures and devoted considerable attention to them. Early this century, Robert Luce (1924) produced a series of fundamental studies of state legislatures. In the 25 years since the first reapportionment decisions by the U.S. Supreme Court, legislatures have received more serious attention. The American Assembly (1966) devoted a major conference and report to them. Various citizens committees (Burns, 1971; Citizens Conference on State Legislatures, 1976) and groups of state legislators (Council of State Governments, 1968) have sponsored studies to improve or strengthen them. The awakening of the reform movement after the reapportionment revolution of the early sixties generated a number of efforts in the states to improve legislative staffing and procedures.

Minnesota, with a strong populist and progressive heritage, has been a willing participant in the cycles of political reform. In 1913, it became the first state to adopt nonpartisan elections for members of the Legislature, and in 1973, the last (except for Nebraska) to abandon them. While it has not embraced annual budgets, the Legislature now meets annually, under a "flexible-session" amendment that allows the Legislature to divide its biennial session into two parts. Legislative leaders in the 1960s enthusiastically expanded the professional staff of the Legislature and transferred the postaudit function in state government to legislative control. The Legislature enjoys a good national reputation as a progressive, hard-working, and honest institution that has confronted difficult state problems and devised innovative ways of dealing with them (Rosenthal, 1974).

In recent years, however, a number of thoughtful legislators and private citizens have worried that one of the best may not be good enough. The complexity of issues on the legislative agenda has increased. The level of public controversy about policy alternatives has also grown. Opinion polls show a loss of public respect for government generally, but state legislatures are even less well regarded than other institutions (The Gallup Report, 1985). In some respects these trends reflect the broader national disillusionment with government following the Vietnam and Watergate debacles. But they also raise troubling and fundamental questions about the capacity of democratic institutions to adapt to new circumstances and to find effective and acceptable ways of resolving public issues.

The objectives of this study are to examine the Legislature as an institution, to understand its essential functions and ways of working, to assess the capacity of its processes for dealing with technically complex and politically controversial policy problems, and to consider ways of strengthening the Legislature and its leadership as the central institution of democratic governance in the state. Thus, the study aims to add to knowledge of the Legislature and legislative processes and to inform public action.

This book begins with an inquiry into what a legislature ought to do in a democratic government and what, as a matter of history and contemporary fact, legislatures actually do. The object of this inquiry is to set some standards against which legislative performance can be judged. These standards are based in political theory and historical practice. They do not offer "bright lines" against which one can measure things like number of staff or the percentage of bills enacted, or the cost of government. These measures of efficiency tend to misapprehend what a legislature is all about. A legislature is a representative institution, designed to act politically on behalf of the people who are represented in it. It has more important things to do than be efficient for the sake of efficiency itself.

The important questions about the legislature as an institution of governance are ones with debatable, not strictly measurable, answers. Are the people well represented? Does the legislature provide adequately for deliberation of important matters and does it make reasonable choices among policy options? Are its decisions accepted by the public, and significant divisions of the public, as legitimate? Has it prudently raised revenues and allocated the resources of the state? Does it adequately hold state officials and agencies accountable for their performance of the policy mandates and execution of the laws enacted by the legislature? Is it possible for the public to hold the legislature as an institution, and its individual members, accountable for their performance? Does it operate so as to ensure that government deals fairly with citizens? These questions go to the essence of the legislative function and frame the debate about how to improve the legislature in a way that allows us to think of the legislature as an organic part of the political system, not merely a piece of government machinery.

Once the functions of the legislature are laid out and discussed, the study moves to an analysis of the way in which the Minnesota Legislature goes about its business. This analysis is based on an examination of the evolution of the Legislature over a generation. The principal method of research borrows from a study of the U.S. House of Representatives conducted in 1963 by Charles Clapp, of the Brookings Institution (Clapp, 1963). Clapp and his colleagues interviewed a number of U.S. representatives who served during one session of Congress to gain an inside view of the congressional experience. Others have also used the in-depth interview of members as a way of gaining insight into the way legislative processes work (Fenno, 1966, 1978; Kingdon, 1981).

The idea behind this approach is that no outside observer using "objective" data will see the institution in quite the same way as those who are direct actors will, and that the reality of the legislature is neither only what a dispassionate observer thinks it is, nor only what those who participate in it think it is. Rather, reality is to be discovered by weaving together perceptions of participants and observers, constantly testing those perceptions against both descriptive and normative ideas of what the legislature is, or ought to be. While this is a debatable proposition, it does offer certain advantages in a study such as this, which aims not only to describe, but to offer suggestions for action.

Changes are most likely to be made in highly structured organizations like legislatures only when their leaders are convinced that changes are necessary or desirable and capable of being achieved. That means that they must recognize a problem and find a solution that seems both reasonable and feasible. The description of the process cannot, therefore, be so abstract that legislative leaders cannot recognize it or so technical that they cannot decipher it. In short it must be recognizable from their experience and framed in a way that compels action. Reform rarely occurs over the opposition of the leaders. When the leaders are reluctant, those who would make changes are most likely to succeed only if they thoroughly understand the institution they are trying to reform and the politics of its leadership.

Heavy reliance on the in-depth interview approach has an obvious disadvantage. It could be too dependent on self-serving testimony from respondents adverse to any significant change. There is also the danger that even experienced leaders will see only part of the elephant and, in spite of their successes, not have a comprehensive view. We have sought to deal with these problems of bias and significance in several ways. We modified Clapp's approach by taking a historical approach rather than a current snapshot. While he interviewed members serving in a single session, we interviewed leaders who had served during the course of a 24-year period. We chose this period for several reasons. First, the 1963 session was the first held after the initial reapportionment decisions and marks the beginning of the modern era for state legislatures. We assumed that the Legislature should be understood as a social organization as well as an instrument of governance, and that today's practices and problems have historical antecedents and roots. A generation spans enough time for customs to form and harden or be modified or replaced. It also marks close to the outside limit for the memory of members or staff currently serving in the Legislature. In fact, only one current member was serving in 1963. Finally, the period involved included a decade during which the Legislature was elected on a nonpartisan ballot, which allowed us to assess the effect of the change to party designation on each house.

Like the Brookings study, we generally conducted group interviews. The usual interview included three or four current or former legislators, although scheduling problems necessitated some individual interviews, and one session included five members. We tried to arrange for members of the same house and of the same caucus, who had served during the same period, to be interviewed together. While this format could not be followed perfectly, the arrangement made for a congenial setting that encouraged candor and mutual reinforcement in the recollection of events and occasional sharp discussion of significant institutional and policy problems and issues.

For each interview, short briefing papers were prepared summarizing the careers of the interviewees and the major events that transpired during their period of legislative service. While the conversation was encouraged to take its natural course, it was guided by questions that were common to each interview. The interviews themselves generally lasted four hours, with a break for dinner between two sessions. All interviews were audio-and videotaped, so that we could ensure accuracy in reporting. Any fears that taping would constrain the discussion evaporated as the conversations proceeded. The tapes remain available for research, but not for quotation except with the permission of the subjects. In the study we have used direct quotations where they seem necessary to establish the authenticity of the points being made and where they help convey a sense of the leaders being discussed.

Another difference between ours and the Brookings study is that we focused our interviews on leaders, members who had held formal or informal positions as leaders of each house. This included the presiding officers and caucus leaders, chairs of major committees, and others who historical research suggested had played significant roles in each house. Given the limitation on resources and time, we felt that such members were likely to have a more comprehensive perspective than others and, as a group, had probably thought more deeply about the Legislature as an institution. Thus we encouraged reflection as well as description and were rewarded with insights that helped us considerably in understanding the facts and opinions we gathered.

In a further effort to overcome the problems in our principal method of developing institutional understanding, we supplemented the interviews with independent historical and empirical analysis of the membership of the Legislature during the period covered. This research helped corroborate information gained in the interviews and made it possible to highlight certain findings or reveal problems and issues that we might not otherwise have discovered.

One of the problems frequently discussed by legislators, as well as critics of the Legislature, is the role of conference committees in setting policy. In particular, there has been considerable public and legal discussion of the extensive use of omnibus bills containing nongermane amendments by conference committees in the Minnesota Legislature during the last decade. We therefore conducted special studies of the operation of conference committees and a detailed examination of the "garbage bill" syndrome: the tendency to insert unrelated measures into conference reports (McCormack, 1985).

The interviews covered a long period of legislative history and helped give us a broad view of the decision-making process. Since that process is central to what a legislature does, we also wanted to examine it close up. This was done through a series of case studies of legislative decisions made during the 1985–86 session. Our focus for inquiry was the use of technical and political information by the Legislature in arriving at decisions on a range of subjects. This allowed us to look at how the Legislature performs in its broader political environment of publics, agencies, interest groups, and media.

Of all the decisions made by a legislature year in and year out, none is more important than the state budget. The budget has been almost consistently a matter of partisan and general public debate in Minnesota, so we have paid special attention to the legislative budget process.

To correct for too much reliance on leaders in the interviews, and to make sure we asked all of the best-informed people in the state—namely those who have served in the Legislature—about life and problems as a representative of the people, we conducted a survey of all members who had served from 1981 through 1985 (Backstrom, 1986). The survey asked a battery of questions about how members see their roles and frustrations, spend their time, obtain information, and view the quality of the institution and their lives as members of it.

Since this is a study that seeks to offer proposals for change as well as to describe the situation that exists, we conducted other special studies of two proposed reforms and a problem. The proposed reforms are reduction in the size of the Legislature (Gray, 1985) and adoption of a unicameral system (Grau and Olsen, 1986). The problem was the use of the legislative veto as an instrument of administrative oversight (Frickey, 1986).

2

What The Legislature Does

Theory and Practice

When assessing public institutions, it often helps to return to first principles. The power to make law and the role of legislatures have been central concerns of political philosophers and writers of constitutions.

In 1748 Montesquieu stated the classic democratic doctrine on the importance of a representative assembly of lawmakers:

> The legislative power should reside in the whole body of the people.
> But since this is impossible in large states, and in small ones is subject
> to many inconveniences, it is fit the people should transact by their
> representatives what they cannot transact by themselves. (Montesquieu,
> 1748:154)

The father of the separation of powers doctrine believed that "every considerable place" should have its representative. The great advantage of representatives over direct democracy, he reasoned, was their capacity to discuss public affairs. Representatives need not await instructions from their constituents before acting, but they ought to be accountable to them (Montesquieu, 1748).

John Locke (1688) held that the legislative power, wherever exercised—by monarch, oligarchy, or a republican legislature—was the supreme power. The proper location of the legislative power in the constitution was therefore the central issue to be decided. Locke saw the legislative power as "sacred and unalterable" once placed by the community; for from that point, no edict, from any source, can have the force and obligation of law, unless it be by "sanction from

9

that legislative which the public has chosen and appointed'' (Locke, 1688:188). Without this sanction, he concluded, the law could not have that which is absolutely necessary to its being a law: "the consent of the society over whom nobody can have a power to make laws, but by their own consent and by authority received from them'' (Locke, 1688:188).

Montesquieu and Locke spoke of the legislative power and its importance. As constitutional systems have evolved, elected representative bodies have been assigned most, if not all, of the power to make laws. It is worth noting that the word *parliament* is rooted in *parler* to speak or parley—to confer. The early parliaments were just that: conferences or parleys with the king, who possessed the legislative power. Early colonial representative bodies were often called general assemblies, general courts, or houses of burgesses or delegates, and seen as advisory to the governors as viceroys of the king. As American practice evolved, they came to be called legislatures (some are still officially called assemblies or courts) and assigned the bulk of the constitutional power to make laws.

John Stuart Mill (1859) argued that these representative bodies, periodically "elected by the whole people, or some numerous portion of them," should possess the ultimate controlling power in the state. But that said, one should pay careful attention to the actual functions the legislature should perform. It should, he said, control all the operations of government, but it ought not directly perform those operations. It should vote the taxes, but not prepare the estimates. What a representative body does best, however is deliberate, indeed talk.

Legislatures, Mill concluded, are unfit to administer government, though they can watch and control it. The same attributes that make legislatures incompetent to run the government make them all the more qualified for their real job:

> [T]hey are not a selection of the greatest political minds in the country
> . . . but are, when properly constituted, a fair sample of every grade of
> intellect among the people which is at all entitled to a voice in public
> affairs. Their part is to indicate wants, to be an organ for popular
> demands, and a place for adverse discussion of all opinions related to
> public matters, both great and small; and along with this, to check by
> criticism, and eventually by withdrawing their support, those high
> public officers who really conduct the public business, or who appoint
> those by whom it is conducted. (Mill, 1859:323)

James Madison, writing in paper No. 51 of *The Federalist* (1789) a half century before Mill, asserted that legislatures were "the grand repository of the Democratic principle of government." In *The Federalist* paper No. 49, he referred to legislatures as "The guardians of rights and liberties of the people," and in No. 73, picked up the refrain, noting "the superior weight and influence of the legislative body in a free government." Like other republicans who had struggled through the centuries against royal prerogative and executive power,

Madison argued that "In republican government the legislative authority is necessarily supreme" (No. 71).

Thomas Jefferson also extolled the legislature as the central instrument of representative government. In 1816 he wrote Samuel Kercheval:

> For let it be agreed that a government is republican in proportion as every member composing it has an equal voice in the direction of its concerns (not indeed in person, which would be impracticable beyond the limits of a city or small township but) by representatives chosen by himself and responsible to him at short periods. (Jefferson, 1816:288)

Drawing sustenance from political theory written at the dawn of modern parliamentary power and gaining strength from the advocacy and applications of men of affairs who created, explained, and led them, legislative assemblies became, by the end of the nineteenth century, "the core of modern representative government" (Friedrich, 1950:325).

Putting their ideas into modern language, the legislative branch of government is the one essential organ of representative democracy and the one that distinguishes this form of government from all others (Adams, 1970:199). It has certain inherent functions, without which it cannot perform its proper constitutional role. Basically these functions are:

1. To represent the public and to be accountable for its performance to those who elected it.
2. To deliberate, educate the public on policy issues, make law, and legitimate policy choices.
3. To control the public purse by levying taxes.
4. To hold the administration accountable for implementation of policy.

Stated so simply and so broadly, the functions of the legislature seem almost obvious. However, a closer look at each function reveals real problems of both theory and practice in how we make each of these functions operational. Moreover, as we look at all of the functions together, we begin to see conflicts among them and paradoxes in what we expect of the legislature. If we are to judge how well a legislature functions, we must first examine closely what it is supposed to do.

Representation and Accountability

The Process of Representation

The concept of representation is an idea of the modern age of political thought (Pitkin, 1967:2). Modern political theory argues, as Jefferson did, that governments gain legitimacy to act on behalf of the people by having their top officials selected and held accountable through free, competitive, honest, periodic elections. Elections link representation to democracy. They are indispensable in establishing the bond of trust between citizens and government (Pitkin, 1967; Fenno, 1978). The authority of the legislature rests on its representation of the people. In Mill's (1859:323) phrase, they should contain "a fair sample of every grade of intellect among the people which is at all entitled to a voice in public affairs."

But, who, in fact are entitled to a voice? What is a fair sample of them?

In its simplest form, these questions ask who votes and how are their votes counted. The Supreme Court of the United States in the Reapportionment Cases (*Reynolds v. Sims*, 377 U.S. 533 (1964)) answered that each person should have one vote, and the votes should be weighted equally. By each person, however, neither Mill nor the Court really meant *every* human being in the nation. Lunatics, children, convicted felons, and aliens are commonly excepted. As we look closer, voting is limited in other ways. Those who vote for legislators must often meet minimum residence requirements, apparently on the assumption that living in a constituency for a time is a prerequisite to understanding what the election is all about. Uniformly in the United States, voters must be registered—enrolled as voters on official lists kept by the government.

There is, therefore, a considerable difference between the basis of apportionment of legislative seats—the whole number of persons residing in a district—and the number of people actually entitled to vote. Of those eligible to vote in any given election, a good percentage do not. In primary elections in which legislators are nominated, a majority do not vote. Only a little more than half vote in general elections, and the number voting for legislators is somewhat smaller than the number who vote for statewide officers or president of the United States and members of Congress.

In Minnesota and many other states, the single-member district system is used, which means that only the one candidate polling a plurality of votes is elected to serve in the Legislature. In contested Minnesota legislative elections in 1984, for example, the median vote for winning candidates was 55.6 percent. If we look at the votes cast for all winners, it amounts to 63.5 percent of all votes cast for legislative candidates. Using a specific example, the legislators from Anoka County elected in 1984 were chosen by a total of 59,027 voters, which was 70 percent of the number of votes cast for legislators, but just 55.8 percent of the number of registered voters and substantially less than half of the population of the districts in the county. Clearly one legislator does not represent all of those living in the district who are entitled to a voice in public affairs, except in the formal sense of being the person elected to serve that official function. Elections only tell us who will hold office, not whom they will represent.

Another way of looking at the representation issue is to acknowledge that election from districts is an imperfect process, but some organizational scheme has to be used to select legislators, and any approach, other than strict proportional representation using multimember districts and compulsory voting, will distort public preferences among candidates. Thus, even though all voters cannot expect their candidates to win every election, they should expect the overall composition of the legislature to reflect roughly the distribution of the statewide vote for all candidates of the political parties. That depends on a number of factors such as: variable turnout in different districts, the number of contested seats, and, perhaps most important, the extent to which legislative district boundaries are deliberately drawn to favor one party over another. Again looking at Minnesota in 1984, more voters cast their ballots for DFL legislative candidates, but the Independent-Republicans controlled the House of Representatives by four votes.

At the margin, such distortions may be of little concern, except where their cumulative effect in individual districts consistently produces a legislative majority for the electoral minority. At the extremes, however, the conscious use of district boundaries to deny political power to groups — especially racial minorities — brings the legitimacy of the regime into question and may well conflict with constitutional and legal requirements for equal protection of the law (*Thornburg v. Gingles*, 478 U.S. 30 (1986)). The Constitution is more tolerant of political gerrymandering, but there are limits beyond which a political party may not stack the electoral deck (*Bandemer v. Davis*, 478 U.S. 109 (1986)).

Distinguishing between tolerable and intolerable distortions of majority and minority electoral strength is not easy, either philosophically or as a practical matter. There is a distinction to be drawn between a legislature that is *representative* and one in which the members are *typical* of the population of the state. Representation is not just a mechanical function but a political process, involving the ability, regardless of the election returns or the socioeconomic makeup of the district, to speak and act in the interest of the people. It is this attribute to which the theory of representative government speaks. There is occasional concern raised, however, that the legislature is not a mirror image of the population. Its membership does not contain proportionate numbers of women, people of different professions and occupations, racial or ethnic minorities, poor people, etc. One often hears the complaint that there are "too many" lawyers or teachers or housewives or "too few" businesspeople and farmers in the legislature. And there are many people who do not identify, for purposes of political representation, with a geographic district or a political party, but with an interest group. Thus a system based on parties and geography is likely to underrepresent their interests and distort considerably the distribution of interests in the polity.

It is this perceived need to ensure that group interests are not submerged in the electoral and formal representative system that nurtures the formation of pressure groups whose purpose it is to represent specialized interests before the legislature and to mobilize voters and campaign contributions as means of encouraging elected legislators and their electoral opponents to recognize the group as an interest to be served.

Representation as a political process is more than an exercise in reflective demographics. The only universal mandate a winning candidate for the legislature has is to occupy a seat in one of the chambers. No member is compelled to vote on any matter or to vote in a manner guaranteed to please the district or any part of it. One concept of the representative function, however, is basically one of agency: the legislator is seen as the agent of the electorate and has a duty to reflect the will of the electorate even if it conflicts with the legislator's own judgment. Some would have gone so far as to bind legislators to instructions from the district. Many legislators style themselves as delegates, whose job is to speak and act faithfully as they think their electorate would if it were acting directly on the matter at a referendum. Much of the sentiment favoring initiative and referenda stems from the feeling that legislators do not, perhaps will not, represent the will of the people, and that a means is needed to ensure that the popular will can be expressed without the distorting refractions produced by the election and party systems.

A contrary view of the representative's duty was championed by Montesquieu and, especially, Edmund Burke (1774), whose famous address to the electors of Bristol argued that what the representative owed constituents was "not his industry only, but his judgment; and he betrays, instead of serving you, if he sacrifices it to your opinion. . . . " It may be coincidental that Burke was defeated in the next election. This notion of the representative as a trustee is much celebrated by writers such as John F. Kennedy (1957), whose *Profiles in Courage* chronicled several U.S. senators who defied the wishes of their states to speak out and cast votes of conscience.

The trustee representative tends to argue for a more organic concept of the public than the delegate. For the latter, the duty is clearly to act the way the constituency wants one to act, now. For the trustee, representation involves a trust relationship. The duty of the representative is to act in the best interest of the constituency for the long run. It may even be to act in the best interest of the larger polity—the state or nation—on the grounds that the interest of the entire political community ultimately will be to the interest of the constituency, and if not, the smaller interest must yield to the greater.

In trying to deal with these abstractions of the representative function, it is sometimes easy to forget that elected representatives are real people. They are governed by more than theory. They have ambitions and appetites, emotions and intellect. Communication between representatives and constituents is imperfect, to say the least. Some legislators see themselves as so much a part of the communities from which they come that they seem to think as their constituents think, or to have developed such bonds of trust that, while their judgment might occasionally be questioned, it is easily accepted as honestly reached. Our survey of Minnesota legislators who have served since 1980 found that 85 percent of them view their roles and responsibilities dominantly as trustees, while only 11 percent regard themselves as delegates (Backstrom, 1986).

The consensus of studies of legislative and constituent behavior seems to be that representatives are not pressed into a single mode (Loewenberg and Patterson, 1979). Their own personalities and the character of their constituencies may have a lot to do with the way they view their roles and the ways in which they actually behave. Even legislators who see themselves in the image of Edmund Burke have been known to take a dive when the feelings of the home folks are abundantly clear. The most determined delegate may have such trouble determining what the district's sentiment is, if it has any at all on the matter at hand, that resort to personal judgment may be the only way to decide, short of flipping a coin.

Some studies of legislators have suggested a third model that may be closer to reality than either of the classic theories: the representative as politico, alternating between the two polar roles, finding ways to balance the interests of constituents (and thus maintain one's electoral base) and the demands of conscience and larger interests (Keefe and Ogul, 1964; Kingdon, 1981; Cavanaugh, 1982; Davidson, 1969; Kozak, 1984).

The point of all of this is to suggest that performing the representative function is not so clear-cut and simple as it sounds. The representative must contend with some concept of duty to represent those who voted for and against his or her election, those who did not or could not vote, and those in wider or different constituencies to whom some measure of responsibility is felt.

Individual representatives articulate the interests and demands of their constituents, at least some of the time. The legislature as a whole reflects the diversity of the state or nation and provides a forum for the reconciliation of constituency interests and conflicts between local and statewide or national interests. Loewenberg and Patterson (1979:4) write: "It is the glory of the institution that it can both integrate . . . and express . . . variety."

In this broader view, representation involves more than election of officials. Election is a vital link in the system, but it is not representation, per se. Elections help legitimate and facilitate representation that is responsive to the interests, wishes, and demands of the people. Elections powerfully reinforce representative behavior. They guarantee a popular voice in the process, but governments are truly representative only when the people have some control over what they do. This *substantive* concept of representation (as opposed to a mechanical sense of it) emphasizes the *activity* of representatives more than the method by which they were selected. It means "acting in the interests of the represented, in a manner responsive to them" (Pitkin, 1967:209). This implies a constant process of responding and an attitude of responsiveness. Such a process requires more than simply following opinion polls and affirming all requests. It entails educating constituents by explaining policy proposals and criticisms, and explaining one's own official behavior (Kingdon, 1981; Mayhew, 1974). The role of elections is, then, not only to select officials, but to provide an ultimate control over them and to facilitate the processes of substantive representation. The representative has a lot of latitude to seek ways of serving constituent and state or national interests, but he or she must finally account for what has been done in the name of the people.

Accounting to the Electorate for Their Performance

Accountability is the concomitant of consent of the governed. At some point, representatives who have been entrusted with the power to act on behalf of the people must return to those who elected them and account for their performance, whether they regard themselves as delegates, trustees, or politicos. Representative government works on a short leash.

Legislators are both personal and symbolic representatives. They are of course responsible for their own behavior. But they also are the only means available to the voter for registering an authoritative opinion on the performance of the party to which the member belongs, or on the performance of the whole house or the whole legislature. In this sense, the legislator represents the government to the constituency, rather than the other way around.

The theoretical notion that legislators should be accountable for their performance, and also for the performance of the government of which they are a part, has a hard time finding a practical voice in American politics. First of all, individual accountability is difficult enough to accomplish. Constituent knowledge of the representative's legislative behavior is, at best, imperfect. Further, news accounts of the legislature and its activities are less than complete and may never mention most members of the legislature. Voting records are not widely distributed and general knowledge of individual bills is usually limited to those in which specific people have an interest. So any constituency sense of performance is impressionistic and subjective. Legislators report selectively on their activities and often target their communications to groups likely to reinforce rather than criticize behavior.

Ultimately, accountability depends on electoral opposition, an opponent who will take an adverse position to that of the incumbent and force discussion of significant policy issues. Even then, the realities of elections make it uncertain that the reelection or defeat of an incumbent or a member of the same party means that the electorate is actually endorsing or rejecting specific policies or an agenda. Some candidates are quite skilled at building support for themselves as diligent and honest public servants, quite apart from how they vote on policies before the legislature. They successfully separate themselves from the party and from other candidates on the ballot. On the other hand, in elections in which candidates for president, members of Congress, and governor appear on the ballot with state legislators, the electoral decisions on the latter may be only a pale reflection of the electoral judgment on the higher offices. In such cases, the verdict tells little about the opinions that produced it. And individual legislators who may otherwise have earned the disapproval of their constituents may have escaped through affiliation with the party standard bearers.

Individual accountability may also be avoided by retirement, leaving the voters no opportunity to speak on the incumbent's performance. The party system to some extent vitiates this situation by providing new candidates who generally tend to represent the same or similar policies.

Party accountability may work slightly better than individual accountability. The political party serves as a means for agglomerating issues and simplifying electoral choices. Where candidates emphasize their party designation, they symbolize for the voter a general tendency toward certain policies, even though they reserve the right to act independently of party on some matters. To this limited extent, each legislative election can be seen as a referendum on the party in power and its stewardship of the legislature or of the larger government. Off-year elections, in particular, are often interpreted in this way. But not all legislative candidates campaign as representatives of the party. Some distance themselves from it, although they will certainly vote with its caucus on the organization of the house. Many legislative elections are uncontested, especially where there is a popular incumbent. In recent Minnesota legislative elections there have been enough uncontested seats to decide which party will control the House of Representatives if the contested seats are evenly decided. The distortions in the representative process also make it possible for the party whose candidates receive more votes statewide than the other party to end up with a minority of seats in the Legislature. One can never be sure that a change in the majority or in its margin of control is a decision that reflects a public judgment on the Legislature or on the entire government.

Vox populi may pronounce a Delphic message, but it is decisive. We know who got elected. We do not always know why. This brings us to a central conundrum of representative government: the electoral mandate. Elected officials often assume, and some proclaim, that they were elected to fulfill a mandate from the voters. They may be right. If they so act, they may also be able to find out if their reading of the electoral mind was correct. The true mandate is to be found not in the prior election, but in the next one. For it is in the process of holding representatives accountable for their work, however imperfect that process is, that an implied mandate is confirmed.

Legislative accountability in the American system remains an enigma. Its problems are exacerbated by both the separation of powers and bicameralism. Clearly it is unfair to hold the legislature accountable for much of what is done by the governor, even when the branches are controlled by the same party. Members of one house are able to avoid accountability by blaming the governor or the other house for problems. They are also able to avoid ethical as well as political responsibility by acting in a manner calculated to be popular, though unwise, with the assurance that the other powers will prevent such actions from becoming effective.

Intervening for Citizens

American legislators, in particular, have assumed a representative function that has become central to their political existence: intervening with administrative agencies to ensure that ordinary citizens have access and are treated fairly. Critics of this ''casework'' function would argue that what legislators often want for their constituents is not *fair* treatment but *favorable* treatment. It may also be argued that legislators who are highly effective caseworkers can escape accountability for their performance and that of their party on major policy concerns. On the other hand, if one's constituents prefer care and feeding to consistency with their policy preferences, the caseworking legislator can argue that one is the soul of accountability!

In many respects, casework does more to build a legislator's reputation with the home folks than positions taken on policy issues. It has become the bread and butter of the elected legislator. The American practice goes beyond the mere ombudsman function of investigating complaints of governmental abuse. It entails providing access for constituents and others to administrators far in advance of any trouble. Legislators commonly serve constituents as ''gofers'' in collecting information for them. They regularly use their offices to set up meetings for vendors of goods and services with agency officials. And they use their positions on committees to raise questions with agency heads about specific cases or types of cases. It is not unusual for a legislative hearing to be focused on a particular case or for a legislator to use the hearing as leverage on the agency to force it to respond favorably to the constituent or group concerned.

Casework is a major source of information to members of the legislature. That it is anecdotal and idiosyncratic or even unreliable does not reduce its power in the legislative process. Casework forms much of the world view of the practicing legislator and as such influences positions on policy questions. Cases become, therefore, important stuff in the deliberative process of the legislature and its committees, for they carry with them the power of example.

As population has grown and public issues have become more complex and government bureaucracy has become more routinized, impersonal, and remote, the casework function of the legislature has provided an important human intermediary between the citizen and government. In this sense, casework plays an important role in the legitimation of government by helping people get a hearing for their problems from someone who is prepared to do something, if only to see that the right door is opened. Much of casework consists of little more than providing helpful directions to the perplexed citizen confronted with a bureaucratic maze. Casework is also integral to the representative function, as it involves the legislator in speaking on behalf of constituents.

Closely related to casework is "bringing home the bacon." Legislators tend assiduously to serve groups of constituents by securing projects and programs that help them economically. Funding for institutions located in one's district is high on a member's agenda, as is gaining support for locally favored public works. This "pork" helps establish the member's reputation as one who can deliver for the district, and builds political support that may cross party lines and ideologies.

Pork-barrel politics is important to the legislative process by making possible coalitions based on convenience or necessity when they cannot be formed through persuasion. A member can trade a vote on an issue about which he or she cares little for a benefit to the home district about which a number of people may care a lot. In its extreme forms pork-barrel politics is not an edifying spectacle. It has been severely criticized by the public-choice school of economists, who regard these "distributive coalitions" (Olson, 1971; Buchanan and Tullock, 1962) as inefficient and, therefore, unwholesome. Democratic governance, however, is not an exercise in efficiency or deductive logic. It indeed involves reconciling competing gratifications. That process, as we have seen, sometimes involves tradeoffs that produce majorities or even consensus, rather than brush-offs that conform to a cost/benefit calculus.

Deliberation, Education, Lawmaking, and Legitimation of Policy

Deliberation in the Legislature

Representation is not a static phenomenon, accomplished by the representative merely showing up. Rather, representation involves action. In a legislative body, the action most often takes the form of discussion with other representatives, the object of which is to persuade them to accept a point of view. If a representative cannot persuade others to accept a viewpoint and vote accordingly, the next best step is to persuade them to accommodate the viewpoint or to do those represented no harm. This process of deliberation is not only fundamental to the representational process; it also serves to integrate the polity by providing voice for interests and clues to ways in which various interests can be accommodated.

Legislative action is usually symbolized by a vote, but legislative votes are more than mere mathematical agglomerations of single preferences of members. Votes follow talk—talk that at its best represents "reasoning on the merits of public policy" (Besseltee, 1979)—which includes information, argument, and persuasion. "Common counsel is not aggregate counsel," wrote Woodrow Wilson:

It is composed out of many views in actual contact; is a living thing
made out of the vital substance of many minds, many personalities,
many experiences; and it can be made up only by the vital contact of
actual conference, only in face to face debate, only by word of mouth,
and the direct clash of mind with mind. (quoted in Besseltee, 1979)

Deliberation is, as T.V. Smith (1940) observed, central to ''The Legislative
Way of Life.'' Unless a clear and constant majority of the body hold the same
view on every significant matter, deliberation, consultation, negotiation, and
compromise are indispensable to performance of the policymaking function of
the legislature. Such a majority could prevent deliberation through closure of debate, then vote and go home, having in theory represented those who voted for it
quite efficiently, and send the minority home having failed in its essential function. But the ethic of parliaments insists that the minority be heard even though it
cannot prevail.

A legislature is not a court, although legislators must often judge causes
placed before them. But those who advocate their causes before the legislature
are not bound by conventions of law, as in the case of attorneys arguing in court,
who zealously and tenaciously defend their sides, leaving it to the neutral judge
to decide. In a legislature the advocates are also judges, and they cannot be im-
pervious to the arguments of colleagues, who will in turn judge their arguments.
The rules permit switching sides or adopting the arguments of others.

Action without deliberation, or very little of it, does occur. In Minnesota, the
most common instance is in the approval, in conference reports that compromise
differences between House and Senate, of new measures that have not been considered previously by either house. Something close to default in deliberation
tends to occur at some special sessions called to deal with an emergency. Bills are
typically precleared through consultation with the legislative leaders and the governor so that disruptive hearings and debate can be avoided. Governor Rudy Perpich has regularly insisted that bills be worked out in advance of a special session. The 1987 special session, for example, was called to enact legislation
designed to block unfriendly takeover of the Dayton-Hudson Corporation. There
was some committee deliberation as the bill was being developed by Dayton-
Hudson's attorneys and state officials, but the entire session itself lasted only a
couple of hours, and legislators spent little of that time debating the issue before
passing the bill by overwhelming majorities.

Cases of no deliberation are the exception. In fact, the rules and customs of a
legislature are designed to promote deliberation. Bills are subjected to repeated
readings. The first reading essentially gives the membership notice that it has
been filed and referred to a committee. The second is usually an opportunity for
detailed debate and amendment following committee action. The final reading
requires consideration of the bill as amended for final passage.

The committee system furthers the deliberative process. Substantive committees include members of the minority party, and membership is usually distributed to recognize geographic regions, party factions, or other interests with which members are identified. In committee or on the floor, the minorities usually do not win, but they are generally allowed to speak. Frequently, they are able to temper legislation by argument or through coalitions that threaten to become majorities.

Bicameralism is an additional institutionalization of the deliberative process. It forces all legislation to be acted on at least twice by bodies with somewhat different electoral bases and political perspectives. While the second look is often cursory, there is at least the opportunity to join the debate.

Deliberation delays action. It often appears inefficient if not completely disorderly. However, it is the mind and soul of representative government.

In the modern legislature, deliberation involves more than discussion by the members of matters all understand. In the early days of representative government, the issues tended to be broad but clear: Should Parliament levy the taxes requested by the king? Should it be possible for people to make wills? Should there be a national bank? As representative government became better established and the power to make positive law became firmly implanted in the legislature, issues became more complex and technical. Legislatures codified the common law, declaring what the law was by statute rather than waiting for the courts to "find" it. As the role of government grew, legislatures found themselves involved in extraordinarily involved matters, such as the regulation of insurance, protection of public health, and the establishment of standards of professional licensure. These are not subjects about which ordinary folk commonly talk unless confronted with a crisis that demands it.

Legislators, like the general population they represent, relied on the specialization of labor to deal with the business at hand. The committee system provided a means by which some members could become educated through the experience of continued dealing with particular areas of subject matter. As the number of matters to be discussed in a session increased, the most detailed and serious deliberation in the legislature moved from the floor to the committee rooms. The main body of representatives were themselves represented by colleagues serving on committees.

These committees often met privately, even excluding other legislators from attending committee meetings as observers. Only the members of the committee were privy to the deliberations. Since all members could not share in all of the deliberations on a bill, most members tended to defer to senior committee members whose judgment could be trusted on both the substance of issues and their political implications. Deliberation had become specialized and compartmentalized.

In addition to the committee members, the deliberative process now includes the witnesses who come before the committees and lobbyists for private interest groups, who provide members with technical and political information on policy questions. In this sense, the legislature, or at least its committees, have become part of a broad public deliberation, which includes the interested bureaucracies and groups and the press. Increasingly, the pressure from those interested in policy, as well as pressure from the members of legislatures themselves, has led to open meetings of committees, including work sessions at which the committee members "mark up" legislation, preparing it for action on the floor.

With increasing volumes of legislation and with the increased technical complexity of public policy, exemplified by modern regulatory and environmental legislation, the ability to deliberate has been hampered by the lack of independent sources of information and analysis for legislative committees and members. Legislative staffs have been expanded from clerical help to a cadre of professional legislative analysts to help members draft bills, analyze proposals, and prepare amendments. Staff have become an integral part of the deliberative process, operating as analysts, advisers, and occasionally as advocates of policy. They provide the legislators with other points of view. They assist the members in framing the issues or in reformulating and justifying a policy to reflect the decisions of a committee or an individual leader.

In the modern legislature, then, the deliberative process resembles a number of whirlpools (Griffith, 1965) composed of specialists in and outside the legislature itself. These whirlpools of deliberation move and occasionally merge with the broader legislative current. On great issues, they may at times suck the entire body into the discussion, but most of the time the debate is among the specialists in and outside the legislature.

Even so, the legislative process is designed to provide an opportunity for those who were in the minority in committee to attract other supporters on the floor through procedural motions or amendments. Floor debate, like open debate in committee, is also calculated to stir the interest of other publics, which might rush to the aid of the legislative combatants with messages of support from the constituencies or interest groups. Those on the losing side may use the rules to delay action to give their forces time to gather, or seek to make their points more effectively when the second house takes up the matter.

It should be apparent that the function of deliberation is an integral activity of the representative. Unless we could assume that every member comes to the legislature equally and fully informed about every matter to come before it and fully instructed on how to vote by an equally well-informed constituency, the representative office could not be performed without some exchange of information and views and an opportunity to assess how measures at hand might affect the interests one purports to represent. Deliberation in a legislature is not a notably orderly process when there is a controversy of any magnitude. The structure and rules permit losers to raise the issues again and again in an exercise designed to allow the majority ultimately to rule, but also to ensure that the minority has had a full opportunity to persuade the legislature and, failing that, to make its case to the public and educate voters for another day.

Educator of the Public

Not only does deliberation inform the legislature, but legislative debate and discussion informs the public. In this sense, the legislature is a school for democracy. It educates its members in both the substance of policy issues and the rituals and procedures of lawmaking and public debate. But it performs a loftier function as the principal organ of policy education for the public at large.

Education of the public is not exclusively a legislative function. All sorts of officials are engaged in education, through speeches and actions. The courts play a conspicuous role through the drama of trials and the written opinions of judges. Executives and administrators are constantly meeting with groups and issuing reports and documents that explain problems and proposed solutions to them. The media, through its news reporting and editorializing, is an almost ubiquitous mass educator. All manner of interest groups, visual and performing artists, and teachers and formal and informal educational organizations participate in the education of the electorate and the broader public.

Few institutions, however, are better equipped than legislatures to illuminate the many facets of a policy issue or to reveal through public discourse and open conflict the interests at stake. Woodrow Wilson (1885:195) argued that:

> [E]ven more important than legislation is the instruction and guidance in political affairs which the people might receive from a body which kept all national concerns suffused in a broad daylight of discussion.

To a considerable extent, the educative function of the legislature is a by-product of deliberation, rather than the principal end of the legislature. But education is frequently a necessary prerequisite to making a policy choice. Legislators may, for instance, be convinced from their own studies of a problem, either as individuals or through the collective investigation of a committee, that new law, or a change in old law, is essential. However, making the change may entail altering the behavior of powerful institutions or of significant segments of the public. The adoption of the no-fault approach to automobile accident insurance offers such an example. Before a legislative majority for this concept could be assembled, it was first necessary for its supporters not only to educate their colleagues of its merit, but to use the processes of hearings and legislative commissions and reports to convince a substantial body of opinion that it was a good idea.

Political education also takes place in political campaigns; public demonstrations designed to influence the legislature; floor debate; public appearances and endorsements; appearances on the electronic media and statements in the print media; committee investigations; explanations to constituents in person, in letters, and in newsletters; and even in hustling pork and handling cases. As a school for democracy, a legislature is anything but systematic and objective. With the possible exception of the media, the legislature is, nonetheless, broader in its inquiries and it often offers more depth and exposes a wider range of opinion (both informed and off-the-wall) than any other public institution.

Making Law and Legitimating Policy Choices

The product of legislative deliberations is public policy in the form of statutes. Other parts of government—courts and administrators—produce policy that has the force and effect of law, but only legislatures can enact legislation, i.e., create it themselves without any limits but the Constitution. While Parliament did not originate as the lawmaking institution of the realm, American legislatures have, by their very name and by acceptance of the separation of powers doctrine, been conceived as the principal sources of law for the states (Pole, 1966).

The legislative function is particularly well suited to a deliberative assembly of representatives:

> [Ever] since the sixteenth century legislation was believed to be the
> most striking manifestation of political and governmental power.
> Legislation entailed the making of rules binding upon the whole
> community . . . [The] making of a rule presupposes that there is a
> series of events which have certain aspects in common. In other words,
> there must be a "normal" situation. This means that time is available
> for deliberation to determine what had best be done regarding such a
> situation. Representative, deliberative bodies require time, obviously,
> and therefore legislation seems to be peculiarly fitted for such bodies.
> (Friedrich, 1950:264)

Making law does not, as history amply illustrates, require a legislature. Legitimating laws and the policies they contain does. In the abstract, the public accepts laws and policies made by the legislature because the legislature acts for the public in its representative capacity. Legislative decisions, however, are rarely unanimous, and even if they were, the distortions in the processes of electing and organizing the legislature makes improbable the notion that the voice of the legislature is indisputably the voice of the people. A lot of people have not participated in either process. Many who have may be quite dissatisfied with the result. Like the soldier in Cromwell's army, they demand to know why they should be subject to laws they had no part in making. In other words, it may be law, but is it legitimate?

Legitimacy of rule is essential to the ultimate survival of a regime. Over time, the divine right of kings was supplanted by the right of the majority to rule. The right of the majority to decide policy questions, however, depends heavily on a respect for the rights of the minority in both the processes of policymaking and in the substantive outcome. A majority may have the *power* to suppress the minority, but most democratic theorists would stoutly deny that it has a *right* to do so. A constitutional democracy normally has explicit safeguards of both substance and procedure to prevent majority tyranny.

In a legislature, policy is made by the majority. It is made legitimate by the minority. This does not mean that the minority must agree with the policy, although broad consensus on the result is one way in which policy is legitimated. That consensus may not be immediate. It took almost 50 years for Social Security to become a consensus policy. But consensus and the legitimacy it confers may be sought in the fashioning of a piece of legislation by its original authors. The demonstration that a policy has won wide support in the legislature is instrumental to building a public consensus and facilitating the acceptance of the law.

What is essential to the legitimacy of policy is that the minority accept that it was made without trickery or abuse of process and that the policy not purport to be the last or only word on the matter. Policy must be liable to future perfection by majorities yet to be formed. Thus, minorities generally are able to accept as legitimate policies made for the time being.

Even policies that are subject to later change can be hard to swallow, however, if they are made arbitrarily, are capricious in character, or are produced through some abuse of process. Procedure is important in a democracy. Its meticulous observance by majorities seems at times a petty inconvenience that slows the machinery of government and merely delays the inevitable triumph of the majority. But in many cases, the ability of the policy to stick may depend on the way in which the minority is treated during its consideration. "The history of liberty," wrote Felix Frankfurter (*McNabb*, 1943:337) "has largely been the history of observance of procedural safeguards." Procedures, rules of conduct, and rituals take some of the heat out of the system that would be generated by raw conflicts over policy. They help make agreement possible and allow major disagreements to be postponed or converted into procedural issues. This not only helps stabilize deliberation; it makes the results of the legislative process easier for the losers to accept.

An important aspect of legislative procedure, as of judicial procedure, is the opportunity for those concerned about an issue to be heard. One test of whether a system is legitimate is if it provides a way for people to give voice to their concerns without being subjected to personal risk or penalty. Legislatures, therefore, spend a lot of time in hearings and debate even though most minds are decided and the issue is in no real doubt. This sacrifice of efficiency for voice contributes to stability and legitimacy of policy.

Thus, one of the central functions of the legislature is to transcend its shallow moorings in an electorate that may have little advance knowledge of the specific issues their representatives will confront and to make policy legitimate by representing the whole corporate and organic public. That legislatures sometimes fall short of such a noble aim should not be surprising, for the legitimating function calls on legislators and their party leaders to practice politics as a system of ethics as well as a system of power.

One can find recent actions of the Minnesota Legislature in which abuse of process produced decisions that were not regarded by the minority as legitimate. For example, the 1986 decision by the majority in the House to insert into an appropriations bill, without hearing, a measure to reduce welfare payments to dependent children by 30 percent was offensive to the minority not only for its consequences, but because it circumvented the regular legislative process. In 1987, the leadership had to withdraw a bill that would have color coded ballots after the minority objected to the substance of the measure, but especially to its being brought before the House without notice, hearing, or committee action.

There are other cases in which the minority essentially acquiesced in the abuse of process, finding the result sufficiently to its liking that it could accept it as legitimate. This has occurred most often in the practice of producing "garbage bills" in the conferences between the two houses. Although extraneous measures are frequently inserted into conference reports that were not previously considered by either house, the overall result remains sufficiently to the liking of most of the members that they are willing to ignore the flaunting of the rules. Such practices, however, tend to undermine the willingness of the public at large to accept as legitimate the products of the legislature. Disrespect for the legislature as an institution of governance is a pernicious affliction. It tends to undermine policy on a wide front and impairs the quality of public service.

The citizen participation movement and the consumer movement are to some extent manifestations of the idea that the policymaking bodies of government are unable to legitimate the policies they make because some essential interest had insufficient voice in the process. In this sense, legitimacy depends on the right to be heard and, in some instances, on the extent to which the resulting policy actually accommodates the interest concerned. To the extent that the legislature is viewed by a larger public as unable to act legitimately, the power of the unelected advocate of the complaining interest is enhanced.

Legitimation of policy is not the responsibility of the legislative majority alone. The minority has an ethical role to play as well. While it may be well said that the function of the minority is to oppose the proposals of the majority, it has also an obligation to accept as legitimate, even if wrong-headed or silly, policies that are fairly made. Such an acceptance robs the minority of no right to continue to criticize the content of the policy or to make it an issue in the next election. But a decent regard for the work of the majority protects the minority's own interest as a future majority.

In the American system of separation of powers, the legitimation function has another dimension. Our system, by creating a politically independent executive, places the legislature in constitutional opposition to the executive, even when the two branches are controlled by the same political party. In a wide range of activities, the legitimacy of the actions of the executive depend upon the concurrence of the legislature. The most obvious situation is the appointment of high-ranking executive officers who must be confirmed by the senate. In other ways as well, the legislature confers legitimacy on the actions of the executive. It may authorize the governor to take certain actions, such as reducing budgetary allotments to agencies. It may endorse actions or proposals by single house or joint resolutions. Or it may give an official or program a seal of approval as the result of an investigation and report.

Controlling the Public Purse

If there is any one function, other than representation, associated with the historical development of the legislature, it is the power of the purse: the power to determine how much may be spent for what purposes, and how taxes will be levied to support the expenditures (Friedrich, 1950; Pitkin, 1967). The right of the people to control through their representatives their common fiscal burdens and benefits is fundamental to the concept of representative government. In England, Parliament does not prepare the estimates or initiate the budget requests; that is the prerogative of the government; but no money can be spent without the consent of the House of Commons. The failure of the government to win the consent of Commons to its budget will result in the government's resignation.

Modern American executives prepare budget recommendations, but the legislature must appropriate all money that may be expended. Except in three states where the legislature may not increase the governor's budget, American legislatures have a free hand in amending the executive's proposals, or even in ignoring them and producing a budget of their own.

More legislative time and energy is expended on fiscal affairs than on any other single subject. Rosenthal (1981), in his study of *Legislative Life*, found that fiscal issues tended to dominate the perception many legislators have of their legislative experience. He reported the following observations:

> As a matter of fact, after the decisions have been made on how to spend money, I'd just as soon go home. (A Florida legislator)

> If you've got your hands on the money, that's the only language anyone understands in state government. (An Ohio legislator)

If you grab them by their budgets, their hearts and minds will follow.
(A Kentucky legislator)

Most members learn early in their careers that the most important committee assignments are to the spending and taxing committees. Membership on them is a measure of power. It is from these committees that legislative leaders frequently rise.

Until the Hoover administration, the Congress assumed responsibility for the preparation as well as the enactment of the federal budget. The same pattern persisted far longer in many state legislatures, although some adopted an executive budget fairly early in the 20th century. But historically, the idea that the president or governor should present a budget bill to the legislative branch and thereby set the main terms of debate on fiscal matters is a new idea that developed due to the increased complexity of government finances and the fact that the spending departments and the treasury were executive agencies.

At both national and state levels, the legislative power over the purse has been gradually eroded. Governors have been assigned the responsibility of preparing budget estimates and recommending budget priorities. Legislatures have reclaimed some lost ground through laws that establish budget format and process, the creation of legislative staffs to analyze the budget and tax policies, and, in 29 states, the movement to an annual budget, replacing the biennial budget system that was almost universal in state government until after the Second World War.

Changes have also occurred in the way in which legislatures appropriate funds. A number of legislatures continue the traditional practice of making line-item appropriations, designating the specific activities or objects for which the appropriations may be used. The complexities of modern government suggest that this approach to legislative control of expenditures is far too rigid and poses enormous problems in practical execution of the budget. Program budgeting in some form has been substituted in most states. In this system the legislature votes appropriations for whole departments as lump sums, with some additional policy guidance on how to spend the money. The historic passion for the line item reappears, however, in specific instructions to spend or not to spend funds for particular activities.

Minnesota law provides an interesting limitation on the legislative power over the budget. Occasionally, the biennial budget, which is enacted in the months before the biennium begins, becomes unbalanced when revenue collections do not reach levels assumed when the budget was enacted. If the Legislature cannot or does not agree on how to increase taxes or reduce expenditures to bring the budget back into balance, the governor may "unallot" appropriated funds by making across-the-board cuts until the budget is again balanced. This was done in 1986 when the conferees from the House and Senate were unable to agree on spending reductions.

This provision is consistent with the trend in legislative-executive relations to increase executive power in fiscal affairs. Generally, this trend is one that gives governors some discretion in cutting public spending, even though the legislature has appropriated funds. At the federal level, the Supreme Court has upheld the Congressional Budget and Impoundment Control Act of 1974, which prohibited the practice of executive impoundment of funds appropriated by Congress (*Train v. City of New York*, 420 U.S. 35 (1975).

Legislatures have been jealous of their fiscal powers, and have delegated little of what might be considered their plenary authority to executives. In a few cases standby tax authority has been delegated, but the character and level of the taxes has been specified as well as the trigger event that allows the executive to impose them.

The power to spend and tax, limited only by the constitution, is based on the representative and deliberative character of the legislature. It is essential, in a representative democracy, that there be "no taxation without representation" and that taxes not be imposed without a full discussion of their incidence and rate. Again, the legislature performs the function of educating both itself and the public on the need for the expense or the tax, and through the representative process at least ensures that those affected have had some voice in the decision.

Holding the Administration Accountable

The Watchdog Function

Many modern writers on legislatures and Congress have argued that, given the enormous growth in the size and scope of government, the most important function of the legislature is oversight of executive activity (Mezy, 1986; Huntington, 1968). The legislature tends to enact policy in broad language that speaks to the objectives sought. But because of the complications of applying these sweeping grants of power to specific and often unforeseen situations, administrators must be given a wide berth to interpret and apply the law. If the legislature is to perform well its function of deliberating on changes to policy, it must be informed about whether its earlier intentions have been carried out. Put too simply, is the policy mistaken or poorly conceived, or has it just not been properly executed?

Mill (1859:321) argued that a representative assembly could not decide all matters of administration, so its "proper role" was to watch and control the government:

> to throw the light of publicity on its acts; to compel a full exposition and justification of all of them which any one considers questionable; to censure them if found condemnable, and, if the men who compose the government abuse their trust, or fulfill it in a manner which conflicts

with the deliberate sense of the nation, to expel them from office, and either expressly or virtually appoint their successors.

Modern bureaucracy confronts the representative legislature with its most formidable challenge. Federal and state bureaucracies are large and diverse. The origins of some agencies are to be found in antique statutes, their mandates for action long embalmed in laws and policies that predate by decades (or even centuries) the service of any living legislator. Agencies take on lives of their own, operating in the penumbra of their statutes, filling in the gaps in the law, and gathering a clientele that supports their activities.

At the state level, official records of legislative debates comparable to the *Congressional Record* are not maintained. Bills are rarely accompanied by committee reports. Thus, unless it is clear on the face of the statute or from contemporaneous accounts what the legislature intended, it is extremely difficult for a court, an agency, or the current legislature to divine the intent of the earlier legislature.

Separation of Powers and Administrative Accountability

In American state government the bureaucracy is supervised by officials elected by a statewide electorate. These constitutional officers—the governor, secretary of state, auditor, treasurer, and attorney general in Minnesota—often purport to speak for "all the people." In that sense, executive bureaucracies are not just instrumentalities created to carry out policies adopted by the legislature; they also are representative organizations by virtue of the requirements for appointment and the role they play as extensions of the policy aims of their chiefs. Unlike the British bureaucracy, which serves the government and is held to account by the minority through challenges to policy and relentless interrogation of the government's ministers in the House of Commons, the state bureaucracy is organizationally responsible not to the legislature, but to the governor or another independently elected official. Agencies retain some responsibilities to the legislature through statutory instructions for reports or other performance. And some agencies retain close informal ties to legislative committees or to individual legislators who serve as their patrons or protectors.

When the administration is an instrument of the legislative power, as in a parliamentary system or in the council-manager system of local government, the lines of responsibility for carrying out legislative intent are clear. So is the responsibility for oversight. Parliament itself cannot be in opposition to the executive, because it creates the executive branch as its instrument. If it votes to reprimand the government, or fails to support it on a critical matter, Parliament must choose a new government, because the existing one cannot function without the confidence of the House. The parliamentary opposition has, therefore, an obligation to its constituencies to criticize and challenge, both to expose the weaknesses in policy and administration that could cause the government to lose support and collapse, and to serve the broader institutional purpose of forcing the government to defend and continuously account to the public, through Parliament, for its performance.

In contrast, the American system of separation of powers maintains that the administrative agencies of the executive branch are no part of the legislative branch. The Minnesota Constitution contains a strict separation of powers clause, which declares that the branches of government are separate and distinct, and that one of them shall not perform any of the functions of the others (*Minnesota Constitution*, article III, section 1). While separation of powers is often more honored in the breach than in the observance, it remains a formidable obstacle to a principled and consistent system of legislative oversight.

First of all, separation of powers intentionally places the legislative and executive branches in constitutional opposition to each other. Two hundred years of constitutional acculturation has produced a system in which it is implicitly understood that the legislature as a whole — not just its minority — has the duty of maintaining a critical distance from the governor. Thus, even the governor's own party has no obligation to support the administration or defend its actions or vote for its budget. While the legislature usually pays considerable deference to gubernatorial proposals, and the governor is almost sure to have members — often, but not always the leaders of their common party — who are understood to be the administration's "spokespersons" in the legislature, even these spokespersons are not bound to support the governor against all opposition. "The governor proposes, the legislature disposes," remains the basic operating rule of American state government.

To this extent, one might argue that legislative oversight in American legislatures is superior to that found in parliamentary systems. All executive policy proposals are likely to be subjected to critical and independent review through the legislature's chief deliberative mechanism, the committee process. No new policy or program proposed by a governor is likely to go into effect without being subject to legislative scrutiny if it requires new legislation or new money. The rub comes when the legislature tries to evaluate how well the administration has done what it was authorized to do, if it has not done it at all, or if it has done things it had no authority to do.

Unlike prime ministers, governors and presidents answer not to the legislative power but to the people directly. They claim a mandate separate from that of the legislature. Their electoral constituency is different. It is possible for a governor to represent a different part of the public than the legislature does, even when the governor is of the same party as a majority of both houses. Since it is a singular office, the governorship does not contain a minority view that must be accommodated or at least heard. And it is to the governor that the bureaucracy reports on its administrative performance.

Legislative Leverage on Administration

Lacking direct control over administration, but having a clear and legitimate interest in how well the administration performs its authorized duties, the legislature must resort to using its political leverage to compel oversight. Its principal leverage, of course, is the power of the purse — the ability to reduce or redirect appropriations. The legislature may also conduct investigations as a basis for future legislative action, and this power is used when there is some reason to believe that an abuse of power or authority has occurred in an agency. Most legislatures, including Minnesota's, have also asserted their power to routinely examine performance and to be concerned with the efficiency of government, again as a basis for policy or financial action. The common manifestation of this interest is government operations committees and legislative audit offices that conduct both financial and performance audits of agencies and programs and report their findings to a committee of the legislature.

These processes, however, are cumbersome at best. The legislature is organized to promote deliberation in specialized policy areas. Members tend to be selected to serve on these oversight committees because of interest in the policies those agencies develop. The committees and their members establish continuing relationships with the bureaucracies the committees create, empower, and fund. With a few exceptions, the relationship between committees and agencies and the clientele the agencies serve develops into an "iron triangle" of mutual support that transcends the separation of powers. Committee members often have little interest in confronting or criticizing their "pets." Moreover, legislators frequently take the posture that their main job is to make policy, not to oversee its administration. Such work, to be sure, is often unglamorous, anonymous drudgery. It also tends to require staff resources rarely available in state legislatures. Finally, it takes sustained time to conduct even a friendly evaluation of an agency to determine whether it could perform more efficiently or effectively.

The legislature has at its disposal, then, several ways of holding the administration to account for its performance. It can determine the way in which bureaucracies are organized and assign functions to specific agencies, or remove them from one and give them to another. It can reorganize and abolish agencies. It can withhold funds or restrict the use of funds to or from certain purposes. The budget process can be used to inquire into the detailed operations of any agency. The legislature can investigate complaints. It usually establishes rules of administrative conduct, such as conflict-of-interest laws. It may retain the power to approve certain appointments. It can conduct audits of agency performance. And it can require reports from the governor and administrative agencies. It can also enact "sundown" laws that limit the life of agencies, requiring them to rejustify their existence at intervals, and "sunshine" laws that require agencies to make decisions in public.

There is an integral connection between effective oversight of administration and other legislative functions such as the power to make law and control of the public purse. Fenno (1966:173) points out that successful legislative scrutiny has to be connected with some retaliatory power:

> Legislative committees need to confront executives face to face and deal with them in a more extended way than a question period, but they also have to convey some sense of legislative muscle. . . . The executive would not listen unless the legislature could convey the idea that it would retaliate in some way if the executive did not take account of what it was saying. Without that legislative lawmaking stick behind the door, effective scrutiny is very difficult — at least in our system.

Viability of the Legislative Veto

Perhaps the most difficult area of legislative oversight of administration is in the field of regulatory activity. Legislatures face the dilemma of writing laws so specifically that they are inapplicable to future circumstances, or so broadly that it is hard for the most conscientious administrators to tell what was intended. The result is a delegation of power to administrators to make rules that have the force of law based on often vague statutory criteria.

Legislatures have responded to this dilemma by inventing the legislative veto. This device requires the rule-making agency to submit its proposed rules to the legislature for review. If one or both houses (or in some versions, a committee) disapproves the rule, it is voided; if no action is taken within a specified time, the rule becomes effective. The rationale behind the legislative veto is that it ensures that the rules made by agencies carry out the intent of the legislature contained in the statute.

The practice is riddled with constitutional and philosophical infirmities. As a matter of constitutional law at the federal level, it violates the "presentment" clause of the U.S. Constitution because the congressional veto has the effect of a statute without being presented to the president for his approval or veto (*Immigration and Naturalization Service v. Chada*, 103 S.Ct. 2764 (1983)). The Minnesota version of the legislative veto appears to conflict with the separation of powers clause of the state constitution because it involves legislators in making executive decisions (Frickey, 1986).

Philosophically, however, the practice is flawed, even if its constitutional difficulties were overcome. The legislative veto allows the legislature to define its intent retroactively rather than to accept responsibility for doing it prospectively. Rather than making law for classes of cases, the legislature acts as if it were a court, applying the law to individual cases. When it comes to determining its own intent, the legislature is even less reliable than the courts. A statute may have been enacted by a generation of legislators long since defeated or dead. A new majority, thoroughly unsympathetic with the earlier view of the statute, may be in power when a rule based on the old law comes before it. It may lack the votes or the will to repeal the law, but it can undermine its effect by exercise of the legislative veto over any regulations produced by the agency. The agency, however, is left with the legal obligation to try to enforce the law as written and may be subject to legal attack for its inability to do what the earlier legislature told it to do.

The easiest way, philosophically, to resolve the problem is for the legislature to establish more specific standards for administrative agencies to use in rule making. Practically, that is not as simple as it sounds. There are new arenas of legislative concern where it is impossible to foretell just what needs to be done. Perhaps the answer, then, is to set standards and require an agency to return for new instructions by statute when it finds the problem it must address exceeds its original authority. This makes it harder to get complex issues off the legislative agenda and into the administrative process. Alternatively, legislatures could proceed to enact regulatory legislation as they have in the past, require that proposed rules be reported to them for a period before they become effective, and proceed by the regular bill process to amend the authorizing statute if they find the administrative interpretation repugnant. A committee to monitor administrative rules would, of course, help spotlight problems.

Of all the functions legislatures are supposed to perform, holding the administration accountable for its implementation of policy enacted by the legislature is, perhaps, the one most plagued with problems. It is a function on which the legislature spends relatively little time, and one about which members, administrators, and other observers of the legislature are most dissatisfied. Effective oversight depends heavily on the career interests of individual legislators (Fenno, 1966; 1978).

The weakness of the oversight process affects other functions as well. It tends to weaken the deliberative process by depriving the legislature of important information about how government works or fails to work. It also undermines the legitimation function, because a weak system of oversight implies that the legislature accepts most of the government as it is.

Understanding What the Legislature Does

The civics text chant that "the legislature makes the laws, the executive enforces, and the judiciary interprets them," leaves out far more than it explains. The legislature, as we have seen, performs a number of functions that are important to democratic governance, of which making law is only one. These basic functions are all important, but they are not always in harmony with each other. The representativeness, responsiveness, and accountability of a legislature can surely attenuate deliberation and complicate its ability to make policy choices or legitimate them. There is often tension between the value legislators place on representing their districts' interests or individual casework and the task of reconciling conflicting interests to produce a budget for the state. The pressure to make choices can squelch deliberation. Legislators may work hard to represent their districts but seek to evade accountability for the overall performance of the legislature. In some cases being representative may conflict with responsibility to exercise sharp administrative oversight. On the other hand, a legislature may do battle with the governor over tax and spending policy one year and cede extensive fiscal power to the executive branch in the next session to shift responsibility for an unpopular fiscal policy.

It is not surprising to find a gap between theory and practice. It is troubling, however, to find so much of the discussion of problems with the legislature focused on one or two functions, such as representation or policy choices, without much appreciation of how these functions are related to the others. All the functions reflect important values about democratic governance and need attention in any balanced analysis of the legislature as an institution. It is even more disconcerting to see reform proposals based on appeals to efficiency, analogizing a legislature to a board of corporate directors, without regard for the political and public functions that may not necessarily coincide with conventional definitions of efficiency.

Recognizing that a legislature has many functions to perform and that they are sometimes reinforcing, sometimes in conflict with each other helps us assess legislative performance and proposals ostensibly designed to change or reform the process. Such proposals generally have an end value in mind. They may be designed to improve the process by making the legislature more representative, open, responsive, or efficient. But these are not neutral ends about which no reasonable person could disagree. The essence of a legislature tied to popular consent is that it is bound to disagree about ends, to find almost any grand-sounding idea problematic because someone's oxen are likely to be gored by it. Improving legislative performance of one of its functions may well undermine its performance of another. Similarly when we criticize a legislature for being unable to produce good public policy, we should ask, ''good for whom?''

Mezey (1986:2) argues that public policy should be informed, timely, coherent, effective, and responsive, and that legislatures are not well suited to making such policy because members need no expertise and the very functions that a legislature must perform make it difficult for it to act coherently and effectively. In response, Cooper (1986) points out that such attempts to rationalize policy as merely the most appropriate means to a particular end misapprehends and even trivializes what a legislature does. Important policy issues before legislatures are as frequently about ends as they are about means. ''The point is that politics is not engineering'' (Cooper, 1986:24).

What individuals and groups want or expect from their legislature varies with their interests and their conceptions of the proper role of the legislature in the political system, as well as with the priorities they believe the legislature should place on its respective functions. Thus, evaluation of reforms needs to be rooted in the perspectives, values, and interests of the observer. "There is no 'model' of a proper legislature to which men of good will can repair" (Huitt, 1964).

This study does not try to present a model. It does reflect the judgment that the legislature is of central importance to the system of representative government. It places a high priority on the functions of deliberation, choice, and legitimation; control of the public purse; and accountability. That is not because I regard representation and administrative oversight as unimportant, but because they are less central at this time to the vitalization of the legislative system. The great struggle for reform in representation occurred in the early sixties and climaxed in the reapportionment decisions of the Supreme Court. While small battles continue on problems such as racial gerrymandering, the big fight to make legislatures function remains fundamental and, as such, influences all others.

I have tried to deal with the functions we have focused on in the context of the others, and in the context of the evolution of the Minnesota Legislature as an institution of governance over the past generation. That requires a close look at how the Legislature has changed, how it goes about its business, how it makes decisions, and how its members perceive it as a place to work. I have assumed that good policy is defined less by its objective rationality or efficiency as a means to a proper end than by its acceptability to the people of the state as a fairly dispositive resolution of an issue. Thus, an acceptable policy is one that does not repetitively appear on subsequent legislative agendas.

Understanding the Minnesota Legislature — what it does, how it works, and how it came to function as it does — is the main objective of this study. That understanding provides a firm basis for clarifying the dilemmas and crystalizing the alternatives for change or reform. I expect, and welcome, disagreement with specific reform proposals, but am convinced that the debate over the future of the Legislature can proceed at a higher level and that proposals for reform are likely to be more meaningful, responsible, and workable if they are based on a clearer notion of what legislatures are supposed to do in a democratic system and on accurate knowledge of legislative behavior, rather than simply on popular stereotypes of the Legislature or utopian visions of possibilities for change.

3

The Changing Legislature

If a citizen visited the capitol in St. Paul in 1989, a quarter of a century after last observing the Minnesota Legislature as part of a high school tour, there would seem to be little change. The sepulchral halls of Cass Gilbert's gleaming Renaissance building still echo each footstep and voice, the grand marble stairs rise to the Senate chamber and the governor's rooms, the bathrooms are hard to find. In their columned chambers, the representatives and senators would, except for the presence of more women, look about the same.

The House has had 134 members, instead of 135, since 1972, but members still sit at small, old-fashioned desks and the speaker still presides beneath a great portrait of a brooding Lincoln. Members can now speak from microphones installed on their desks, where once they had to move to a microphone that an aide plugged in to one of several outlets in the House chamber. Gone also are the brass spittoons that once challenged the nonrhetorical accuracy of members. In the Senate, an alert observer would notice that the presiding officer is not the lieutenant governor, but a member of the Senate. And in both chambers, television cameras are trained on the speakers.

A closer look would, however, reveal substantial change in both houses of the Legislature. Some of these changes are the results of constitutional amendments, court decisions, and other laws. Others have come about due to shifts in political practices, self-imposed changes in the rules of one or both houses, and the influence of external events and conditions on the Legislature. The sum of these changes has made the Legislature a different institution than it was in 1963.

The reapportionment revolution that resulted from decisions of the U.S. Supreme Court in 1962 (*Baker v. Carr*, 369 U.S. 368) and 1964 (*Reynolds v. Sims*,

377 U.S. 533), remade the political geography of the states. Implementation of the one-person, one-vote rule in Minnesota shifted seats in both houses from the rural areas of the state to the Twin Cities and their suburbs. The requirement of decennial reapportionment and shifts in population within the state produced, by the time of the 1983 session, rough parity between the number of legislators representing the Twin Cities metropolitan area and those from the rest of the state.

Shifts in Party Control

Beinning in 1914, when the state adopted a nonpartisan election system for members of the Legislature, until the system was abolished in 1973, the Senate was consistently controlled by rural conservatives. The House, except for periods during the governorships of Floyd Olson and Orville Freeman, had also been dominated by conservatives. Since 1973, as Figure 1 shows, the liberal and Democratic-Farmer-Labor (DFL) caucus has controlled the Senate. Since 1963, the House has shifted control five times between the DFL and the Independent-Republican (IR) Party. The increased strength of the DFL in the Legislature is not only a result of reapportionment, but of the statutory change approved in 1973 to require that candidates for the Legislature be designated on the ballot by party affiliation.

Flexible Sessions

Repportionment ushered in an era of unparalleled reform of state legislatures. Many states adopted new constitutions. Others, like Minnesota, substantially revised and updated their constitutions. An important change in the Legislative article in the 1972 revisions provided for flexible sessions of the Legislature (*Minn. Const.*, Art. IV, Sec. 12). This amendment provided that the Legislature could meet for a total of 120 legislative days during each biennium, as opposed to the old system, which required a single session once every two years. This change allows the leadership of the Legislature to schedule some part of the session in the second year of the biennium. In practice, this has produced a long meeting of the Legislature during odd-numbered years and a short meeting in even-numbered years, although both are technically parts of the same session. Since the constitution prohibits the Legislature from reconvening in regular session after the third week of May, special sessions have become frequent necessities to complete work that fails to meet the deadline. De facto annual sessions also mean that legislators tend to spend more time at the Capitol between sessions than they did a generation ago.

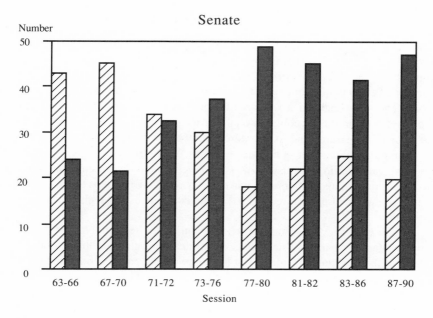

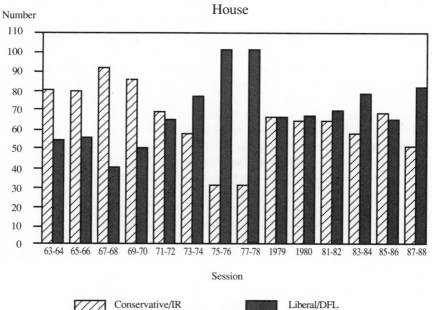

Figure 1. Party Division in the Minnesota Legislature

Professional Staff and Open Meetings

Another pervasive legislative reform is the development of professional staffs. In 1963, neither house had a strong staff that was concerned with the substance of legislation. The chief clerk of the House and the secretary of the Senate were not concerned with policy, but with housekeeping and procedures during the sessions. The joint Legislative Research Committee, consisting of a senator and a representative from each congressional district, supervised studies conducted by the director of research and four research analysts. In the fifties and sixties standing committees did not meet between sessions. When there were problems needing study, an interim commission was appointed, composed of an equal number of representatives and senators, to make policy recommendations to the next regular session of the Legislature. Today, regular committees and legislative staff fill this need.

A generation ago, most staff served only during the session. Now both bodies have substantial permanent staff and some professional staff groups — notably the Office of the Legislative Auditor, the Legislative Reference Library, and the Office of the Revisor of Statutes — serve both chambers. The Legislature continues to employ a fairly large number of temporary employees who work only during sessions.

Some aspects of the staffing pattern are unique to Minnesota. Each party caucus in each house has a partisan staff, which provides political support and constituent services to the caucus under the direction of the caucus leaders. A central staff unit in each house serves both committees and individual members in providing technical and professional assistance on policy proposals and bills. Each committee has clerical and administrative staff, but usually does not have its own professional staff. The exceptions are the taxing and appropriating committees, to which professional analysts are assigned. In the late sixties the House Appropriations Committee and the Senate Finance Committee were the first standing committees to have professional staff regularly assigned to them. There remains, within this structure, considerable ambiguity about the political and professional responsibilities of staff, particularly in the House, where turnover in partisan control has been frequent.

Another major reform was the adoption, in 1973, of the "open meeting" rules for regular committee meetings in each house and for conference committees composed of conferees from each house. Prior to the adoption of these rules, committee meetings could be, and often were, closed to the public and media and occasionally to other legislators who were not members of the committees.

Political Volatility

In Minnesota, as elsewhere in the country, the political context within which the

Legislature works has been transformed as the loyalty of voters to the major political parties has declined. These factors, combined with demographic shifts and migration patterns, have caused the state to become more volatile in its voting behavior for both state and national legislators. Party control of the governorship has changed five times in seven elections. Since 1960, only Governors Wendell Anderson and Rudy Perpich have been elected for consecutive terms. While a majority of the state's U.S. congressmen are DFLers, both U.S. senators have been Republicans since 1978.

Movement politics has often been more important than parties in shaping the legislative and broader political agendas. The environmental movement, the peace movement, the women's movement, the religious right, and, more recently, the farm movement have all enjoyed moments of political power and legislative enthusiasm. Movement politics, which tends to be thematic rather than programmatic, principled rather than pragmatic, introduces tensions to the legislative process that it is not especially well adapted to manage. Problems are hard to solve through legislation when protagonists are unwilling to compromise their demands.

During the same period, there has been a proliferation of interest groups, which tend to focus on a narrow agenda. In the first generation after the Second World War, legislative lobbying was dominated by the major interests traditionally concerned with state legislation: the railroads, organized business, labor unions, and the Farm Bureau. For the most part, these groups dealt directly with policy issues before the Legislature. They drafted bills and amendments, buttonholed members, entertained them, and fed them information about the matters that concerned them. Beginning in the late sixties, the decline of political parties, the availability of technologies for communicating with blocs of people interested in narrow issues, and changes in campaign finance laws helped stimulate the growth of specialized group and corporate political action committees (PACs). The number and diversity of interest groups increased. Today, many of these groups spend substantial sums on indirectly influencing legislation through attempts to manipulate public opinion and increasingly focus their attention on political campaigns. As the cost of campaigning has increased and the availability of volunteers has declined, PACs have become major sources of legislative campaign contributions.

Together with the influence of television, political action committees have changed the nature of campaign finance and campaign strategy for legislators. Interest groups have become openly active in recruiting candidates to seek legislative office. As a result, some legislators have a stronger political base in group politics than in their local communities or districts. Television has become the medium of choice for public political information and has influenced the way in which the Legislature works, when it works, and how the public perceives it. Legislative leaders use television as the principal medium through which they define issues and as a platform for challenging their legislative opponents or the governor.

Against this backdrop of political change, the agenda of policy issues has also become more complex, and their resolution is often beset with controversy. In the period covered by this study, the Legislature has had to come to grips with financing of public education, tax reform, containment of health costs and reorganization of the health care industry, environmental regulation, the decline of agriculture and industries based on the state's natural resources, the impact of national and international economic restructuring on the state's economy, rural and urban economic development, abortion, child abuse, welfare reform, and the future of its land grant university, to mention only a few.

Changing Levels of Legislative Experience

Issues of this magnitude, controversy, complexity, and cost must be faced not only against a tableau of external change, but by an institution whose members are themselves constantly changing. From 1963 to 1988, 556 different people served in the House of Representatives and 234 served in the Senate. The average length of service for representatives was 7.8 years, just short of four 2-year terms. Senators served an average of 9.9 years, a little over two full terms. Half of all House members served 6 years or more, and half of the Senators served 8 years or more.

Different patterns of legislative service have occurred after each decennial reapportionment. Figure 2 illustrates the differences among the sixties, seventies, and eighties for members of the House. Figure 3 reports the patterns of service in the Senate. During the sixties, 265 people served in the House. Slightly more than one-fourth of them (71) were members for a single two-year term. This contrasts with the seventies and the eighties, when only one-fifth of those who served in the House lasted only one term. On the other hand, a substantial number of senior representatives—84 members with 10 years or more of experience—served during the sixties, offsetting the large number of people serving one term. It was these senior members who gave the House the appearance of stability it enjoyed during the sixties.

In the seventies only half as many representatives as in the sixties served longer than 16 years, and the number declined to half of that figure in the eighties, when only 7 members had been reelected eight times. But while the proportion who had 10 years or more experience dropped from almost one-third in the sixties to one-fourth of the members serving in the seventies, by 1987, a cadre of senior members had been rebuilt and the proportion of members with 10 years or more of legislative experience had almost returned to the level of the 1960s. The difference was that there were fewer members with more than 16 years of service, but a higher percentage with 10 to 16 years behind them.

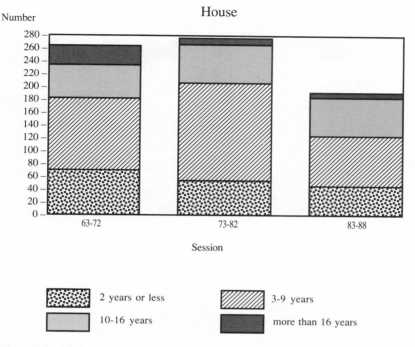

Figure 2. Legislative Experience of Members of the Minnesota House of Representatives

The cumulative level of experience in the House dropped to its lowest in 1973 and 1975, when the DFL gained control and many of the experienced conservative legislators who had dominated the House during the sixties retired or were defeated. There was a major generational turnover in the House. The average length of service dropped to 6.9 years for the decade, down from the 8.1 years of the sixties. Since 1983, the average length of service has climbed back to 7.4 years for all members serving.

Turning to the Senate, 2 of every 5 senators who served during the sixties and seventies had 10 years or more of senatorial experience. Some had, of course, also served in the House prior to their election to the Senate. The Senate retained a stable number of members with 10 years or more of experience through the sixties and seventies, although the number of very senior members dropped to 7 in the seventies.

The Senate has become a more experienced body in the eighties than it was in the two prior decades. Over half of those serving in the Senate in the eighties will have 10 years or more of experience in that body (assuming that those elected in 1986 complete their full term). There are fewer 20-year veterans in the current Senate than were there in the sixties, while there are as many with more than 16

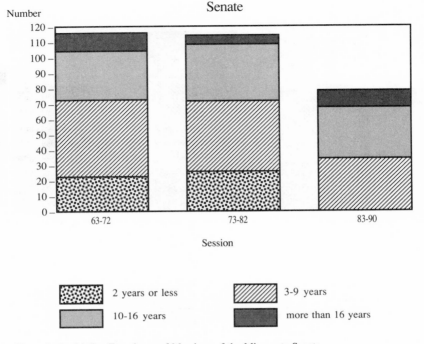

Figure 3. Legislative Experience of Members of the Minnesota Senate

years. Today, 1 of every 7 senators has been elected to four full terms, in contrast with only 1 in 13 during the seventies and 1 of 11 during the sixties. In general, the eighties has been the time of greatest stability in the Senate. The average length of service for an eighties' senator is 10.2 years. In the sixties it reached 9.2 years, but had declined in the seventies to 7.6 years.

Figure 4 shows the average experience members of the House and Senate had when they were elected to each term of office from 1963 to 1987. This is the time when experience counts in the organization of each house and assignment to committees. Looking at each session separately shows that the average level of experience declined from 9 years in the House and 6 in the Senate in 1963 to less than 4 years in the Senate and 6 in the House by 1975. But by 1987, the experience level of the House had recovered to stand at slightly more than 8 years. In the Senate it had risen to 6½ years.

Averages, however, do not tell the full story. In any session, new members normally are not assigned leadership tasks. New members are also a measure of turnover and stability in the Legislature from one session to another. High turnover means that there must be a substantial effort by the leadership to educate the new members and a considerable effort on the freshmen's part to "learn the

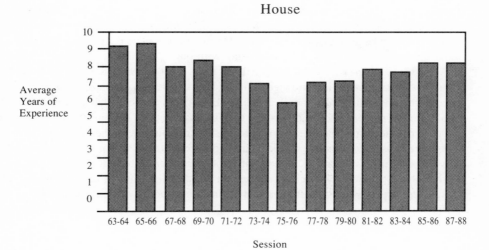

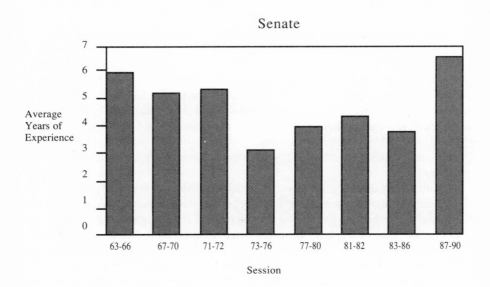

Figure 4. Prior Legislative Experience of Legislators When Elected to Each Term of Office

ropes," so they can become effective participants in the legislative process. Where turnover occurs is also important. If retirement and defeat replace a group of experienced committee members with freshmen, it may be difficult to keep up the same pace in the committee in dealing with policy problems.

Legislators generally acknowledge that it takes most members about 6 years to gain an effective working knowledge of the Legislature and to establish the contacts with and confidence of colleagues, lobbyists, and agencies that are essential to effective performance. Legislating is more than voting. It involves development of leadership capacities and craftsmanship in dealing with the intricacies of both the substance of policy and legislative procedures. It is important to have in every session a substantial number of experienced and able members among whom to distribute the burdens of leadership and detailed work. If key committee or leadership positions must be given to inexperienced members, the process tends to be slowed due to missteps and problems as they try to accelerate their progress on the learning curve.

Figure 5 shows the number of newly elected senators and representatives in each session of the Legislature since 1963. Twenty-three new senators—one-third of the total membership—were elected in 1963. There has been a significant deviation from this level of turnover in the Senate only twice. In 1973, 30 new senators took office as the control of the Senate switched from the conservatives to the DFL. The lowest turnover in 24 years was in 1987, when only 9 freshmen were seated.

There has been greater fluctuation in new membership in the House than in the Senate. Because House districts are half the size of Senate districts, the marginal impact of reapportionment on them tends to be greater. Consequently, there has been an increase in turnover following each reapportionment. The increased turnover in 1963, 1973, and 1983 reflects, in part, the effects of reapportionment, although other factors were also at work in those elections. Each reapportionment involved a change in control of the House. The greatest turnover occurred in 1975, when the "Watergate massacre" of the Independent-Republican party in Minnesota produced 55 new representatives—41 percent of the total membership.

Although control of the House has switched six times since 1973, turnover has tended to be low in the years when only representatives face the voters. Gubernatorial elections tend to increase turnover in the House by about 10 to 15 seats above the level of the last off-year. Control of the House has changed in only three gubernatorial elections, 1962, 1978, and 1986. In 1962, however, liberals lost control of the House even though the DFL candidate for governor, Karl Rolvaag, was elected after a recount in the closest gubernatorial election in Minnesota history.

One of the characteristics of both chambers in the early sixties was the number of members with 10 years or more of experience. Figure 6 shows how the number

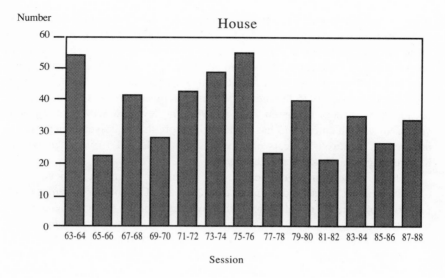

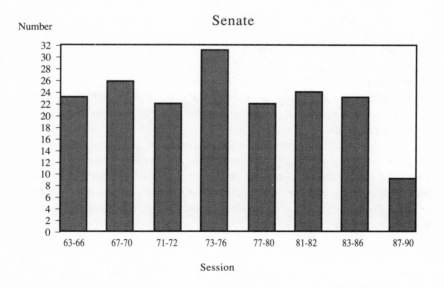

Figure 5. Number of Freshmen Legislators by Session

of senior legislators in each house has changed over the course of a generation. In 1963, 30 House members—over 1 of every 5—had served for 10 years or more when the session began. Fourteen of them had been in the House for over 20 years, of whom 3 had served more than 30 years. By 1975, only 13 members had served more than 10 years when the session convened, and none had 20 years of prior service. Since 1975 the number of senior representatives with more than a decade of experience had risen to 31 in 1987, but few now serve as long as 20 years. No session since 1975 has started with more than 3 20-year veterans, and no one had achieved 30 years of service since 1974 until 1987, when Willard Munger began his 31st year in the House.

In 1963, 12 senators, 1 of every 6, had 10 years or more of experience. Four of these senators had served for more than 20 years. The number of senior members rose to 15 in 1971, but dropped sharply in each of the next two Senate elections to a low of only 8 10-year veterans when the 1977 session began. A substantial number of the senators elected in the great turnover of 1971 stayed on, so that by 1981 the number of senior members had returned to 12 and by 1987 had reached 17. Veterans of 20 years were common in the sixties and earlier, but such long service has been unusual since 1971. One member of the 1987 Senate, Jerome Hughes, the senate president, had served 20 years, but by the end of the term in 1990, 5 more senators will have two decades of service.

As in the House, a substantial shift of seats following a reapportionment could again reduce the experience level of the Senate. Otherwise, Senate seats seem fairly immune to any coattail effect from gubernatorial or presidential elections. Only three gubernatorial elections in the last two decades have coincided with Senate elections, those of 1970, 1982, and 1986. Wendell Anderson's 1970 victory did not produce a liberal triumph in the Senate, but the conservative majority was cut from 45 to 34 members—a margin of control of a single vote. In 1982, the DFL lost two seats in spite of winning the governorship. In 1986, the DFL picked up five seats.

A principal reason for concern about the number and proportion of senior members in each house is to be able to fill key leadership positions, especially committee chairs, with experienced people who are familiar with the legislative issues coming before the committees, and the agencies and groups that will advocate and oppose policies. Figure 7 shows the experience level of committee chairs in each house since 1963.

Senate committee chairs were substantially more experienced in the sixties than in any later period. The average experience of Senate committee chairs dropped as the conservative majority diminished, and has grown as the DFL stabilized its control in recent years. It reached its low mark, as would be expected, when control switched to the DFL in 1973. Since that time, the experience of Senate chairs has gradually recovered and now is near 1963 levels.

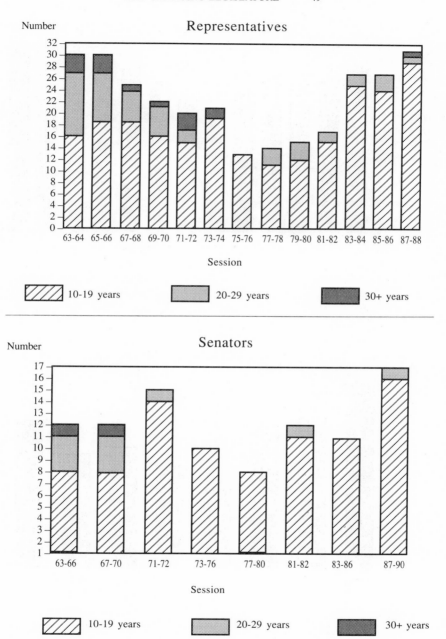

Figure 6. Number of Senior Legislators by Session

House Committee Chairs

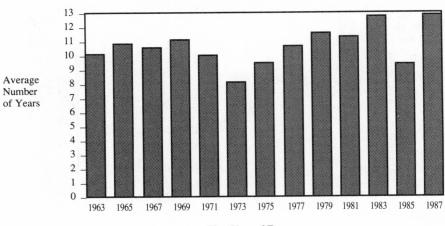

Senate Committee Chairs

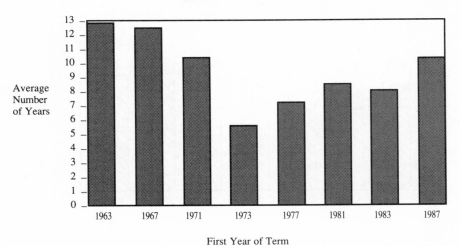

Figure 7. Experience of Committee Chairs in the Minnesota Legislature

From 1963 through 1972, House committee chairs were slightly less experienced than their Senate counterparts. Since then, they have had as much or more experience. House committee chairs had the least experience in the 1973 and 1985 sessions, when there were major changes in party control and the new majority in the House had relatively few senior members in its ranks.

The average length of service for legislators declined during the 1970s, but has generally been restored in recent years. By 1987 it was only slightly lower than it had been a generation ago. Actual exposure of members to legislative activity has increased for each year served, however, due to the fact that since 1973 the Legislature has been in session every year. Thus, it is possible for a member elected since that time to have more exposure to the legislative process during each term of office than one elected earlier. The quality of exposure is a different matter. That is affected by the pace of action, the depth of involvement in substantive and procedural matters, and the levels of responsibility exercised by the member. Relatively few representatives with less than three terms of experience or senators with less than two terms can expect to chair significant committees, although a few may receive appointments as vice-chairs or as assistant floor leaders. The quality of policymaking cannot but be affected when nearly half of the members in any one session do not have experience in handling major legislative responsibilities. One of the problems that leaders of all periods mentioned was the difficulty of finding enough able members to take on the most important assignments.

Table 1. Mean and Median Ages of Representatives and Senators in Selected Sessions

Year	Representatives		Senators	
	Mean	Median	Mean	Median
1963	48.24	47	50.28	49
1973	42.31	41	44.49	44
1975	40.76	38		
1983	44.48	42	42.73	41
1987	45.91	45	47.43	46

The average age of members follows roughly the same trajectory as experience—falling during the seventies and rising again in the eighties. Table 1 shows the mean and median ages of representatives and senators for selected years from 1963 to 1987. Except for 1983, senators were slightly older than representatives. The change in party control in 1973 had a more pronounced effect on the age of House members than on senators. The youngest House was seated in 1975, the year of highest turnover when half the members were 38 or younger. The youngest Senate, in contrast, was seated in 1983. The Legislature in 1987 was only

Number of Women

House

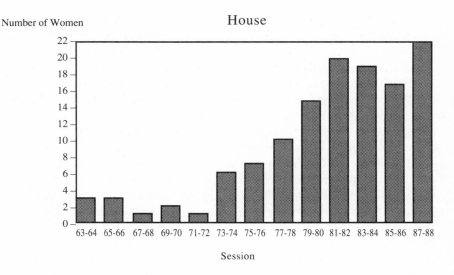

Session

Number of Women

Senate

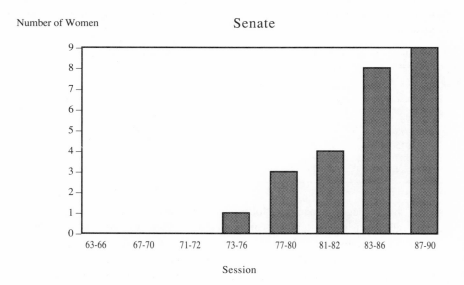

Session

Figure 8. Number of Women in the Minnesota Legislature

slightly younger than in 1963, hardly enough to attribute any changes in behavior to youthful folly.

Changes in Gender and Occupation

Members of today's Legislature are only slightly less experienced than in the early sixties, but they are different in other ways. As shown in Figure 8, only 3 women served in the House in 1963; none served in the Senate. In 1987, 22 representatives and 9 senators were women. Women were elected as majority leaders of the House in 1985 and again at the end of the 1987 session.

When the Legislature met for one 120-day session every other year, a substantial number of attorneys found it possible — even good for business — to serve. They could afford to be away from their practices for these short, intermittent periods. Since the advent of the flexible session, the number of lawyers in the Senate has declined from 24 in 1963 to 10 in the 1987 session, as shown in table 2. In the House, table 2 shows that the number of attorneys has declined from 27 in 1963 to 12 in the 1987 session. At one point (the 1981-82 session) only 9 attorneys were in the House.

The number of farmers in the Senate has been relatively stable, ranging from 12 to 15 members in all but two periods. Only 9 served in 1971–72 and 18 in 1981–82. During the sixties and the early seventies the number of farmers in the House fluctuated between 29 and 37 members. A sharp drop occurred in 1975 and a further decline in 1977 to a low of 18. Since that time, the number of farmers in the House has increased and reached 27 by 1987.

In 1963 only 16 Senators listed a business as their principal occupation, but during the late sixties and early seventies the number of businesspeople in the Senate increased, only to drop off again in the eighties. In 1987, 19 Senators were in business. Except for the seventies, the number of House members with business backgrounds has remained at 39 or more. The high point for members with business backgrounds was the 1985–86 session when 50 were elected. Interestingly, more DFL than IR Representatives listed a business affiliation as their principal occupation during that session.

The greatest increase in occupational representation among members of the Legislature has been in teachers and educators. Only 3 senators in 1963 were professional educators, compared with 9 in 1987. In the House, the number of educators has risen during the same period from 6 to 21.

The other occupational category that has increased dramatically in both houses is legislator, indicating that the member reports that his or her legislative duties are the principal occupation. No senator reported legislator as a principal occupation until 1983, when 1 did. In 1987, 4 senators considered their principal occupation to be their legislative duties. In the House, only 1 legislator was listed until 1975, when 4 appeared. The number then declined with none being listed in

Table 2. Occupations of Legislators

Year	Business	Farmer	Attorney	Educator	Full-time Legislator	Other
House of Representatives						
1963	43	37	27	6	0	22
1965	44	37	26	6	0	22
1967	44	31	32	5	0	26
1969	41	29	30	6	0	29
1971	37	35	32	17	0	20
1973	30	31	25	16	0	32
1975	33	24	19	24	4	30
1977	34	18	11	25	3	43
1979	37	21	12	21	1	42
1981	43	23	9	21	0	38
1983	39	25	11	28	11	20
1985	50	23	11	19	11	20
1987	42	27	12	21	14	18
Senate						
1963–66	25	13	25	2	0	2
1967–70	28	9	23	5	0	2
1971–72	24	12	22	6	0	3
1973–76	29	13	13	8	0	4
1977–80	24	13	12	8	0	10
1981–82	12	18	12	9	0	16
1983–86	14	17	11	8	1	16
1987–90	19	14	10	9	4	11

1981. Beginning in 1983, however, 11 were listed for that session and for the 1985–86 session. Fourteen members considered legislating to be their principal occupation in the 1987 session. While these numbers represent dramatic increases, they are still quite small as a proportion of the whole Legislature. It is also significant that a survey of people who served in the Legislature during the 1980s found that 88 percent felt that legislative service should not be a full-time occupation (Backstrom, 1986).

Today's legislators are better educated than those of a generation ago. Very few do not have some postsecondary education. Figure 9 shows the highest levels of education attained by members in selected years. There has been a gradual increase in the number of members with four years or more of higher education. The dip, during the seventies, in the number with postgraduate degrees reflects, in part, the decline in lawyers in the Legislature. In the eighties more members with other postgraduate training are replacing lawyers at the upper end of the education spectrum. The educational attainment of legislators suggests that more

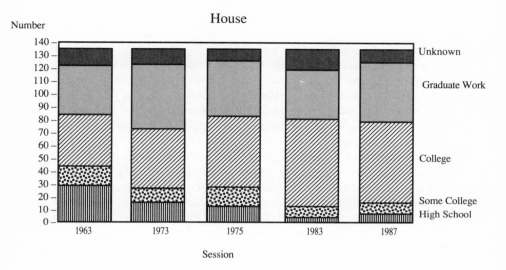

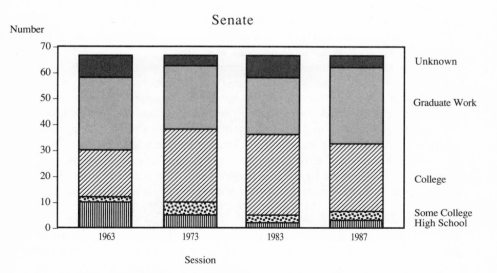

Figure 9. Education Levels of Minnesota Legislators in Selected Years

members today have trained capacities for reasoning, making critical judgments, and independent thinking—all attributes that should be valued in a legislature. These very qualities, however, demand a different style of leadership and a process that makes it possible to use the talent assembled in each house.

The changes in the characteristics of the members of the House and Senate have both reflected and accelerated other changes in the way in which the Legislature works. The influx of less experienced members to both Houses in the 1970s provided strong support for greater openness in the legislative process, especially since a number of them were elected in 1972 on a platform of opening legislative committees to public scrutiny. The loss of senior members, particularly in the House, reduced the Legislature's institutional memory and made possible changes in procedure and decorum. At the same time, it seems probable that the simultaneous retirement of the more experienced leaders and the introduction of party designation strengthened the formal leadership institutions of both houses, accelerating trends toward centralization of power.

Except for the seventies, when turnover was at its highest, the Legislature has maintained a substantial number of members who might be described as legislative careerists, although they also followed other occupations. In recent years, there has been an increase in the number without other occupations. Throughout the period there has been a high number of members who served only a single term, or at most two.

These facts raise complex questions about the notion of a citizen-legislature. In one respect, this concept is analogous to the citizen-soldiers, who put aside their real calling or occupation to serve for an emergency, then return once the need has passed. Similarly, citizens take time out from their regular work to represent their neighbors at the Capitol, but only for a short time and only part of the year. Legislative work is not to be regarded as a career.

While the idea of the citizen-legislator retains great support, historically many legislators were dual careerists, maintaining an occupation but serving 10 or more years in the Legislature—a substantial legislative career. Leaders, especially, have had longer than average careers in the Legislature. It seems clear that effectiveness and mastery of policy rises with tenure. In this sense, at least there may be a substantial public interest in encouraging members to serve longer than three House or two Senate terms. It is therefore troubling to see the large number of members who leave the Legislature between their 10th and 16th years of service, when they should be expected to be at the peak of their effectiveness and power.

Building a legislative career, however, tends to require a sacrifice of one's "real" career in business or a profession. The most serious conflict in legislative and professional careers is reflected in the decline in the number of lawyers serving in the Legislature. This decline corresponds to the increasing demands on the time of members for regular session and other business. Does this mean that the

Legislature has developed to the point that it is impractical for people from some lines of work to consider serving? The increase in the number of members with no occupation but legislator raises a related question: Has the legislative work-load become so heavy that a person can really make it a full-time job? Where these perspectives are combined, it forces consideration of whether Minnesota can have an effective Legislature, with a number of experienced and competent members leading it, if it operates on a part-time basis.

How we answer this question will depend on our understanding of how the Legislature works in practice as opposed to theory, and it is to that inquiry we now turn.

4

The House of Representatives

As the members and leaders of the Minnesota House of Representatives have changed, so have the practices of the House. Though not part of the formal structure or rules, certain practices, customs, and folkways become norms of conduct that define the culture of the House.

In this sense, the House is more than a formal constitutional body that is part of the government of the state. It also is a social organization, with a history, customs, and traditions that include but go well beyond the constitutional description. In the 24 years covered by this study, there were many changes in membership, staffing, physical accommodations, and procedure. Combined with reapportionment, annual sessions, party designation, open meetings, and the introduction of computers to help members analyze issues, all these changes have altered the feel and behavior of the House. But many of the fundamental folkways and customs have survived, or they have adapted to new circumstances, producing a distinctive organizational culture that has changed more slowly than outward appearances might suggest. This culture may tell us more than the formal rules about how the Legislature really works. It helps us assess the possibilities for and limitations on reform or change. Because culture is both a product and shaper of history, it must be understood in the context of time.

The House is Serious but Not Stuffy

One of the first things a new observer of the House is likely to notice is its informality. Its rules concerning decorum are lax, at least in comparison with the Senate. Members have long been allowed on the floor without coats and ties.

They are not admonished for eating or reading at their desks during the session. They address each other by name, rather than as "The representative from [District or County]."

Though the House is no club, membership in it is special and is not taken lightly. The House gives wide latitude to the behavior of its members. The most traumatic event in House proceedings is a challenge to an elected member's right to sit. The unseating of Robert Pavlak in 1979 and the censure of Randolph Staten in 1986 were deep emotional issues for most members, regardless of how they viewed the merits of either case. The House tends to shelter its members from assault by any quarter on their right to sit once elected.

The informality of the House has historical roots. Until the 1970s, no members, except for the speaker and the majority leader, had private offices. Committee chairs used their committee rooms as offices if another committee was not meeting in them. The ordinary member had only a desk on the floor of the House. Except for a small joint staff of legislative analysts and attorneys from the Office of the Revisor of Statutes, then attached to the supreme court, there was no professional staff to assist members in drafting bills, conducting research, or serving constituents. Correspondence was handled through a common secretarial pool. Members met constituents on the floor when the House was not in session. If a member needed to use a telephone, there was a bank of them available in the hall. After he became speaker in 1963, Lloyd Duxbury closed the chamber to visitors an hour before sessions began to give members a little time free of interruptions.

In spite of these difficult working conditions, the House was a relaxed and congenial body. Rod Searle remembered it as a place where there was a lot of mutual respect and camaraderie; there was more fun and humor than in later years. Members were not seated by caucus affiliation, so close friendships developed across political lines. Contact with colleagues was unavoidable due to the fact that, for most members, their work at the Capitol had to be done in the House chamber. There was, therefore, a wide sharing of knowledge and expertise, and informality was as much a necessity as a choice.

While the necessities of the earlier era no longer prevail, the custom of informality has continued. While a few members complain that the House often looks (and is) a bit chaotic, most appear to agree with Speaker David Jennings (1985–86), who could often be found presiding in his shirt sleeves, that too much formality just got in the way of getting the business done expeditiously. Some members even appear to take perverse pleasure in the discomfort their casual ways give members of the Senate.

The Majority Party Runs the House

Of all its unwritten rules, the most important is that the majority party runs the

House. The evolution of the caucus into the most important extraconstitutional factor in the culture of the House has occurred over several decades. The development is all the more remarkable for having occurred at the same time that political parties generally were declining in importance as instruments of governance.

In the nonpartisan Legislature, the main function of the caucus was to organize the House. It was also an important social grouping of legislators who generally shared a political approach to government. In some elections, the caucus itself endorsed House candidates, especially incumbents. Although members were not elected on a partisan ballot, most candidates for the Legislature declared their intention, if elected, to affiliate with the conservative or liberal caucus. A few members, like Lloyd Duxbury, waited until they were elected and had a chance to attend both caucuses before deciding which to join. While most members were also affiliated with the national parties, the conservative leaders were sensitive about being identified as Republicans. The liberals, however, were more openly members of the DFL, and most of them yearned for party designation on the ballot, figuring they would be helped by statewide candidates like Hubert Humphrey and Eugene McCarthy.

A Member Votes with the Caucus on All Procedural Issues

Caucus discipline is required on the organization of the House and on votes on rules and other procedural matters. Members of the caucus are expected to take their cues on procedural issues from their respective floor leaders. It is generally considered better to take a walk (absent oneself from the chamber) on a procedural issue than to vote against the leadership. It is particularly bad form to vote against a ruling by the speaker of one's own party, although such behavior has, in rare instances, been tolerated if there were enough other votes to sustain the speaker.

In recent years, caucus discipline has been expected on substantive legislative issues more often than in earlier years, when it was rarely invoked on specific bills. Roy Dunn, the conservative leader in the fifties, would, according to Duxbury, explain a bill in detail to the caucus, make his own position clear, and then admonish his group to "vote your conscience." Speakers and majority leaders called caucus meetings sparingly after the session was organized. Today, both party caucuses meet frequently, at least weekly once the session is in full gear, and it is not unusual to have daily caucus sessions during the busiest period of the session to keep members abreast of the legislative priorities of their leaders.

Even though it did not bind its members to vote with the majority on specific bills, cohesion on substance of legislation in the conservative caucus was high, in spite of occasionally bitter battles for organizational control between the "progressives" such as Aubrey Dirlam and the more conservative faction led by Duxbury. Until 1962, most of the conservative members represented rural and non-metropolitan districts. A high percentage of these members boarded at the Ryan Hotel, in St. Paul, for the entire session. They ate breakfast and dinner together, drank together after the session, and met there with lobbyists and constituents. They were virtually marinated in politics and legislative policy in this environment, so formal caucuses were unnecessary. By the time an issue had been developed by committee and reached the floor, members knew how they were supposed to vote. The system of discipline was benign, but effective, based as much on social pressure as on the overt exercise of political power. Strong leadership was important, however. When Duxbury retired as speaker, the old factional rivalry resurfaced in the conservative caucus during the 1971–72 session, when the margin of control was down to five votes.

Since the advent of party designation in 1974, Independent-Republicans have continued to enjoy relatively high cohesion in their voting. Although the socialization of the caucus provided by common living arrangements has long since evaporated with more efficient commuting and dispersed housing of members, the IR caucus has either been fairly small, as in the mid-seventies, just short of a majority, or in control of the House by a small margin. Speaker David Jennings argued that small margins contribute to cohesion because all members recognize that a single defection on any issue can impair the effectiveness of the entire group. Thus, while there may be strong disagreement within the caucus, members have been willing to accept tight discipline once a caucus position has been defined. And the social pressure to conform is intense.

The liberal caucus was less cohesive than the conservatives. Its membership consisted of three groups in uneasy alliance: representatives from Minneapolis and St. Paul, the Iron Rangers, and the rural remnants of the Farmer-Labor party. The city representatives went home at night and did not socialize as much with their colleagues who could not travel to their distant districts. Infrequent experience in the exercise of power due to near permanent minority status also gave the caucus leaders little leverage over wayward members. An extraordinary leader, like Fred Cina, could, however, generate enough loyalty and enthusiasm to make the liberal caucus operate as an effective force in the House, especially when working with a DFL governor. The liberals captured control of the House in 1957 and held it through 1962; that was their only period of control between 1938 and 1973.

The DFL caucus has inherited many of the characteristics of its liberal predecessor, but not its permanent minority status. Cohesion has not been the caucus's strong suit, although during the seventies it held such large majorities that defections were of little consequence and could be tolerated by the leadership. Factional defections, such as those by the rural "Wood Ticks" during the 1984 session, when the margin of control was thin, presented the leadership with a serious problem in maintaining control of the legislative program.

While the customs of the House do not generally require loyalty to the caucus on specific legislation, new members learn quickly that they should vote with the leadership of their caucus. One member recalled a "counseling session" with Speaker Martin Sabo after she had asserted her independence on a bill that was important to the leadership: "You rarely can go wrong if you stick with your leaders," he reminded her.

Members Are Not to Be Punished for Voting
Their Districts or Their Convictions

If discipline is regularly required only on procedural votes, and occasionally invoked on specific bills or amendments, it follows that members generally should not be disciplined by their leaders for votes that reflect personal convictions. A vote against the leader may also be tolerated if the matter is crucial in the member's district and adherence to the caucus position would be likely to endanger reelection. In either case, however, surprises are not appreciated. A defector is expected to notify the leader and gain approval for the vote or abstention. Defection may not be approved if the vote is expected to be so close that one or two members could make the difference.

Discipline, in its harshest form, involves removal from a treasured committee assignment or chair. But it can also take lesser forms, such as not being assigned to a conference committee, losing authorship on a bill that is important to one's constituency, or not being invited to join a delegation making an out-of-state visit or attending a national or international convention or study tour. Leaders are expected to discipline members who break ranks on a binding caucus vote, but there are few such votes. Leaders are expected to overlook other defections, and especially they are expected to accept mere disagreements over the course of policy in either caucus or bilateral discussions.

Leaders who do not accept these norms of behavior are likely to lose their hold on power in the House. In 1980, a number of DFLers rebelled against their leader, Irv Anderson, whom they felt had punished them for prior policy disagreements or for personal reasons by denying them the committee positions in 1979 that they had expected by virtue of experience and geography. Twenty-six members bolted the caucus, which had voted to support Anderson for speaker, and formed a coalition with the Independent-Republicans to elect Fred Norton, one of the anti-Anderson DFLers, as speaker.

Norton later paid for his own violation of the unwritten rule that one must maintain loyalty to the caucus on organizational matters by being denied a second term as speaker in 1981. As his faction grew in strength, however, and after the retirement of Anderson and many members of that faction, Norton regained power, first as minority leader in 1985, and finally as speaker in 1987. In part, his action can be seen as violation of one custom to vindicate another. There also appears to be some recognition, even among those who stayed loyal to Anderson, that he had abused his trust as a leader, and that the action by Norton and his faction was justifiable.

The Speaker Runs the Caucus

Almost paradoxical to the informality and apparent casualness of the House, there is widespread acceptance among members of the idea that if they are to get anything done, they need strong, centralized leadership. Thus, almost all of the leaders interviewed for this study accepted the notion that the speaker alone should appoint committees and run the House. One argued, however, that the centralization of appointment power made the speaker too powerful, and instead favored establishment of a committee on committees, similar to the practice in the Senate, to select chairs and committee members.

The culture of the House demands that the speaker be more than a party leader. As the presiding officer, the speaker also has an obligation to the entire body to foster and protect its traditions and to represent the interests of the whole House, not only its majority, in dealings with other parts of the government and with the public. Speakers are expected to be partisans who are fair in their dealings with the opposition. Lloyd Duxbury and Martin Sabo perhaps best personify the ideal speakers, who most closely embodied the cultural expectations of the institution. Both were unquestionably in charge of both their caucuses and the House. Duxbury, who became speaker in 1963, was regarded by his contemporaries with a mixture of fear and reverence. He centralized power in the House in the office of the speaker. His authority was seldom challenged and never challenged successfully. Even opponents, such as Irv Anderson, who later served as DFL majority leader in the seventies, remember "Dux" with affection, even when recalling that "the majority ran [the caucus] with an iron fist . . . [it] was a very closed process." Sabo's recollection was similar: Duxbury "was very quick in the chair, and he was fair. . . . He took me to the cleaners a couple of times." Sabo was likewise remembered with affection by partisans and opponents: "Sabo was the best speaker. . . . He was interested in each and every piece of legislation. Sabo was a leader and an inspiration."

Seniority Matters, but It Is Not an Absolute

Seniority remains an important consideration in the affairs of the House. In earlier times it was a near absolute in making committee appointments, but even in those days it was not the meticulously ranked system that prevailed for many years in the U.S. Congress. Adherence to seniority and deference to committee chairs have not endured. Senior members of the majority party can still reasonably expect a favorable committee assignment, and probably can expect to be chair of a committee or a major division of a committee. But seniority generally has yielded to the power of the speaker to exercise wide discretion in making selections. Every speaker since Duxbury has selected less senior members for positions on important committees including Appropriations, Taxes and Tax Laws, and Education Aid committees. In other words, the speaker does not have to follow a preset pecking order based on length of service, doling out the most important positions to the most senior members.

The customs of the House demand that the speaker give great attention to the balance of the committee membership among geographic and ideological interests. Geographic balance has become one of the most important considerations in the selection of committee members.

As turnover increased and average tenure declined during the seventies, the customary deference shown by new members to their elders also degenerated. When Aubrey Dirlam was elected to the House in 1940, great deference was afforded senior members and the chairs of committees. New members learned quickly that they should vote with the leaders of their caucus and the chairs of their committees and keep quiet, at least until they had completed one full term. According to Dirlam, new members would not even be recognized by the speaker to participate in debate until after they had made a memorable maiden speech.

Dirlam learned early in his legislative career that the unwritten rules of deference to senior members were enforced by social pressures and political displeasure when he offered an amendment to an appropriations bill. One simply did not challenge the chair of the Appropriations Committee on "his" bill. Committee chairs held life-and-death power over bills. A junior member who wanted his or her bills to see daylight, did nothing to irritate the chair.

As deference to seniority has declined, so has deference to the chairs of committees. It is no longer considered unacceptable for a member of a committee who has lost a bill or amendment in the committee deliberations to challenge the position of the committee on the floor. With some regularity, members bring to the floor amendments that were previously defeated in committee. While they do not usually prevail, it is not considered a breach of etiquette, as it once was, to try. This change in custom appears to result in part from lax enforcement of the deadline for the introduction and reporting of bills to the point that such behavior is almost sanctioned by the customs of the House.

The Real Work of the House is in Committee

The focal point of work and debate in the House traditionally was the committee room, not the floor of the House chamber. Experienced members became highly specialized and expert in the areas of legislation assigned to their committees. Among these members there was almost a passion for detailed mastery of legislative formulas and language. Those few who mastered the details were heavily relied upon by others for guidance. In recent years, members appear to rely less on expert colleagues for cues on how to vote, but continue to rely on them to gain understanding of complex legislation or to certify its technical acceptability.

The House system focuses on those in charge. A few members stand out as workhorses and policy experts. Others are virtually anonymous and seem at times to be mere "pet rocks" of the leaders or interest groups. The House committee system, said Senate President Jerome Hughes, produces (in contrast to the Senate) "more competence and less experience." In recent years, the influence of the expert members has been eroded with the introduction of computers in the House Research Department. It is now possible for members with no understanding at all of funding formulas to find out quickly how a committee bill might affect their districts and to order staff to draft amendments to alter the result.

As in the House as a whole, the majority party controls the process and the product. Committee chairs have extensive control over the agenda of the committee, but there is no common practice with regard to their openness to sharing that power with colleagues. Some run a tight ship, permitting little dissent and virtually relegating minority members to the role of protesting observers. Others are more democratic and informal, taking ideas from any source, and distributing credit and authorship widely. While the general rule is that a chair may run a committee with a pretty free hand, the days are gone when committees were closed not only to the public, but often to other members of the House who were not members of the committee. Gone also are the days when it was not uncommon for the chair to have the only copy of the bill being considered.

Cycles of Partisan Retaliation and Retribution

The House is intensely partisan, with the majority caucus firmly in control of committees and the floor. The minority has little role in shaping legislation. The function of the minority is less to work on legislation as such than to challenge the majority by presenting alternatives that are certain to be defeated, whatever their merits, and to lay the political groundwork for the next election. Since 1983 at least, this situation has influenced minority leaders to pay relatively little attention to development of detailed amendments designed to perfect legislation or to attract compromise majorities in committee or on the floor. Instead, both David Jennings and Fred Norton focused their efforts as minority leaders on policy themes that emphasized partisan differences as a basis for the coming election campaigns. The two-year election cycle contributes to the high degree of partisanship, as members are almost constantly campaigning and concerned with fund-raising and interest-group or constituency reaction to policy proposals.

Before the late seventies, the control of the House was relatively stable. The House had been controlled by the conservatives for a decade before the liberal victory in 1972. Party designation, which became effective in the 1974 elections, helped the DFL maintain control until 1978. Beginning with the 1978 elections, control of the House has been unstable, and the majority, when there was one, was quite narrow until the strong DFL victory in 1986. Control has shifted four times since 1978, and neither party has controlled the House for more than four consecutive years. Thus, any election could shift control. Not only did this intensify the partisan combat in the House, but it produced a cycle of retaliation by the successive majorities that has become a central feature of the contemporary culture of the House. As each party assumed power, it used its organizational and procedural power to humiliate the minority, producing a thirst for revenge among those members who could hardly wait for their turn in power to get even.

The roots of this dismal cycle were planted in the successful 1979 fight to unseat Representative Robert Pavlak for election law violations. After Pavlak was expelled, a DFLer replaced him in the special election to fill his seat, giving the DFL a two-seat majority and the ability to elect the speaker. Independent-Republicans felt betrayed by the process, which they felt was used unfairly to unseat Pavlak, solely to shift control of the House. Connie Levi described the Pavlak affair as "the blackest day in the history of the legislature. . . . " Those who remember it, she said, have less confidence in the process. She and other leaders of the IR majority in the 1985–86 House trace the decline in decorum, manners, conduct, and language in the House to that incident.

This reaction was undoubtedly intensified by the fact that half of the Independent-Republican caucus were freshmen. They lacked the "bench depth" to use the rules to oppose effectively the challenge to Pavlak led by Irv Anderson, the wily and experienced DFL leader. Jerry Knickerbocker, one of the more experienced Independent-Republican leaders then in the Legislature, claims that the Pavlak incident poisoned the working relationship between the parties in that session and in later ones. Representative John Himle, who was elected in 1980, pointed out that trust underlies the legislative process, and when something happens that diminishes trust, members retreat to the arena where they can trust each other—the party caucus.

Service in the House Is a Part-Time Job

Since the adoption of the flexible-session amendment, the legislature has been in session every year. This fact has had a powerful influence on the culture of the House. Members elected in the sixties or earlier could genuinely look at their legislative service as a regular but minor invasion of their normal work life. They expected to spend 3 or 4 months every two years in St. Paul, and a few days during the remaining 18 to 20 months attending to legislative business. While more than today served for long periods in the legislature, none regarded it as their primary career. Even the earlier speakers and majority leaders were successfully able to carry on other businesses or professions.

As noted in Chapter 3, with the coming of annual sessions, a small but growing fraction of members have come to consider legislating their principal or sole occupation. While only 1 in 13 regards legislative service as a primary occupation, 1 in 7 ranks it as at least a concurrent secondary job (Backstrom, 1986). The realities of yearly sessions and more frequent committee meetings, however, conflict with the claims of "real jobs" for the time of some members, especially those in positions of leadership in the House. With annual sessions, "mentally you never leave being in the Legislature," said an assistant party leader.

The occupational classes from which House members are drawn have narrowed. Turnover has increased, although the reasons are not entirely clear. Surprisingly, most members do not complain that legislative duties place undue pressure on incomes and family life (Backstrom, 1986). Many thoughtful members, however, remain concerned about the stresses of legislative life that contribute to family problems, divorces, and instances of alcoholism and drug abuse.

Those in leadership positions report that they spend virtually full time at their legislative jobs. Some members, like Knickerbocker, who served through the transition period, see the growth in the number of careerists diminishing the quality of the Legislature in several ways. They argue that members who regard being a legislator as their sole occupation are more inclined to reflect interest-group positions and pander to public expectations to maintain strong electoral support. As more members see the House as a step on a career ladder in politics, competition among members and partisanship increase. There is less allegiance to the institution or to a broader concept of public interest, and more to self-advancement. As Ron Seiloff put it, the House, as a good stepping stone for a career, makes for impatience.

Leaders who were interviewed were divided in their attitudes toward the future of the citizen-legislator. Charles Weaver regarded the citizen-legislator as a thing of the past, but noted that legislative pay was currently too low to attract members of as high a quality as had once been able to serve. He agreed with Knickerbocker that full-time members are too reactive to the electorate. He observed that trying to be responsive to constituents tends to kill thought about major policy questions, and reduces the thoughtfulness of the discussions in committee and on the floor.

Respect for the Institution Is Low

As these comments suggest, perhaps the greatest change in the culture of the House in the last generation has been the diminished sense of history and institutional memory that was carried by the more senior members. Instead of institutional memory, there is memory of the short-term interparty and factional disputes of the past decade. Ann Wynia lamented that in the last 10 years the perspective has become too short—only to the next election. Tom Osthoff, a maverick in his early legislative career, pointed out that with tenure, legislators become more respectful of the institution. Some leaders, however—Jennings is an example—argued that one of the problems of the older system was that members served too long and developed too much reverence for the institution and allowed themselves to be distracted by sentiment from their duty to enact policy changes demanded by the public, even if so acting meant overriding some of the old institutional norms.

As the institutional culture of the House has evolved, the House has changed in the way it works and in the way its members and leaders behave. Paradoxically, its informality in procedure and decorum is balanced with a system of tight, central control and intense, often bitter partisan competition. Because so much of the operational quality of the House turns on the speakership, it is to that office the analysis now turns.

The Speaker

From 1963 to 1987, seven men served as speakers of the House of Representatives. Each was a product of his time and political circumstances and each had a distinctive style and approach to the office. Each contributed to the evolution of the office into one of the most powerful positions in state government, second only to the governorship in its influence on public policy. The paths they took to power and the ways in which they used their powers help us understand the office as it stands today and its significance in the Legislature.

Paths to Power

Duxbury and the Rise of the Modern Speaker (1963–70)

Lloyd Duxbury set the standard for the modern speakership. Before him there were several strong speakers, but much of the power in the House had been shared with the majority leader. Roy Dunn, for example, had refused the speakership because he viewed it as a less significant office than the majority leadership.

Duxbury first ran for a seat in the House in 1950. He was not endorsed by the conservative caucus or the Republican party. He never considered himself an active partisan and, although a Republican for national election purposes, he did not believe that party designations were appropriate for state legislators. When he arrived in the House, he received invitations to join both caucuses, but joined the conservatives as "the lesser of two evils." He was appointed to the Appropriations Committee and came under the less-than-tender tutelage of Claude Allen, the autocratic chair of that committee.

Duxbury learned about the legislative process by "sitting around and listening" to the older members. Like most of his nonmetropolitan conservative colleagues, Duxbury stayed at the Ryan Hotel during the session. Legislators met for breakfasts and dinners as if living in a boardinghouse. According to several members from that era, many decisions were made in the evenings at the hotel, over dinner or drinks. Committee meetings were occasionally held at the hotel, and that is where members could expect to meet with lobbyists, who were always ready to pick up the tab for dinner or drinks. A few lobbyists even had established rooms where a legislator could go for a drink or a meal almost any evening.

Duxbury never chaired a standing committee because by the time he had enough seniority, the conservatives were in the minority (from 1957 to 1963). By 1959, Duxbury, a feisty and witty legislator, had learned the ropes from masters such as Allen and long-time conservative leader Dunn. He was ready to take on the progressive wing of the caucus in a fight for the minority leadership and ousted Aubrey Dirlam from that job in 1959. Winning the position, he made it his mission to "ride herd on the liberals." By his account, he "ran them into the ground," and the conservatives returned to control of the House in 1963.

Duxbury then faced a decision whether to run for speaker or majority leader. He had reservations about being speaker, which involved responsibility for the operation of the House. He also savored the role of majority leader, which allowed him to enter into the debates, for which he had great zest. Ultimately, he yielded to others in his faction and stood for speaker, but only after being assured that Richard Fitzsimons would accept the chair of the Appropriations Committee. Duxbury saw this as the pivotal committee in the House, and wanted a chair whose policy and judgment he could trust.

Opposed in the caucus by Dirlam, Duxbury won the bitter battle by a single vote, and had to accept Dirlam as majority leader. The election of the two opponents to leadership positions, however, helped solidify the caucus under Duxbury's leadership. Some hard feelings remained, however, throughout Duxbury's term as speaker.

Duxbury met with every member to discuss preferences for committee assignments, and tried to see that each got one high-priority assignment, within the custom of the House that chairs must be assigned on the basis of seniority. Duxbury honored the custom, but made sure that if a chair was weak, he had a strong "speaker's man" on each committee to carry the important bills. Duxbury discussed minority assignments with the minority leader, Fred Cina, with whom he had a warm personal relationship in spite of sharp political differences. He made the assignments of minority members himself, however, and made sure that all members knew that their appointments were his alone.

Dirlam: The Speaker as Broker (1971–72)

Aubrey Dirlam had a lifelong passion for politics. In 1937, he sought and received a patronage job as a doorman for the House of Representatives. According to his account, he was not a very good doorkeeper, since he was too interested in the proceedings of the House to give his full attention to the job. The sergeant at arms of the House rescued him by offering him a job as a janitor so he could spend most of the daytime hours watching the Legislature at work. Before the next campaign year, Dirlam's patron died, leaving vacant the seat in his home district. He filed and lost his first race by 138 votes. On the second try, he was elected.

Although his interest remained high, Dirlam reported that he had no real grasp of the legislative process until well into his third term. His passion for the House made him one of its best "utility" members. He served on nearly every committee. Dirlam did not aspire to leadership in his early years in the Legislature, but in 1957, when the liberals gained control in the House, he was elected minority leader. He was then serving in his 16th year as a member of the House. In 1963, he was talked into being the progressives' candidate against Duxbury, who had ousted him from the minority leadership in 1959.

Dirlam lost the speakership by one vote, but was elected majority leader and served in that position until Duxbury's retirement in 1970. Once again, he was challenged in a close race for the speakership, but this time he won—again by a single vote. His opponent for speaker, Ernest Lindstrom, was elected majority leader.

By the time he had become speaker, the conservative majority had been diminished by reapportionment and the rising tide of DFL support in the state. Dirlam's 69-member majority was weakened by a conflict with Lindstrom over campaign financing for the caucus by a group of business lobbyists. The prospect of party designation in legislative elections and the popularity of DFL Governor Wendell Anderson also undermined Dirlam's power. The longest special session in history (159 calendar days), called by Anderson in 1971, further widened the conservative split. During that session, Dirlam found himself acting as a broker in the effort to obtain a majority for a compromise with the governor on school financing and tax policy. When Lindstrom would not designate House conferees to negotiate with the Senate and the governor, Dirlam finally had to take over bargaining for the House with Governor Anderson and Senate Majority Leader Stanley Holmquist in a series of sessions at the governor's mansion late in the special session. The result, which finally passed the Legislature, was the "Minnesota Miracle," which set a new pattern in state financing of education in the state.

In 1973, the DFL took control of the House and Dirlam once again became minority leader. He retired in 1974, after serving 34 years in the legislature. Only two other members ever served longer.

Sabo: The Speaker as Party Leader (1973–78)

Martin Sabo became a political activist in the DFL in the early sixties while attending Augsburg College. He worked in a series of DFL campaigns, and at the age of 22, while still in law school, State Senator Don Fraser and the state party chair encouraged him to seek the DFL endorsement for a Minneapolis House seat held by an incumbent "who was not good for the party." He did so, and was endorsed and subsequently elected.

Sabo had no particular policy agenda in mind when he was elected. He knew little of the way the Legislature worked. He served loyally in the liberal minority and was appointed to the Tax Committee, where he developed a reputation as a diligent committee member. He stayed quiet until 1967, when he was tapped to lead the opposition debate on the sales tax. His impressive performance on that issue made others notice his leadership potential. When Fred Cina, who had led the liberal caucus for many years, retired in 1968, Sabo became a candidate for minority leader. He won by putting together a coalition of some of the urban legislators with most of the rural liberals. His own background as a North Dakota farm boy helped win the trust of the rural members.

As minority leader, Sabo orchestrated an aggressive and effective attack on the conservative majority in the House, which focused on the system of closed meetings used by the majority to dominate the legislative process. He made open government the theme of the liberals, and through the recruitment of able candidates and the advantage of reapportionment, Sabo led the DFL to control of the House after the 1972 elections.

Unopposed for speaker, Sabo had a free hand in the selection of committee chairs and the assignment of members to committees. In 1974, the DFL, riding the crest of the Watergate scandal in Washington and the popularity of Governor Wendell Anderson at home, increased its House majority to 103 of the 134 members. Sabo used his overwhelming majority and his long alliance with the governor to move a long agenda of DFL legislation through the House. He also presided over a major expansion of the staff for the House, which Duxbury and Dirlam had started to build. Sabo increased the number of professionals serving the whole House, but he also placed a strong emphasis on effective staff for the caucuses.

Searle (1979) and Norton (1980): A Divided Speakership in a Divided House

Rod Searle and Fred Norton (who also served as speaker in 1987) hold unusual places among the speakers of the last generation. Each served for only a single year during the 1979– 80 Legislature. Both were products of the 1978 election, which ended DFL domination of the House under Sabo and chose Albert Quie, an Independent-Republican, as governor.

Searle was first elected in 1956 and served a long apprenticeship in the House, first in the minority, then in the majority under Duxbury, and again in the minority during the Sabo years. A member of the Appropriations Committee from his earliest days in the Legislature, he became assistant minority leader from 1975 to

1978. When Henry Savelkoul, the IR minority leader, retired in 1978, Searle's long tenure gave him an advantage over other IR members, most of whom had been elected since 1976, and he was elected party leader and the IR nominee for speaker.

The House elected in 1978, however, was equally divided; the Independent-Republicans and the DFL each had 67 seats. For two months, the House was not organized. Deputations from each caucus, led respectively by Searle and Irv Anderson, the DFL leader, negotiated for control.

Agreement was finally reached. Searle became speaker and Anderson chaired the Rules Committee. The other key element of the agreement that broke the organization deadlock gave the chairs of the Tax and Appropriations committees to the DFL (although Searle, as speaker, got to name the Appropriations Committee chair). Although the DFL was granted a majority of one vote on appropriations, all four divisions of the committee were chaired by Independent-Republicans. The IR also chaired both divisions of the Tax Committee. The remaining committees were equally divided in membership and control between the two caucuses.

Although shorn of his power to appoint half the committee chairs and members, Searle was not rendered quite the political "eunuch," as he characterized his truncated speakership. He could preside over the House and use his good offices to try to achieve consensus, both within his own restive and disillusioned caucus and between his party and the DFL. Searle tried to establish a high standard of decorum and fairness for the divided House, and encouraged an atmosphere of cooperation on major legislation. He also controlled the purse strings of the House because he had to sign the warrants for payroll and expenses of members and committees. On occasion he used this power as leverage against Anderson. While the new governor was a Republican, Quie held himself aloof from the legislative infighting and provided little support to Searle.

The fragile agreement that allowed the House to organize and function was shattered by the unseating of Representative Robert Pavlak on a straight party-line vote (since he could not vote on his own expulsion) and his replacement by a DFLer after a special election gave the DFL control of the House by a margin of two votes (see p. xx). The DFL caucus was, however, bitterly divided over the speakership.

While Irv Anderson held the loyalty of a majority of the caucus, a number of members were adamantly opposed to his election. A faction of 26 of these members, led by Gordon Voss and Fred Norton, reached an agreement with Searle and the Republicans that made Norton speaker and gave the Republicans a stronger role in the committee selection process than they would otherwise have had. Norton, who had served as chair of the Appropriations Committee as a protege of Sabo, thus rose to the speakership without the support of most of his own party. He, too, found himself unable to exercise the kind of power that Duxbury and

Sabo had. And unlike Searle, he was not even recognized as the leader of his own caucus until later in his career, when he became minority leader (1985–86) and, after the DFL victory in 1986, speaker for a second time.

Sieben and the Restoration of the Speaker's Power (1981–84)

Harry Sieben had "always wanted to be a leader." He grew up in a political family, and came to the Legislature with the intention of making his mark. Like those who preceded him to the speakership, Sieben had no specific policy agenda in mind when he was first elected. He set out, however, to make himself useful to his colleagues and the leadership. In 1978, he had thought about leaving the Legislature and running for Congress, but decided to stay on. Then, in the 1979 Legislature, he was appointed to chair the Tax Committee as part of the bipartisan deal for the speakership. He was also elected floor leader for the DFL caucus.

As the 1980 elections approached, Sieben perceived that both parties were "fumbling around," and that there was a real opportunity for new leadership. Although he had remained loyal to Anderson in the party split that resulted in the election of Norton as speaker, Sieben recognized that either man would have trouble leading a deeply divided caucus. In the fall campaign he busied himself in helping elect DFLers to the House in his role as the chief recruiter and campaign chair for the caucus. His activities in the campaign and in the Legislature fostered the allegiance of members who saw Sieben as one who was there when they needed help in campaigns or in the Legislature.

The DFL regained control of the House in 1980, winning 70 seats, and Sieben mounted an active campaign for the speakership. "I . . . carried water for a lot of people" over the years, he recalled; and he began to call in his IOUs. He managed to convince Irv Anderson that the old party leader could not obtain a caucus majority for speaker, and that if Sieben were elected, he would see that Anderson got a position of dignity when assignments were made to committees. No specific appointment was promised, but Anderson threw his support to Sieben, as the best hope of beating his archrival, Speaker Norton. On the first ballot in caucus, Norton and Sieben each had 35 votes. One person switched on the second ballot, to give Sieben the edge, and a third, unanimous ballot was then cast to make Sieben the clear choice of the DFL caucus.

As a result of his approach to his colleagues, Sieben was able to smooth over the breach in the party caused by the Norton defection the year before. Except for his pledge to Anderson, Sieben entered office with no commitments other than to treat everyone, freshmen included, fairly. As a result, he was able, in his first term as speaker, to restore to the office most of the powers that had been exercised by Duxbury and Sabo.

Jennings and Central Control of the House (1985–86)

David Jennings was elected to the House in 1978 and served his freshman year during the Searle-Norton divided speakership and the bitter fight over unseating Robert Pavlak. He was drawn to politics by strong ideological interests. After serving as an aide to a Republican congressman and working in political campaigns, he ran for the House on a program of cutting taxes and spending. He saw service in the House as a short-term opportunity to carry out his political agenda.

Jennings was distressed to find that few in the IR caucus shared his commitment to ideals; they focused instead on the power struggle between the parties. He and other newly elected members were basically spectators in the Searle-Anderson negotiations, too green in the ways of the House to operate as an effective faction within the party caucus. With Searle's retirement in 1980, however, Jennings and others of his persuasion began an effort to capture the leadership of the caucus. He became the group's candidate for minority leader. Though ultimately defeated by Glen Sherwood, a fundamentalist Christian who had defected from the DFL, Jennings had established himself as a rising force in the Independent-Republican caucus.

Sherwood retired from the House in 1982 to pursue an unsuccessful campaign for the IR nomination for governor. Jennings renewed his quest for the leadership of the party and was elected minority leader. In contrast with the almost nonpartisan approach of Searle and the low-keyed manner of Sherwood, Jennings mounted an aggressive and abrasive attack on the DFL House majority and Governor Rudy Perpich. His strategy was an uncompromising attempt to draw a clear distinction between the parties on taxes, spending, and the business climate issues, and then to use these issues as the basis for the 1984 election campaign for control of the House of Representatives. He and Representative Cal Ludeman organized an extensive and well-financed campaign to recruit and elect an IR majority.

These efforts resulted, in 1984, in the first majority for the IR since the advent of partisan elections. The 69 triumphant members of his caucus elected Jennings unanimously as their choice for speaker. Like the strong speakers before him, Jennings used his appointment power to consolidate his position and power. More than any previous speaker, he also used the rules of the House and the disciplined cohesion of his caucus to ensure that his legislative program passed the House. Because he faced a hostile Senate and governor, Jennings tended to stake out fairly extreme positions on matters such as budget and taxes, forcing the others to compromises more favorable to the House than if he had tried to accommodate their interests in the original House bills. He worked closely with his negotiators in the major conferences, at times taking over in direct discussion with the Senate majority leader and governor, following a pattern that had been established by earlier speakers, but making it a more regular occurrence.

To the surprise of both friends and critics, Jennings announced his retirement at the end of the 1986 special session, which he had forced to be called by adjourning the House before conferences could agree on major bills at the end of

the regular session. He was persuaded to enter the campaign for the IR gubernatorial endorsement (against his former colleague, Ludeman), but was defeated in
the party convention. Thus, Jennings served only one term as speaker, but made
a major mark on the office during his short, forceful, and highly controversial
reign.

The Use of Power

These thumbnail sketches of how seven speakers attained the office suggest that
while the office is powerful, power does not flow automatically from it. Each
speaker used his formal and informal powers differently, but there are patterns of
usage that emerge.

Formal Powers

The speaker has a number of formal powers: the power to preside, which includes the power of recognition; the power to rule on parliamentary points and to
assign bills to committees; the power to appoint committee chairs and members,
House conferees in conferences with the Senate, special delegations, and principal House staff positions; and the power to manage the administrative affairs of
the House and to share with the president of the Senate in the management of the
joint administrative services of the Legislature. The speaker also has the power to
sign the final versions of bills enacted by the Legislature on behalf of the House.

Of these formal powers, the most important are appointment, presiding, and
the administrative, or housekeeping function. All, however, can be almost hol-
low shells if the speaker lacks the political base to exercise his formal authority
purposefully.

Appointments   Each of the strong speakers of the past generation has had a virtually uninhibited hand in making committee appointments. This is not to say
that these decisions were made without political considerations. Much to the contrary, they were made with a fine sense of politics. The important distinction is
that the strongest speakers were not constrained by the necessity of holding together a coalition. Thus, the committee chairs they appointed owed their positions to the speaker alone, and not to an independent source of power in the caucus.

The speakers used their power of appointment in subtly different ways. Duxbury had the knack of using the experienced conservative leaders in his majority
judiciously, picking those who could be counted on to keep things in line and do
a good, skillful job. Given the culture of the House at the time, he had to honor
the seniority system, but he could also place able members on committees to
keep him informed and follow his advice.

Sabo had slightly more latitude and he used his appointment power to "make"
leaders. He had an uncanny ability for seeing potential in members who had little

prior leadership experience. His proteges included William Kelly, whom he appointed to chair the Tax Committee; Joseph Graba, who "knew nothing" about education aids, but was tapped by Sabo to head that committee; and Fred Norton, an experienced member of the Appropriations Committee, whom he selected to chair that critical committee. Each was an extraordinarily effective legislative leader, but each had a core constituency of one—the speaker. They did not come to power through the usual way of accumulating debts and credits from colleagues on the committees. Nor were they in positions to bargain with Sabo for their positions. They were the speaker's men. They could be trusted in two important ways. First, they were loyal to the speaker. Second, they were smart and could be trusted to develop sound policies and sell them to the caucus. By using this strategy of appointment, Sabo was able to tap the creativity of the best minds in the House and put them in leadership harness rather than let them languish as frustrated gadflies on the sidelines of power.

Like Sabo, Jennings also placed key lieutenants in committee chairs; but, unlike Sabo, he did not put them on a long leash in the development of policy for the caucus. Instead, his committee chairs were expected to deliver on a centrally developed agenda that was tightly controlled by the speaker. In part, the differences from other speakers were in personality and ideology. But in part they also stemmed from the fact that Sabo was seeking to expand the role and functions of government, and Jennings was determined to rein it in. He could not afford to establish a system in which the committee chairs might "go native" and embrace the expansive interests of constituent groups or bureaucracies.

In his second tour as speaker in 1987, Norton used the committee chairs and the appointments to provide a power balance in the caucus that recognized the main elements of the DFL's fragile consensus among metropolitan and rural legislators. He also used his power to banish old antagonists to the legislative sidelines, displacing Representative Jim Rice from his former position as chair of appropriations under Speaker Sieben with Glen Anderson, a rural DFLer who had been a "Wood Tick" in a 1984–85 session. Later in the session, Norton removed two Tax Committee members who failed to support the caucus position on an important committee vote. Although his style and temperament, like Sabo, was to share power far more broadly than Jennings or Sieben, Norton recognized the importance of the appointment power in creating the kind of leadership system he wanted, and did not hesitate to use it when his wishes were challenged.

Presiding Officer   Searle asserts that it was important for the speaker to inspire a sense of awe in the membership of the House. For the "backbenchers" and the minority, especially, much of the speaker's reputation comes from his/her performance as presiding officer.

From the high desk at the front of the chamber, the speaker looks out over 133 members, whom he/she must know on sight and have a sense of what each might say if recognized. An effective speaker has developed a personal knowledge of how each member is likely to perform; what each needs; how each is motivated. Speakers use the caucus intelligence system built around the assistant majority leaders and their own feeling out of the minority leader and other key members of the chamber to take the political temperature of the House. "You either have a sixth sense of where the votes are or you don't," said Martin Sabo, reflecting on his experience as speaker.

The speaker controls the debate through the power of recognition and enforcement of the rules of the House. Constant contact with the majority leader must be maintained by phone, notes, and gesture. On important matters, a floor strategy is worked out with the floor leaders in advance. The speaker knows whom to recognize for what purposes and in what order. The job, in a nutshell, is to see that the majority wins. There is also an obligation to see that they win fairly.

This sense of fairness means that a speaker must often rule on motions and amendments, some of them propounded for the sole purpose of putting the House's leader on the spot. Although the clerk of the House sits just below the speaker and provides expert advice on parliamentary law, the rules of the House, custom and usage, and precedents, it is the speaker who must choose the ruling and announce it. It is vital to the office and its continuing respect that the rulings of the speaker be upheld by the House. Therefore, the most basic rule for the majority caucus is that members must always vote to uphold the speaker in the event of a challenge to a ruling or in any motion on rules made by the majority leader.

Speakers walk a fine line in their rulings between their roles as party leader and conscience of the House with respect to fair treatment of the minority. For many years, it was rare to see a challenge to rulings of the speaker. Duxbury and Sabo, in particular, developed strong reputations as speakers who made rulings that were both sound and fair. Even minority leaders eschewed challenges to the speaker's authority, feeling that it was something that reflected poorly on the House itself.

In recent years, challenges to the rulings of the speaker have become more frequent. Challenges to Jennings' rulings were almost commonplace. This appears to be a function of two forces that feed on each other. Sieben and especially Jennings were perceived by the minority caucuses as more intensely partisan than earlier speakers. There was a strong feeling that Jennings "cooked" the rules and made individual rulings that unduly favored the majority and augmented the power of the speaker. There was also a strong feeling that his rulings were often arbitrary as well as one-sided. To some extent Jennings contributed to this feeling by flaunting his majority power.

The other force, somewhat exacerbated by the first, is the minority's increasing use of amendments to bills and challenges to the rulings of the speaker as a guerrilla tactic to force the majority into politically embarrassing positions and votes.

The authority of the speaker on rules will be upheld, however, so long as the caucus remains under control. Speakers have extensive discretion in making parliamentary rulings. The written rules of the House and *Mason's Manual*, the officially recognized guide to parliamentary law used by the House, cover only a little of the ground that a Speaker faces. In addition, custom and usage, the uncodified and unpublished precedents established by earlier rulings in arguably similar situations, is available to the speaker and chief clerk, but not without research to the members at large. When Jennings became speaker, the rules of the House were amended to change the priority of authorities to be used by the speaker in making rulings, giving custom and usage priority over Mason's manual. This change was deeply resented by the minority, which saw it as a means of giving Jennings unchecked power to rule about any way he chose, and to be able to cite his own recent rulings as precedent.

The speaker controls debate in more subtle ways as well. Through actions and comments, the tone for the debate is set. The use of humor, rebuke, warnings, and encouragement by the speaker can affect the temper of the House during debate. Through comments on the debate, the speaker can change its course and intensity. A joke can relieve tension. Stern demeanor can signal to the House that the speaker considers the matter at hand to be serious and expects it to be addressed in that manner. Here the power of the speaker's personality is entwined with the formal powers of recognition and ruling.

On rare occasions, the speaker may leave the desk and join in the debate on the floor. Duxbury, Dirlam, and Searle all left the chair on special occasions to speak on issues before the House; Sabo never addressed the House. These are historic occasions and usually involve one of two situations. The first occurs when a matter of great significance is involved and the vote is likely to be so close the speaker is uncertain of the outcome. In coming to the floor, the prestige of the office is put on the line for the cause, a clear signal to the majority caucus and others that the speaker considers the matter to be of the utmost importance. The second situation is less significant. It tends to involve matters in which the speaker has a personal or district interest.

While the distinction between these occasions may be clear in the minds of the speakers, they are not always easily distinguished by members of the House who take their voting cues from the speaker. Thus, when Speaker Jennings went down to the floor to speak against raising the drinking age, many legislators voted with him, although he was at pains to say he was speaking out of personal conviction and not as in his capacity as speaker of the House. The bill was defeated and Jennings had to bring it back for reconsideration to put the state in compliance with federal transportation funding laws.

Chief Housekeeper   The speaker sets the agenda for the business of the House. Although not fully in control of what goes on the agenda, once it is there, the speaker controls the flow of business. By assigning bills to committee, he/she can exercise substantial control over their fate, if there are choices to be made. Although the speaker does not preside over the Rules Committee, the majority leader usually does, and customarily confers closely with the speaker on how to handle issues before the committee.

The appointment of senior staff serving the House must be approved by the speaker. Along with the president of the Senate, the speaker cochairs the Legislative Joint Commission, which is responsible for personnel policy for the Legislature and the appointment of staff who serve both houses. The speaker is the chief administrative officer of the House. Although certain staff directors such as the director of house research and the clerk of the House have authority to hire staff as they see fit, the political employees of the House—the caucus, administrative, and committee staff—are all subject to control by the speaker, although some have shared this power and day-to-day responsibility with the majority leader.

In 1985, when the IR Party took control of the House, Jennings dismissed the House administrative staff and most of the committee staff, replacing them with new personnel. Although a number of the dismissed staff considered themselves as nonpartisan professionals, Jennings exercised his prerogative of replacing them with people who he felt would be more loyal to the new majority or would perform in a more professional fashion. When the DFL returned to power, there was not a full staff purge, but there were a number of changes. The DFL majority also unceremoniously dispossessed Republicans of office space and equipment, leading to a futile protest by the minority leader to the Rules Committee.

This ability to control the size and assignment of key personnel and office space or other facilities is another source of power. The speaker can grant or deny requests of committee chairs for additional staff. Retention of central control also focuses the loyalty of the staff on the speaker and the leadership, rather than the committee chairs.

Informal Powers

Caucus Leader   Although the majority leader or another person has, from time to time, been the formal chair of the caucus, there has been no doubt that the strong speakers have been the real caucus leaders. The stronger the leader, the more likely he/she could operate with relatively few meetings of the caucus. Duxbury rarely called the caucus together. Norton, as minority leader and later as speaker, caucused one to three times a week. Sabo, Sieben, and Jennings had reputations as great explainers to their caucuses. They often described the options on major bills, then gave the reasons why they recommended a particular course of action.

Speakers have differed substantially on the degree of discipline they have demanded. This was in part a function of the size of their majorities. Duxbury held few caucus votes, and then only when he regarded discipline as absolutely necessary. When that occurred, he demanded unanimous discipline on the floor. Sabo, with large majorities, could afford a more relaxed attitude about discipline. Jennings tended to stake out his position on the issues and then dare his caucus to follow. Because his majority was narrow, he, like Duxbury, demanded absolute discipline on a party issue.

The support of the caucus is essential to a speaker's power. House leaders cannot afford to lose on a critical issue. For that reason, speakers must maintain close bonds with their party followers, and have an open ear to their concerns and the nuances of positions on issues, so that a solid vote can be obtained. Duxbury, for example, postponed action on overriding Governor LeVander's veto of the sales tax bill until he was certain he had enough votes. This involves a sixth sense of timing and feel for the temper of the party and the House, as well as a basic organization capable of reliably counting the votes. As Sieben put it: "My power came from the majority of the caucus and that is all. . . . The caucus must trust you." There is some reason to believe that one of the reasons that Jennings adjourned the House in 1986 before it had completed action on major legislation was because of concern that there would be defections from the IR caucus on critical budget issues and that the speaker would be outvoted on the floor. In the 1987 session, the leadership adjusted its position on the budget after hearing from the caucus that new members, especially, were wary of the higher spending targets that Norton and his lieutenants had originally set.

It is in their relations with their caucuses that speakers come to understand most fully that if they are to be masters of the House, they must also be its servants. These are not polar roles. The distinction between master and servant is subtle in the strongest speakers. The clearest path to the speaker's chair is through service to colleagues and caucus. All of those who became speaker "carried a lot of water" for others, and even after becoming speaker, one continues to serve the caucus and the House. Effective service is the obverse face to mastery on the coin of leadership. A speaker who does not understand and perform the service functions of the office — caring for the creature comforts of the members, providing counsel and support for committee chairs, distributing honors and perquisites, rewarding allies and punishing enemies, upholding the position and power of the House in its institutional dealings with the Senate and the governor — would probably never achieve or maintain mastery of the majority caucus, much less the House. In other words, a speaker must be able to deliver as well as direct.

While a speaker's power flows from the caucus, the strongest speakers also gain autonomy from the caucus. Duxbury, Sabo, Sieben, and Jennings were sufficiently established in the trust of their caucuses that they could function without extensive consultation with them, leaving these speakers with virtually free hands in the appointment of committees. Each was a formidable and convincing advocate who had wide respect for integrity, devotion to the interest of the state and the caucus, and fairness in dealing with colleagues. While each operated differently, each nurtured an aura of power and sound political and substantive judgment.

Searle maintained effective control of his caucus during late 1978, when the protracted negotiations for control of the House were being conducted. During the 1979 session his position as speaker allowed him to be an effective advocate and shaper of caucus positions on policy. But the Young Turks elected in 1976 and 1978 chafed at Searle's nonpartisan style and consensus politics. They thirsted for confrontation with the DFL and aggressive pursuit of a clear partisan agenda. His control weakened in 1980, both because he was no longer speaker, and because some members of the IR caucus strongly disagreed with the idea of a coalition with Norton and the dissident DFLers. They felt that the IR members should have allowed Anderson to become speaker and reap the harvest of DFL discord and Anderson's belligerent style of leadership.

Norton (during his first tour as speaker in 1980), on the other hand, was not in a position to consolidate his own caucus, where he enjoyed the support of only a minority of the members. Anderson supporters considered him a traitor to the party. To gain the speaker's chair he also had to forfeit much of his appointment power to Searle and the IR leadership.

Neither Searle nor Norton attained the full level of autonomy enjoyed by their predecessors. To maintain their precarious perches, they had to constantly consult and compromise. They were not speakers in their own right, and often were reduced to presiding and administering the affairs of the House. Dirlam was in a different position. Weakened by intraparty factionalism and a thin margin of control, he nonetheless had the full range of powers and the will to exercise them. He was more than a housekeeper, but was unable consistently to consolidate and lead his majority in fights with a popular DFL governor.

Chief Budget Maker   The speaker is the chief coordinator for the budget process in the House. This requires working closely with the chairs of the Appropriations and Tax committees, keeping informed on the levels of expenditure proposed and the amounts of revenue that will be needed. During conferences, the speaker keeps in touch with the conference chairs, the majority leader of the Senate, and the governor. Where there are major differences between the houses that involve balancing the budget, the two leaders are in the pivotal positions to develop the framework for compromise—tax and spending targets—so the conferees can then work out the details. Essentially, they are the only members of the Legislature who have the entire financial picture of the state in their grasp, and

are therefore in position to exercise enormous influence on the final product of
the session.

In the 1985–86 Legislature, a change in the rules gave Speaker Jennings even
greater control over the budget than was exercised by his predecessors. A new
Budget Committee was established, with the speaker as its chair. The committee's task was to establish an overall spending and tax ceiling for the session.
Once a ceiling was approved by the House, the speaker was then given authority
to rule "out of order" amendments that would "bust the budget." When the
DFL returned to power in 1987, Speaker Norton replaced the Budget Committee
with a new Ways and Means Committee. While larger than its predecessor, and
less obviously the instrument of the speaker alone, Norton named himself to the
chair, and give the committee a mandate of coordinating the budgetary process
for the House. The work of this committee is essentially completed early in the
session, when it sets spending targets. As the session grinds to a close, the
speaker alone coordinates the work of the tax and appropriation conferees and
becomes the pivotal figure in negotiations with the Senate majority leader and
governor when an impasse must be resolved.

The practical effect of the speaker's budget power is the enhancement of the
myth of the office by setting the speaker apart from all other members of the
House. It also gives the speaker an aura of expertise in the single most important
policy deliberations of the session. This monopoly of information forces other
leaders and the majority caucus to rely on the speaker for information and judgment as the budget is being cobbled together in the final days of the session. A
speaker who wishes to do so can keep the minority totally in the dark by refusing
to appoint minority caucus members to the tax and appropriations conferences,
an action Jennings took in 1985.

Masters of the House

Ultimately, it is not the formal powers that make the speaker powerful, but the
informal powers and functions, gathered up and pyramided by the "Masters of
the House." A "Servant Speaker" is left with the shell of power defined by the
formalities of the office. The masters of the House were first of all the masters of
their caucus and its politics. To a considerable degree, this mastery was earned
by years of labor. Respect was extended for knowledge of substantive policy and
the legislative process; the ability to serve the ends of the caucus or its factions;
and services to colleagues, from helping to draft or push legislation, assisting
with constituency services, or providing critical backing on some matter of great
importance to the recipient, to helping with fund-raising and campaigning.

In reviewing the careers of the seven speakers, it is possible to characterize
their performances as masters of the House or as its servants. These are, of
course, not absolute distinctions; as mentioned earlier, each speaker was a mix-

ture of both. Of the seven, Duxbury, Sabo, and Jennings would appear to be consensus choices as masters of the House. All three had full and consistent control of their caucuses. All were held in awe by their colleagues as extraordinary legislative craftspersons. Duxbury and Sabo were not only solidly in control of their own caucuses, they were also deeply respected by the opposition for their knowledge, toughness, and fairness. Jennings did not, however, enjoy the affection of the opposition, a fact which made his leadership more brittle than that of the two earlier speakers.

Sieben might also be classed as a master of the House. He was, by all accounts, a very effective speaker. One leader who served with several speakers felt that Sieben was "distinguished by his ability to relate to legislators as individuals." Another recalled Sieben's exceptional powers of persuasion in discussing legislation and strategy with the caucus. But he was faulted for not giving the House his full attention, particularly during his second term, due to the demands of his law practice. Sabo and Jennings, for all practical purposes, had no other vocations, and Duxbury served in a time when the Legislature was far less demanding of the time of its leaders. A comment about Sabo sums up the ideal that members like to hold of the speaker: "Sabo was the best speaker. . . . He was interested in everyone and every piece of legislation. Sabo was a leader and an inspiration."

Dirlam is difficult to classify clearly. He came to the speaker's chair better prepared, in many ways, than any other. He had served on every major committee and had been majority leader for almost a decade. But he presided over a divided caucus that held a narrow majority. In many respects he was the last of the old-order legislators who served during the nonpartisan era. Unlike Duxbury, who preceded him, and Sabo, who followed, Dirlam assumed the speakership at the end of his career rather than at its peak. Because his caucus lost in the next election, he never had the opportunity to consolidate his power. He was more than the mere servant of the House, but not quite its master.

Martin Sabo and David Jennings stand out as speakers who had well-developed leadership programs they sought to accomplish. Like Lloyd Duxbury, both came to power after having served as minority leader. Unlike Duxbury, both were unopposed in their caucuses for the speakership. There is, however, a significant difference in the way they rose to power and developed their programs.

Sabo was the quintessential consensus builder as leader. He publicly sublimated any personal program in order to build the DFL legislative program out of the interests and endeavors of other caucus members and the governor's program. He used the committee system extensively, selecting able chairs and crafting the membership to produce program ideas. Then he folded the initiatives of his chairs and their committees into a broad program of policy initiatives and institutional reforms. In many respects, Duxbury had followed a similar pattern of leadership and provided the model for Sabo, except that Duxbury maintained his political distance from the governors with whom he served, regardless of party. Speaker Sabo also had the luxury of large majorities, which allowed him to guide his caucus with fairly loose reins. There were enough DFL votes to pass almost any good proposal, even if a number of members defected on a specific measure.

Sabo was speaker at a time of remarkable harmony in the DFL and in state government. The DFL was, for the first time in a century, in control of both houses and the governorship throughout his tenure as speaker. He enjoyed a warm friendship and close collaboration with Governor Wendell Anderson. While he and Nicholas Coleman, the majority leader of the Senate, were not close political or personal associates, they were able to work together on major matters without serious conflict.

Sabo's style was low-key, but firm. He was extraordinarily well-informed on substantive issues, and was perceived by both his own caucus and by the Republican leadership as open-minded and fair. Younger members of the House regarded him with respect approaching awe, much as an earlier generation of members had felt toward Duxbury. Politics was Sabo's career, and politics involved the creative use of power to produce ''good'' policy. He was a man of the House, nurtured by it and in tune with its ways, tolerant of its customs, enthusiastic about the potential of his colleagues, and eager to improve it and its products. Sabo, said one of his contemporaries, was ''a tremendous individual. He recognized talent in others, he was innovative, understanding, loyal. He made committee chairs solve problems and agendas, forced them to take responsibility.'' Another said that he ''was a strong speaker due to his command of the issues. . . . He loved and believed in the Legislature as a partner in government.'' Both Duxbury and Sabo were House ''patriots.'' They felt strongly about its role in state government and cared deeply for it as an institution.

Jennings, in contrast, served no long apprenticeship learning the ways of the House. He sought the minority leadership in his second term, and achieved it in his third. He became speaker after serving only six years. Unlike the other speakers, who initially came to the Legislature with only vague good intentions, Jennings had a program when first elected. He never viewed himself as a career politician. His earliest experience in the House, as a freshman member during the coalition Legislature of 1979–80, produced a distaste for the folkways and consensus politics of the House, which he perceived as impeding his programmatic goals. Jennings saw the Legislature itself as part of the problem he wanted to do something about. He viewed it as a necessary instrument of power, but not as a great good in itself.

Jennings' approach to leadership was almost the reverse of Sabo's. He had a slim majority of four votes. He could not afford defections on important questions. He confronted a DFL governor and Senate. To be effective he had to challenge his opposition head-on and force them to respond to his initiatives and give him a large part of what he wanted in return for some of what they wanted. He had fashioned the legislative program for the Independent-Republican caucus, initially as a minority program and then as a campaign platform for the IR House candidates in 1984. The prestige gained in leading his party to victory, plus the need for unity, gave him the needed leverage to marshal his forces behind his program. He selected committee chairs and members for their loyalty and ability to carry their committees on the major issues. He gave the committees their programs rather than wait for the committees to develop them.

Searle and Norton (in 1980) were, more by force of circumstance than choice or personality, servant speakers. They learned quickly that the power to preside, while important, is no match for the appointment power in establishing the authority of the speaker. As one leader put it: "Searle got good press and the podium. The DFL got the power." Norton got a little more. Both men basically were left with the shell of power defined by the formalities of the office. They presided but did not rule.

The degree of mastery exercised was surely a function of legislative and political skill, but it was also a product of several independent forces and factors. These include the size and/or cohesion of the speaker's majority in the caucus and in the House; the intensity of the issues dividing the legislature; and the extent and direction of external pressure on the House from the governor, the Senate, and interest groups. While some leaders, particularly Jennings, argued that leadership was an easier job with a narrow majority than with a large one, that seems true only in the sense that it may produce more social pressure for cohesion. Even that is problematic. Sieben did not enjoy greater cohesion when his majority was reduced, and Dirlam had to contend with a major rebellion in his caucus led by his majority leader. The bare majority held by the DFL in 1980 probably facilitated the caucus's bolt from Anderson to Norton and its alliance with the Republicans.

Floor Leadership

Like an orchestra conductor, the speaker of the House calls up the sounds he or she thinks will be most persuasive during floor debate. Before one can conduct effectively, however, the orchestra must have its key and pitch set. The majority leader, like the concertmaster, sets the tone of floor debate and has the further job of organizing the majority caucus so that it can prevail when the matter is brought to a vote. Here the orchestra metaphor breaks down. In the House of Representatives there is always a competing group, the minority, which is trying to outplay and overwhelm the majority tune. And under the rules of the game, the minority's dissonant notes must be heard. Thus, the majority leader must not only organize and rehearse his or her own players, but develop layers of contingent strategy for repulsing the attacks of the opposition and surmounting defections from one's own party by those who respond to a different beat.

Ultimately, no speaker has enough power to run the House successfully without an effective majority leader. In many ways the majority leader has the most difficult job in the House. The position is elected by the majority caucus, not the House as a whole, as in the case of the speaker. While this distinction is a subtle one, it is of central importance. It makes the majority leader an officer of the party caucus, while the speaker is an officer of the House. On some matters the speaker is expected to transcend party. The majority leader is not.

In some state legislatures, the relationship between speaker and majority leader is established by the method of election. Candidates for speaker often indicate in advance who their majority leader will be — it is part of the package bought by the caucus. In Minnesota, however, the caucus has traditionally separated the election of the majority leader from that of the speaker; and the candidates for the two positions rarely have run as a team, at least in their initial elections. It is not uncommon to have candidates for majority leader announce their interest in that position and seek it independently of the contest, if any, for the speakership. A candidate for speaker may, after sensing too little support for that office, fall back to seek the majority leadership, as Robert Vanasek did in 1986.

In the years covered by this study, only Jennings was either in position or disposed to nominate his majority leader. Duxbury and Dirlam both had to accept as majority leaders legislators who had been their rivals, occasionally bitter ones, for the speakership. In such cases, the ability of the two former rivals to work together was a measure of their political professionalism. Duxbury as speaker and Dirlam as majority leader served together for almost a decade without becoming close collaborators. Each did his job. Duxbury described their relationship as one in which they "worked well together. We kept our noses out of each other's business." Dirlam refrained from any direct challenge to Duxbury during their years of leadership. When he became speaker, he was not so well served by his majority leader, Ernest Lindstrom, who challenged him directly within the conservative caucus on a matter of campaign financing for caucus members and on the appointment of conferees for the 1971 special session.

Sabo apparently did not involve himself deeply in the selection of the majority leader, and although he and Irv Anderson held the respective offices throughout the six years of DFL ascendancy in the House, their working relationship deteriorated toward the end of the period. In some respects this was due to the quite different temperaments of the two leaders, but it also involved the natural conflict in ambitions between the two men. The majority leader is usually the heir apparent to the speakership, and while succession is not automatic, its prospect, as in the case of the relationship between the president and vice-president or governor and lieutenant governor, can make the best of friends natural enemies if the junior partner has unfulfilled higher ambitions.

Searle's speakership was encumbered by the fact that he in effect had no majority leader, as there was no majority. Sieben and Knickerbocker were floor leaders of their respective caucuses. Sieben worked well with Willis Eken, who had shown no interest in the speakership, but actively sought the majority leadership. Even so, there were tensions between the two. Eken noted that the speaker and leader tend to develop somewhat different power bases in the caucus and that it is difficult to keep on the same wave length in communicating with the caucus and in sharing responsibility for what happens in the House. In his second term, Sieben had difficulty balancing his responsibilities as speaker with the demands of his law practice. This left a vacuum in the system that was difficult for Eken to fill without overstepping the limits of his role.

Of all the leadership teams in the last generation, Jennings and his majority leader, Connie Levi, seem to have had the smoothest working relationship. Hand-picked by Jennings, Levi considered herself a loyal lieutenant of the speaker. Jennings, she acknowledged, was the clear leader of the caucus. ''My role was to consolidate support and move the issues. I also did a lot of personnel and administrative stuff.'' Levi did not aspire to the speakership, and she developed a strong relationship with the caucus: many of the IR members referred to her as their ''den mother.''

Like Gilbert and Sullivan's policeman, the majority leader's lot is not always ''an happy one.'' As Sabo sees it, the job has no defined duties. Ambitious leaders are restless to do more, but are institutionally unable to prevail over the speaker. Success in the job depends to some degree in fitting the role cast by circumstances. Some leaders—Eken and Robert Vanasek, majority leader in the 1987 session, are good examples—function as balance in the leadership by coming from a different party faction than the speaker, or from a different geographic region of the state. This at least lays a basis in the caucus for broader access and confidence. The selection of a rival to the speaker, like Dirlam, may actually help sometimes in building consensus by giving the losing faction in the speaker's contest a sense of real participation in the leadership. In some ways, the fact that a majority leader has some degree of political independence of the speaker can increase the credibility of both when they later unite to ask the caucus for support on policy matters.

The majority leader has occasionally been the nominal leader of the caucus, but since Duxbury's time the speaker must perform that function. In recent times, some majority leaders have even given up presiding at caucus meetings, recognizing that the speaker is actually in charge.

The majority leader has two primary formal touchstones of power: the chair of the Rules Committee and the right to be recognized at any time during floor debate. As chair of the Rules Committee, the majority leader works with the speaker to control the flow of legislation to the floor and to regulate the conditions under which it will be considered. On the floor itself, the majority leader organizes and orchestrates the debate for the caucus, serving as chief advocate (a role that may be turned over to a committee chair or bill sponsor), signal caller, motion maker, and disciplinarian.

The floor responsibilities require the greatest strategic and tactical skill. Above all, majority leaders must be able to count, or they find themselves uncomfortably in the minority. First of all, this means they have to mobilize their own caucus and have an accurate count of any defections. On close votes, they need to know how members of the other party plan to vote and where they can pick up additional votes if they are needed. In many legislatures, a whip system is built around assistant majority leaders from regions of the state. The assistant leaders in the Minnesota House tend to be more honorific than in some states, but they are occasionally used to round up votes and to maintain a running count of support and opposition.

Dissidents may be brought into line by personal persuasion and the provision of information, or they may require pressure or inducements. These may come in the form of appeals to the interest of the caucus or to personal loyalty. If these appeals fail, it may be necessary to use threats and promises. The main power of the majority leader lies in the ability to help a member pass a cherished measure. The leader may keep a recalcitrant member's favorite bill locked securely in its original committee by passing the word to the committee chair, or keep it bottled up in committee until the member becomes more reasonable. The leader can also tap a member for a prominent role in the floor debate. It may be possible to trade support of one bill for another, or to gather support by agreeing to amendments that add or delete sections of concern to the undecided or opposing members. In tight situations, leaders may resort to promising support for appointments favored by a member, location or naming of a facility, or arranging other benefits or events that the member wants.

The majority leader also sets the standard of debate and legislative behavior for the House and especially for members of the majority caucus. In this sense, the floor leaders are role models for other members and set the norms by which the House functions in session and in a committee of the whole. Majority leaders, for example, are expected to continue to represent the interests of their districts. They are not, however, expected to use the power and influence of their office to force other members to vote with them on a matter of district or personal, as opposed to party, interest. It is all right, in other words, for the majority leader to see that a measure in which he or she is interested is inserted into a bill. It is not all right to insist that other members must support that amendment as part of the caucus package. Here style and image are crucial to the continuing respect and power of the leader.

Because the House involves such direct, personal contact among members under pressure of time and interest groups, personalities and political style are important. Leaders who ask their caucus members to lay it on the line for them must be ready to reciprocate. While the speaker and majority leader often have access to campaign funds and can distribute them to deserving colleagues, they dare not develop reputations for playing favorites. A leader who develops a reputation for arrogance, vindictiveness, or arbitrary punishment of members out of proportion with the offense (like striking them from a committee assignment because of one "bad" vote) is likely to breed resentments that can later ripen into revolt. While Irv Anderson was greatly admired as a floor general and masterful debater and respected as a wily adversary, his punishment of legislators because of policy or personal disagreements with them led to the caucus rupture in 1980 that denied him the speakership. Rather than operating to smooth over differences, Anderson's approach to conflict tended to polarize the caucus. The consensus assessment of Anderson was that he had the will and capability to be a great leader, but his personality would not allow him to exercise his abilities as a leader must. "Irv had bitter enemies who would never vote for him," is the way one of his admirers put it. Another who had supported him added, "Irv Anderson was difficult to deal with in any opposition. . . . he would punish enemies and get even *forever*." An enemy was more direct: "The liberals had a personal hatred of Irv Anderson."

Eken was almost an opposite model. Relaxed, affable, and a skilled negotiator, he was more likely to use persuasion on reluctant supporters than force, but he could put on the pressure when necessary. He remarked that he tended, in tight situations, to rely more on threats than promises. A threat is easier to deliver on, as it can be carried out alone. Working with Sieben, Eken managed to keep together a fairly narrow majority. Ironically, he seems to have been more successful in his leadership during the last half of the administration of Albert Quie, a Republican, than in the first two years of DFL Governor Rudy Perpich's second, nonconsecutive term. The difference may lie in the relative effectiveness of the minority leadership in the two periods. In the first, Glen Sherwood was the compromise choice of a divided IR caucus. Sherwood's style was low-key and nonconfrontational. In contrast, David Jennings as minority leader led aggressive attacks on DFL policy and the Perpich administration.

The Minority and Its Leadership

If the majority leader must work with ambiguous power, the minority leader's base is ethereal. In the Minnesota House, unlike the U.S. House of Representatives, custom does not give the minority much recognition. The minority caucus is allowed some staff members, but there is no minority staff for committees. Central research and legal staff are available to all members, of course, but they can be virtually commandeered by committee chairs once the session is in full swing. The minority leader is entitled to recognition as leader of the opposition, but there are few resources available to the opposition beyond that.

The minority leader is elected by the minority caucus. Unlike the speaker and majority leader, the minority leader has no prizes to distribute. The speaker usually consults with the minority leader in the selection of minority members for committees, but the quality of this consultation is fully within the discretion of the speaker. In the U.S. House, for example, the minority leader's recommendations for committee assignments are invariably followed. In Minnesota, the more common practice is for the speaker to tell the minority leader the number of members the minority will have on each committee and ask for recommendations. The speaker may also indicate the kind of geographic or other balance desired for committees. The minority leader's recommendations are not binding on the speaker, and speakers have frequently assigned or reassigned minority members as they saw fit. Jennings practiced this power more aggressively than his predecessors, moving some of the most senior and experienced DFL members off committees they once had chaired or in which they were acknowledged experts. Sieben also made assignments that did not coincide with the minority leader's recommendations. All the minority leader can do is take the floor or call a news conference and fulminate.

The minority is not guaranteed membership on conference committees. In the 1985 and 1986 sessions, for example, Speaker Jennings appointed no minority members to either the tax or appropriations conferences, although there were DFLers who had voted in favor of the House bills. This practice differs from congressional experience, where the ranking minority members may usually name minority conferees.

This lack of formal power means that the minority leader is in a poor position, even if only a few votes shy of control, to try to have a major influence on legislation at the committee level, where the speaker has stacked the deck to ensure that all important committees will report legislation that is to the leadership's liking. Consequently, the minority leader's overriding concern is to get out of the minority in the next election, never more than 20 months away.

Two basic strategies are available as alternative or complementary approaches to this central task. The first involves the development and advancement of an alternative program or theme to that of the majority. Although almost certain to be shot down in committee and on the floor, it can be used to embarrass the majority in public, to amass voting records that can be used against majority party incumbents, and to attract the support of the media and interest groups outside the Legislature. In some cases, the alternative themes may also have a constructive effect in the Legislature by attracting a few wavering members of the majority into temporary coalitions that are capable of at least modifying legislation, if not defeating it.

The most successful practitioners of thematic opposition in the past generation were Sabo and Jennings. Sabo established ''open government'' as the theme of his opposition to Dirlam's majority. He used every opportunity to assail the speaker and the House leadership for closed committees, closed conferences, and "back-room politics." His special target was the Rules Committee, which had no minority members and always met in closed session. Jennings developed the business climate issue into a frontal assault on DFL propensities to expand government programs and increase taxes to pay for them. He persistently raised the issue in every context possible and clearly identified the Independent-Republicans in the House with lower taxes and less government. Both minority leaders struck responsive chords in the electorate and the media. Their efforts were rewarded by finding themselves in the majority and the speaker's chair after the next election.

A variation of thematic opposition is akin to the British or Canadian parliamentary opposition's view that the duty of the opposition is to oppose. Minority leaders who are gifted in debate and parliamentary tactics, as were Duxbury, Fred Cina, Sabo, and Jennings, can build and maintain a loyal following (and provide good theater) by simply holding the feet of the majority to the fire. An effective minority leader will select issues on which the majority will be vulnerable in both substance and procedure to put the speaker and majority leader to the test. The object of the exercise is not only to raise policy questions and force the majority to record itself against reasonable-sounding amendments and substitute measures, but to relentlessly prey on weaknesses in the cohesion of the majority and in the leadership capacities of the speaker and majority leader or committee chairs.

The role played by the minority leader in following this strategy is calculated to enchant the rank and file in the caucus, entertain the galleries and the press, and push the speaker and majority leader to or over the brink of frustration. Most speakers, however, have recognized the minority leader's role as one that requires a lot of latitude, and have been accommodating up to the point of not endangering their ultimate control of the House.

The second strategy is to focus sharply on the mechanics of electing a majority at the next opportunity. This means setting up task forces, as Fred Norton did in 1985–86, to define issues for party candidates; develop campaign schools on how to speak, prepare literature, canvass districts, and address the issues; and especially to recruit viable candidates in targeted districts where majority party incumbents seem vulnerable. The caucus and its leaders also work to develop a substantial central pool of funds to help legislative candidates. This is accomplished through caucus fund-raisers held during the session, when it is easy to encourage contributions from lobbyists.

Jennings and Representative Cal Ludeman simultaneously followed both approaches. Ludeman put together an extensive recruiting and candidate training and support effort to help elect IR House candidates in 1984. Representative John Himle worked with a group of business leaders to build a large central campaign fund to support legislative candidates who had a chance to win if well financed. In preparation for the 1986 campaign, Representative Wayne Simoneau headed the House DFL caucus recruitment effort, touring the state to recruit and groom strong candidates in targeted districts.

Because of the lack of appointments and other currency of politics to distribute, the minority leader has a harder time than the speaker or majority leader in papering over ideological and policy differences among party members and producing cohesion in the minority caucus. There is always the danger of raids on the minority by the speaker—an assignment to a conference committee, a trip to a convention, the acceptance of a treasured amendment important to the folks back home—that undermine trust and cohesion in the minority caucus. Policy and personality differences can, without the grease of patronage and the fear of losing power, make coalescence around a common theme virtually impossible for a minority caucus. If the minority leader also lacks the charisma and skills needed to inspire and unify the caucus, then election mechanics is the only viable strategy available. That strategy is undermined, however, to the extent that the minority appears aimless, uncertain, or a faint echo of the majority—"Me, too, but not so much."

The Committee System and House Leadership

The work of the House is done primarily through its committees. Membership on an important committee is a great prize for a member and an opportunity to make a mark on state policy. Of all the committees, the money committees—Tax, Appropriations, and the Education Finance Division of the Education Committee— are regarded by those who have held leadership positions as the most important. Speakers have always paid closest attention to the appointment of effective chairs and able members of these committees. While other committees, such as Judiciary, Government Operations, or Environment and Natural Resources, may occasionally handle important and politically sensitive legislation, the money committees deal year after year with the most difficult, complex, and controversial issues that divide the parties in the Legislature, the houses of the Legislature, and the Legislature and the executive branch. The Legislature, Aubrey Dirlam asserted, "must do only one thing: appropriate enough money to run the state."

The role of committees and their chairs has changed over the years. Before the rise of the strong speakers, some committee chairs were autocrats, exercising life-and-death power over bills assigned to them. Only the chair of the committee had secretarial assistance. Duxbury recalled the time when a committee chair who opposed passage of a bill assigned to his committee simply left the country with the only copy of the bill in his pocket.

While the style and extent of sharing of power still varies with individuals, the modern model was set by Richard Fitzsimons, whom Duxbury insisted take the chair of the Appropriations Committee. Fitzsimons took the assignment with the understanding that the subcommittees would act as staff for the committee. He established a system of collective decision making in which the subcommittees were held responsible for the quality of their work. While the subcommittee system spreads the workload in a busy committee like Appropriations, the effective result of the system is to delegate to three or four members of the majority party the power to decide budget issues for large segments of the government, such as health and welfare agencies, or the education system.

Basically, it is up to the subcommittee chairs, perhaps with some guidance from the committee chair, whether and how to make use of the expertise and ideas of minority members. As Mary Forsythe, who was Appropriations chair in 1985–86, pointed out, however, the majority party on the committee knows that it must expect to have the votes to report from committee the bills for which it will be responsible on the floor. Minority members can expect that, whatever the merit of their ideas, the bills that emerge from committee will bear the names of the subcommittee chairs or other members of the majority party.

The advent of staff support and instant computer analysis of funding formulas has undermined somewhat the hegemony of the chairs. Most experienced leaders also complain of a decline in the quality of committee work. It is no longer unthinkable, as it was when Dirlam did as a young second-termer, to offer an amendment to an appropriations bill being managed by the committee chairman. Although Dirlam's amendment passed, he was taken off the floor and lectured on the impropriety of challenging the finished product of the Appropriations Committee. In recent years, it has not been uncommon to see the author of a bill — even a money bill — or the chair of a committee offer amendments to a bill sent to the floor by that committee. As respect for the authority of the committee chairs has weakened, it also seems that there is less to respect in their work.

This change not only is the result of technology and the increased pressure of time on the committees, but it reflects a broader cultural attitude toward authority and participation in policymaking. It also reflects the substantial decline in the amount of experience of some of the key committee chairs and members. Particularly when control of the House shifts, important committees may be led by members with no prior leadership experience in the House and relatively little familiarity with the details of the problems before the committee. The absence of a "ranking member" system, as in the U.S. House of Representatives, means that a minority member is not necessarily being groomed for the chair when party control changes.

Minnesota legislative committees are not staffed in depth. Few have professional staff permanently assigned to them and under the control of the chair. There is no minority staff. As a consequence, there is weak continuity from session to session.

William Schreiber, Tax Committee chair in the 1985–86 session, commented that the best committee work in his experience occurred during the 1979–80 sessions, when the tie in party strength, which was reflected on the committees, meant that no bill that was not acceptable to both sides could pass from committee. Thus, any bill clearing a committee was certain to pass. Forsythe disagreed, saying she thought the Appropriations Committee did "rotten work" during that period, because the two parties had fundamentally different agendas on spending issues. The compromises could pass, but they were unsatisfactory to either side. It is conceivable that both assessments are correct—each in its own arena.

Almost every speaker has tinkered with the committee system, but none has changed it fundamentally. Jennings came closest by tending to use the committees more as mechanics whose job it was to tighten the nuts and bolts of centrally designed policy than to perform the more traditional task of actually designing the policy agenda.

Committee life, however, has a logic and force of its own, which a speaker can influence, but not fully control. Even a stacked committee must hear witnesses and tolerate debate that may sway one or two members. That happens often enough to significantly alter the outcome. Norton espoused a different approach to committee work, arguing that committees should be given their heads; that better work comes from sharing power broadly within the committees and the House because it makes better use of the talents and ideas of more of the members. The model for this approach is the idealization of Sabo's regime, which in reality was probably less participatory than remembered, but which did make extensive use of a large number of members and committees in developing a consensus program for the majority.

Many of the legislative leaders interviewed for this study volunteered the opinion that the House had become "too partisan" in recent years, and lamented that the talents of minority members were often wasted as a result. A few urged a return to nonpartisan election, but others pointed out that the old system was only marginally less partisan and that majority caucus control, if anything, was tighter then than it has been since party designation. Most leaders resisted the idea of providing committee minorities with separate staff, as is done in Congress, feeling that the central research staff could provide the minority with adequate assistance.

The Costs and Benefits of Centralized Leadership

The evolution of the House of Representatives and its leadership system has produced three paradoxes in the way the House performs its functions:

   (1) Since the 1960s, the state's political parties have become weaker and less disciplined as electoral organizations, but House leadership has become more centralized and polarized.

   (2) The complexity of issues confronted by the Legislature has increased, but the quality of deliberation on these issues has declined, in both commit-

tees and in the House as a whole.

(3) In spite of a number of reforms designed to strengthen the Legislature and legislative processes—open meetings, professional staffing, reapportionment, etc.—the members of the House appear to have less respect for their leaders and for the House as an institution than in earlier times.

Each of these paradoxes raises troubling questions for those interested in the improvement of the capacity of the Legislature to perform its functions in an information age.

The keys to the centralization of power in the House lie in the speaker's appointment power of and control of the caucus. While the autonomy of the speaker in making appointments is remarkable, it tends to fit well with the general political culture of the state, where openly jockeying for position and trading of offices for support is considered unseemly. There has, on the other hand, clearly been an evolution in the way this power is exercised, from Roy Dunn's admonition to his caucus to "vote your conscience," to Fred Norton's removal of two Tax Committee members for failing to adhere to the caucus position in committee action on the tax bill.

Beyond the power to appoint and remove, and the usual control over perks, the power of the caucus leaders has been enhanced substantially by the changes in campaign finances that have made fund-raising by the caucus more efficient than individual efforts, especially for nonincumbent candidates. This ability to supply funds, information, and advice for campaigns is more important than ideology in producing loyalty and cohesion among members of the caucus, particularly the newer members. And because turnover among members has increased, most people who serve in the House do not serve long enough to develop an identity independent of their caucus. Ironically, when party discipline in the electorate at large has been in decline or even disarray, it has increased in the Minnesota House of Representatives.

Institutionally, the increased power of the speaker and the caucus has eroded the power of the committees and the members who chair them. Experienced legislators report that the quality of committee work has declined. In recent years, there were frequent reports of committee chairs who "had their orders" from the leadership on major bills, and whose function was not to perfect legislation through committee deliberation, but to get it passed.

While staff resources available to committees have increased, the staff generally have been used not in a creative process to generate and improve legislation, but in a more reactive mode, to answer questions, to deal with technical issues, and to prepare draft language or marshal evidence to support the view of leaders or committee members. As the minority are effectively denied staff support comparable to that available to the majority, they tend to be suspicious not only of the majority and its motives, but of the work of the staff, no matter how professional it may be. A survey of House members who served during 1981–85 reported that

34 percent of them found committee staff of little help in deciding how to vote. Whatever the reservations members have about committee staff, they are far less satisfied with the central House staffs, which, though nonpartisan, are perceived to be even less helpful. Seventy-one percent of the members responding to the survey reported that the House Research Department staff was of little help in deciding how to vote, and 67 percent said that they considered it to be less than adequate. Fifty-six percent said they thought the staff of the Office of the Revisor of Statutes was inadequate (Backstrom, 1986). The reasons for this attitude are unclear. "Inadequacy" for example, could merely indicate that members want more staff service, not that they regard individual staff members as inadequate.

Studies of legislatures and Congress generally find that members rely heavily on each other for expertise in understanding legislation and in deciding how to vote. This seems to be almost inevitable, due to the necessary specialization resulting from committee assignments. As in other states, some members in the Minnesota House diligently master the subjects before their committees and become experts on whom their colleagues rely for guidance, especially on technical matters. It is common to hear that Representative so-and-so is the "only" member who really understands the education aids formula or some other arcane but important part of the legislative system. More than half of the membership, however, reports little reliance on colleagues as a source of assistance in deciding how to vote (Backstrom, 1986). The governor and caucus leaders remain the principal influences on the decisions of members of the House.

The quality of committee work, or at least the respect for it and the committee chairs, is reflected in the increased frequency of amendments to committee bills offered from the floor and in the number of them adopted. In some cases, these bills have become a necessity, and are in fact offered on behalf of the leadership, to correct errors or problems that were not dealt with in the committee. For example, major amendments to the tax bill were required after the bill left committee during the 1985 session.

The polarization of the House around the positions taken by the caucuses emphasizes the differences between parties on policy issues rather than legislative skill or problem solving. In a sense, the de facto function of the House in the overall legislative process has become one of crystalizing the partisan issues in legislation, not resolving them, except in the most formal sense: there is a vote, which the majority always wins.

As a result of this polarization, the processes of deliberation and legitimation suffer. Deliberation becomes inexpedient, as it can result in compromises that muddy the distinctions between partisan positions and blur the focus on the responsibility of the majority for the outcome. The legitimacy of action is undermined by the needs of the majority for a clear-cut victory and of the minority to be able to claim not only that the policy is unwise, but that in addition it was railroaded to passage with little or no regard for fairness to its opponents. The process and procedures, rather than being used to minimize conflict and broaden the popular base for legislation, are used instead to dramatize and sharpen the conflict and narrow the base. Thus, contrary to findings of earlier studies of legislatures that their function was to identify political conflicts and subject them to a process that reduced them to a minimum (Wahlke, 1970), the function of the Minnesota House of Representatives is to magnify the conflicts and dramatize them as a basis for electoral politics.

The institutionalization of caucus polarities in the House has a number of other notable effects. One of the most serious, in its effect on both the content of legislation and its perceived legitimacy, is that the talents of minority members are virtually ignored. It is occasionally possible for a member of the minority to initiate significant legislation, but the ability to carry it to enactment is entirely at the sufferance of the majority. The demands of party tend to relegate the work of minority members on committees to irrelevance, unless they in effect cross over to the majority side or their votes are needed because of defections from the majority party. Because the minority do not have access to effective staff resources at the committee level, they usually must devote themselves to the development of policy alternatives that are intended more as symbols than as serious legislative proposals. Their shortage of analytical resources also tends to diminish the effectiveness of their opposition to the proposals of the majority. The impotence of minority status surely is one factor that causes some members to voluntarily leave the House, either to seek other offices or to retire from political life.

Another effect of the polarization and the ways in which it has manifested itself is a decline among the members of the House in their respect for the institution, its procedures, and its leaders. House procedures are not well respected, in many cases by the leaders themselves. There are simply too many recent examples of leaders using the rules, bending them, or ignoring them to achieve their short-term ends. The list includes the tactics of Irv Anderson to secure the party-line vote expelling Robert Pavlak in order to gain control of the House; the amendments by the IR majority in 1985 to change the order of authority and give Speaker David Jennings the ability to rely on custom and usage in preference to *Mason's Manual*; Jennings's peremptory adjournment of the House in 1986; and Norton's termination of the debate on an elections procedures bill in 1987. Whatever the merits of these and other examples, they reflect a syndrome in which the minority expects unfair treatment by the majority.

This expectation of unfairness insidiously undermines the civility and coherence of the House. Disrespect for the office of the speaker, even as its raw power is acknowledged and resented, leads to frequent challenges of rulings and resort to guerrilla theater by the opposition party. This, in turn, tends to produce a determination by the leadership to crack down harder on disruptive and dilatory tactics, measures certain to be interpreted by the embattled minority as an effort to stifle dissent.

The expectation also contributes to the cycle of retaliation, described earlier, which has tended to characterize the frequent changes in control of the House since the Pavlak ouster. The mass firing of House staff and the changes in the rules in 1985 and the shuffling of offices in 1987 are examples of this cycle. While Norton, in both manner and method, took some actions to reduce inter-party tensions, and although William Schreiber was less adversarial than Jennings in his approach to minority leadership, the minority still tends to feel unfairly treated. In many respects, leaders feel more strongly about procedural and personal slights than other members. They have served longer than others and they carry with them the institutional memory of the House. That memory appears to contain a large element of bitterness, inducing a desire to get even once those in the minority come to power.

The major benefit of the partisanship of the House is that it provides a clearer public focus on the responsibility of the caucuses for legislative actions. The speaker symbolizes the majority caucus's position on policy questions in a way that helps make differences with the other party clear. There is little doubt about who is in charge in the House. The strong caucus system, therefore, tends to enhance the accountability of the majority party and provides a clear opportunity for the public to express its preferences on policies as well as personalities during the midterm election, at which only House members are chosen. While the quadrennial election of governor and Senate also afford that opportunity, the result is less clear-cut than when the House alone must face the voters.

Minnesota practices party government in its House of Representatives, even though both parties are in decline among the electorate at large. The great advantage of this system is that it makes it possible for the leadership of the House to advocate and pass, at least through the House, a clear program. When the governorship or the Senate is held by the other party, the positions taken by the House tend clearly to delineate the differences between the parties. This, in turn, can sharpen the issues for the voters in the next general election. It also can make governing the state very difficult when control of the branches of government, or even the houses of the Legislature, is divided. The political polarization makes compromise more difficult because compromise diffuses credit and blame.

During the early years covered by this study, party leaders and speakers generally served for long periods of time. Duxbury was speaker for eight years. Sabo served for six. A member was elected speaker only after many years of experience, and often after service as minority leader. Since the end of the Sabo speakership, short tenure in leadership positions has been the norm. No one has served more than four years in a combination of top leadership positions. The last three speakers—Sieben, Jennings, and Norton—have stepped down from office, declining to run for reelection or resigning from the House. The turnover in minority leadership has been even more frequent. While this may be an aberration, it raises a question about House leadership as an institution, for during this same period, the leadership of the Senate has remained stable, at least on the majority side. Two or even four years may be an insufficient time for a speaker to develop the touch needed to govern the House and learn how to deal effectively with the Senate and the executive branch.

The turnover in leadership contributes to instability in the relationships between the majority and minority caucuses, as almost every session involves mutual testing of both policy and procedure, generating a more volatile environment for the conduct of legislative business. It has also produced inconsistency in the way rules are administered by successive speakers, so that norms of conduct and debate have not been clearly developed. No speaker has served long enough in this decade to develop a style that members can identify with and to produce the stories that orient newcomers and provide guideposts for the experienced members as they practice their legislative craft.

One possible reason for the turnover in leadership may be the work load. The principal offices of leadership in the House are full-time jobs. Although the House is in session for only a few months of a biennium, the tasks of the speaker, the majority leader, and the minority leader require their full attention. They represent the House and their parties, attend to myriad administrative details of managing the House and its staff, prepare for interim meetings of committees, receive delegations, speak to groups, attend interstate and international meetings of legislators, represent the state in meetings with members of Congress and the federal executive, and prepare for the next regular session of the Legislature. It is unrealistic to expect that they can maintain another occupation while serving as leaders. It is significant that the most effective leaders have devoted their full time to the job.

Others in leadership positions, particularly the chairs of the Tax and Appropriations committees, also devote large amounts of time to legislative duties apart from the months when the Legislature is in formal session. While these duties are not yet full time, they do require far more time than that spent by the average legislator on public business. The per diem approach to such service provides some compensation, to be sure, but it often does not replace income foregone by absence from a business or profession. The loss to the state of the services of experienced members who retire as they reach the peak of their legislative careers because they can no longer afford public service should be a matter of deep concern. Some means should be found of fostering parallel careers in public service for citizen-legislators whose colleagues have recognized their talents by placing them in positions of leadership.

Even under the most favorable circumstances, the experience level of the House is likely to be lower, on average, than the Senate. To a considerable extent, the House provides training and experience for the Senate. In 1987, 36 percent of the members of the Senate had seen prior service in the House. The problem for the House is not in the loss of members who decide to run for the Senate and continue their public careers in the other chamber. It is in the loss of members who have served for five or more terms in the House and who might continue that service in positions of substantial responsibility if the disincentives to stay were not so great. Among those disincentives are compensation, but for experienced minority members, the consignment to ineffective posturing is probably an even more serious problem.

5

The Senate and Its Leadership

In some respects, the changes that swept Minnesota politics in the 1960s and 1970s had a greater impact on the Senate than on the House. In 1973, the Senate converted, politically, to a permanent liberal/DFL majority after 60 years of conservative control. Reapportionment reflecting the changing population distribution shifted the geographic balance in the Senate from rural domination to rough parity between rural and metropolitan districts.

Organizationally, the caucus became a more important influence on the substance of legislation than during the nonpartisan period. The majority leader emerged from near obscurity to become a major figure in the legislative process. In 1972 the state constitution was amended to remove from the lieutenant governor the duty of presiding over the Senate, and to allow the Senate to elect its own president. As in the House, a professional staff was developed to serve the leadership, the caucuses, the committees, and members.

The Culture of the Senate:
Oligarchy, Consensus, and Formality

The Greatest Club in Minnesota

Unlike the House of Representatives, the Minnesota Senate is almost sedate in its proceedings. The traditions of formality established early in its history have endured, substantially unchanged from the description offered by Gordon Rosenmeier, who served 34 years (1937–71) in the Senate, many of them as its dominant figure:

The Senate was very formal. There was a strict protocol regarding
conduct and discipline. A senator never addressed another by name or
directly, but always through the chair. A member would never walk
between the senator speaking and the chair. Senators always wore a
jacket on the floor.

Nicholas Coleman, who was less reverent about the Senate than Rosenmeier,
remembered the early days as a bit less uptight, recalling seeing some members
with whiskey instead of water in the paper cups on their desks. Coleman, too,
however, regarded the Senate as fairly formal, though less so by 1978 than in
earlier years.

Stanley Holmquist perhaps caught best what it means to be a senator when he
called the Senate "the greatest club in all of Minnesota." Far more than the
House, the Senate is clubby. Much of this tone was set in the era before party
designation. The Senate was ruled for 60 years by the conservatives, their hegemony unbroken by the liberals. Even the great statewide sweeps by Farmer-La-
borite Floyd B. Olson and the Democratic triumphs of Franklin Roosevelt did not
dislodge their control of the "upper" house of the state Legislature.

For most of this era, the social center of the Senate was the St. Paul Hotel,
where most of the conservative Senators took rooms every two years for the session. The members ate and drank together and discussed legislation with each
other and with lobbyists. Every week during the session, there was a dinner for
which a lobbyist picked up the check and in return made a short presentation.
With only a trace of hyperbole, William Dosland claimed that "more legislation
passed over the bar at the St. Paul Hotel than over at the Capitol."

Nonpartisan elections from the safe rural districts produced a large number of
senior members, many of whom had not faced a serious opponent after their initial elections. The safest districts, of course, produced the most senior members,
who eventually became the most powerful. New members expected to serve a
long period of apprenticeship before rising to a position of power in the Senate.

The inflexibility of the seniority system, as applied in the Senate well into the
1960s, frustrated members who were elected to the Senate after long service in
the House. Rosenmeier explained:

> . . . the system was simply based on continuous [Senate] tenure. You
> could not tack House tenure onto Senate tenure. A classic example is
> that of Claude Allen. He got into the Senate and wanted to get on the
> Senate Finance Committee. He had been chairman of House
> Appropriations and we wouldn't let him on, much to his distress. . . .

As there was no professional staff until after 1970, experience was the most
important source of knowledge about the substance of legislation as well as the

rules and procedures of the Senate. This added to the power of the senior members and those who developed expertise in particular areas. They expected and received the deference of their colleagues.

A Sense of Continuity and Independence

Senators looked on themselves as the branch of government with continuity. As Holmquist put it, "We live forever while [the governor] is here only one or two terms." The conservatives saw themselves as running the Senate, and through it, the state. Theirs was almost a judicial attitude, according to Holmquist. Senators tended to regard the Senate as the moderator of government and looked at the House and the governor as subservient to them.

The smaller size of the Senate, combined with four-year terms and less turnover in membership, contributed to the development of a higher regard for individual independence from caucuses, leaders, and governors than was found in the House. While the Senate was clearly managed by an oligarchy composed of a group with strongly shared values and policy interests, there was an almost obsessive respect for the right of each senator to vote as he or she saw fit. Dosland recalls being drilled by senior members to vote his "soul and mind," and that it was assumed that each member had a right to make his or her own decisions. Moreover, there was no punishment for voting contrary to the wishes of the inner circle of senior senators who generally controlled things:

> [W]e had no caucuses in the sense of a policymaking group. . . . We had a meeting of what we called the Majority Group and that met, I've forgotten how often, but say every two weeks or something like that. . . . And the rule was that no person could be told how to vote, nor would any vote be recommended in that meeting. . . . All we did there was talk about issues. Don Wright would report on the tax situations as he saw it, what was going to be finally decided, but nothing was even said about how he expected the caucus to vote and nobody could ever tell.

The only binding decisions of caucus were on the organization of the Senate and the adoption of rules. There, discipline was expected to be absolute; but beyond that it was highly unusual—some say unknown—for senators to be asked how they would vote by a colleague who was managing a bill. Holmquist could recall only one incident of deviation on a rules question. In 1971, when the conservatives had only a one-vote majority, Senator Carl Jenson, a conservative, offered an amendment to the rules, which then passed with liberal support. Jenson was taken aside by senior colleagues and "straightened out and it never happened again."

All Senators are Equal, but Some Are More Equal Than Others

To say that every senator was expected to vote his or her conscience reflects well the myth system of the Senate. It is, however, a bit too benign a view of what actually happened or how the Senate worked. There was general agreement that the Senate was "run" by three senior members for many years: Rosenmeier, Donald Wright, and Donald Sinclair. How were they able, without formal power—none was ever the majority leader—to exercise such dominance? All three were strong and persuasive speakers, and contrary to the House, the floor of the Senate was a place where decisions were sometimes made on the substance of law. Rosenmeier in particular was regarded with awe for his knowledge of legislation and his mastery of the rules. He and his cohorts were helpful and solicitous toward new members, helping them with legislation and coaching them on the rules. New members were often seated near experienced members of the caucus, who took the freshman under their wings for tutelage in the ways and manners of the Senate. The "curmudgeons" took leadership positions on issues, so others knew where they stood. Richard Fitzsimons, who had been a powerful member of the House as chair of the Appropriations Committee, was subsequently elected to the Senate. Of Sinclair, he recalled: "You did what he told you to do. There was total conviction of his honesty and integrity. He ran a relatively open committee, but his very presence subdued the proceedings."

These powerful leaders were able to punish the obstreperous and reward the compliant in a wide variety of subtle ways that left no doubt about who was really in charge. Holmquist told a revealing story of how Rosenmeier exercised his dominance:

> As a freshman I authored a constitutional convention bill, with
> Rosenmeier's blessing. But when it came before the Judiciary
> Committee it was short one vote because a member who was for it was
> absent. When the bill came to the floor, Rosenmeier opposed it although
> he had testified for it in committee. With his opposition, it was
> defeated. Senator Charlie Root moved indefinite postponement, which
> passed. I then moved the report of the committee and amended the
> indefinite postponement motion to call for an immediate vote.
> Rosenmeier declared I had circumvented the committee process and it
> all went down.

Another former senator, when asked how the "three curmudgeons" managed to exercise such control, also referred to their legislative and procedural prowess, their help to others, and then said, "Looks. When you got out of line, they just gave you a look."

Reapportionment and the rise of the DFL as the majority in the Senate ended the careers of the old conservative oligarchy, but much of the culture established during that period has lingered. The Senate today is less stuffy and formal, but still far more formal than the House. Eating while on the floor is forbidden. Only senators are permitted in the retiring room; not even House members may enter. Debate is more formal. Coats must be worn. The chair must be addressed. There is a considerable respect for traditions. There is a sense that being a senator and being in the Senate is important, perhaps more important than being in the House. Seniority still matters, but it is no longer the first rule of the Senate. Few senators seem ready to centralize power in the majority leader or create a leadership position similar in power to the speaker of the House.

Pluralism and Consensus

The result of these strong traditions of individual autonomy, courtesy, and benign oligarchy is that the Senate is markedly pluralistic in its political behavior. Members of the minority are more likely to be effective as sponsors of bills or amendments, both in committee and on the floor. Ronald Sieloff, who spent his Senate career in the minority, did not feel that he was particularly inhibited in achieving what he wanted to do. George Pillsbury, who served three terms in the minority, agreed. The idea that all senators are equal tends to pervade the Senate and produces a level of collegiality and mutual respect not seen in the House.

The House lives by its majority. The Senate seeks consensus, though there surely are issues on which the majority and minority caucuses divide. Taxes and spending policies are the most common grounds for party differences and party-line votes. But on most matters, committees and the Senate as a whole work toward broader agreement.

There is still an oligarchy, but within it power is shared. The majority leader clearly is first among equals. But a great deal of power resides with the committee chairs.

Leadership in the Senate

Leadership patterns in the Senate fall into two periods, separated by the advent of liberal control in 1973. Many of the customs of the period of conservative dominance have continued into the DFL era, but there are also some significant changes. The most important characteristic of Senate leadership is its pluralism. Power over the most important matters—appointments, control of the agenda, and management of the process—is shared among the members of the leadership group.

The Organizing Committee and the Committee on Committees

The key to how the Senate is led is the Organizing Committee, or the Committee on Committees, of the majority caucus. The Organizing Committee was created in 1931. With the election of Floyd B. Olson as governor, the conservatives were reduced to a one-vote majority in the Senate. According to Rosenmeier, his father, who then chaired the Rules Committee, and other conservatives feared that the lieutenant governor, Henry Arens, as presiding officer of the Senate might make committee appointments favorable to the governor if the majority group was not prepared to present a slate and support it unanimously:

> Of course they were all afraid of Olson because he had been arguing for public ownership of this and that. It turned out he was not anywhere as eager to carry it out as he was to talk about it. . . . But because they had to protect that one vote, they were all afraid of Arens, a fear that was not really justified, they didn't know him, they couldn't let the president of the Senate appoint the committees. So, in order to protect . . . that one vote, to count up the committee structure, they created the organization committee outside the organization.

So the Organizing Committee was put together as an informal group to convene the majority and to prepare a slate of committee appointments based strictly on seniority. By the late fifties and early sixties, it had become the central force in the leadership system.

Once it was clear that the conservatives had a majority, the Organizing Committee was "elected." Initially it had only three members, but was expanded in later years to consist of the senior member from each judicial district in the state.

In 1954, when he was first elected to the Senate, Stanley Holmquist was the only conservative senator from his judicial district. This automatically gave him a seat on the Organizing Committee. Rosenmeier was concerned, however, about the idea of a freshman being on the committee, but reluctantly acquiesced due to the tradition of having each district represented on the committee.

The Organizing Committee was dissolved once the initial committee assignments were made by the president of the Senate (in accordance with the recommendations of the Organizing Committee) and the president pro tempore (always the most senior senator) was named. In its place a Committee on Committees — usually the senior senators of the conservative majority — selected conference committee members and interim committees.

When the DFL took control of the Senate in 1973, it did not retain the Organizing Committee, but retained the practice of the Committee on Committees. Its sole functions are to select the chairs and members of Senate committees and prepare the rules for the operation of the Senate.

During the conservative regime, seniority alone was the criterion for selection as a committee chair. Every senator with more than two terms was guaranteed a committee chair. The number of committees might be expanded or reduced, if necessary, to ensure full coverage. The most important committees, Tax, Finance, Government Operations, and Judiciary, went to the most senior members. Rosenmeier, who frequently was the chair of the Organizing Committee, acknowledged that the seniority system sometimes produced chairs who were less effective than might be produced by some other methods, but in such cases the committee tried to select other members to strengthen the capacity of the committee. Until the number of lawyers in the Senate declined to a point that made it impractical, the Judiciary Committee consisted entirely of attorneys. There was, in fact, an effort to let all lawyers in the Senate serve on that committee.

The majority leader under the conservative regime was, until Stanley Holmquist sought and won the position, primarily a factotum who kept track of the agenda and called up bills for a vote in the order suggested by the Rules Committee. As such, the majority leader had little influence on the decisions of the Organizing Committee. Both Nicholas Coleman and Roger Moe, the DFL majority leaders, exercised far greater influence in the selection of committee chairs. They were not as reticent about making suggestions to the Committee on Committees as their predecessors were, and their advice was normally followed.

Once the organization of the Senate is complete, the only function of the Committee on Committees is to select members to serve on conference committees and interim committees and commissions. The majority leader has become the most influential force in its deliberations, but does not formally control the decisions. Thus, unlike the House, where the speaker has unchecked authority in the selection of committees members and conferees, the leader of the majority caucus in the Senate draws his or her power not from position, but from personality and custom.

Though the leader does have greater influence in chair assignments now, seniority remains the single most critical factor in assigning chairs. Factional and personal politics count more in the selection of vice-chairs, which are more important for their symbolic value to those who are named to them than they are for their impact on legislation. Geography counts most in the balancing of memberships. During Coleman's tenure as majority leader, for example, the caucus agreed to combine the Committee on Agriculture with the Committee on Natural Resources in order to balance urban and conservationist interests with rural and development-oriented interests and force some conversation between them. Basically, however, the Committee on Committees, according to Judiciary Committee Chairman Allan Spear, "tries to make folks happy and not make a lot of them unhappy." The decisions remain collective decisions but they are heavily influenced by the majority leader.

The Rules Committee

The Rules Committee is chaired, as a matter of custom, by the majority leader. Historically, the majority leadership evolved from the chair of the Rules Committee. Even today there is no parking space at the Capitol reserved for the majority leader. The sign reads "Chairman of the Rules Committee." The modern committee membership consists of the assistant majority leader, chairs of the standing committees, majority caucus whips, and members of the minority caucus leadership. Minority membership was not allowed until 1973 and still is not necessarily proportionate to the number of minority senators, thus giving the majority leader clear dominance over any matter brought before it. The committee's function is to schedule legislation for floor consideration and to propose changes in the rules of the Senate.

The Rules Committee is an important instrument in the leadership of the Senate, as it brings together all of the major actors and provides a means of coordinating their work and determining priorities for action by the Senate. It also provides the majority leader with an important channel of communication to and from the committees.

The Majority Leader

Holmquist Invents the Office (1967–72)

Stanley Holmquist and Nicholas Coleman remade the office of majority leader into a powerful legislative force. Until Holmquist assumed the job, it was of little real significance in the running of the Senate. Holmquist's predecessor, John Zwach, was regarded as an errand runner for Rosenmeier, Wright, and Sinclair, the three men who collectively led the conservative caucus. Rosenmeier, for example, always insisted that there was no real majority leader in the Senate, that such a title was not to be found in the rules and that its very existence implied that one member was "above" other senators. "We didn't acknowledge any leadership. I remember I was horrified when Stanley Holmquist introduced himself as the leader. I recall I had to get up and explain to him he wasn't my leader." He and other conservatives even eschewed the term "caucus," preferring instead to refer to themselves as "the majority group." At any rate, it is fair to say that for many years the majority leader did not really lead, but served as a floor manager for legislation brought to the floor through the Rules Committee.

In 1966 Zwach retired from the Senate to run for Congress. Holmquist, who was not considered a member of the in-group, indicated his interest in the position. Holmquist acknowledges that Rosenmeier could have been chosen had he wanted the position, but he had no desire for a position the very existence of which he denied. Ironically, Rosenmeier's challenge to the notion of the post led, in Holmquist's skilled hands, to strengthening it.

Holmquist used the chair of the Rules Committee as a means of consolidating power in the leader. As the session draws to a close, all bills except tax and appropriations measures must come to the Rules Committee, where the majority leader can exercise a considerable influence on their fate, simply by deciding whether they are scheduled for debate. In addition, the majority leader is in a position to control the referral of bills to committees in the first place, and can use this power to send bills in which he or she is interested to the Rules Committee.

In the Senate's more relaxed and tolerant atmosphere, Holmquist never felt constrained by his position from taking positions on issues. Since there were no caucus positions, he was quite free to do so; but because he was majority leader, his position was not infrequently assumed to be the position of the majority group. He was also able to build coalitions with minority members by recommending them for conference committees and seeking their help on legislation.

Holmquist recognized that as majority leader he could not exercise power unless he appeared to have it, especially on crucial matters. That meant he could not afford to lose an important vote. The critical test of Holmquist's leadership came on the issue of overriding Governor Harold LeVander's veto of the sales tax. Although it was still considered unethical to ask senators how they would vote, Holmquist knew that he had two defections in his caucus, and would have to secure some votes from the liberal side to override the veto. He managed to prevent the issue from coming before the regular session. In the caucus following the session, he told his colleagues that a special session would be called, but that he would not bring up the veto until "I have 45 votes in my pocket." He then proceeded to break with custom and ask each member how they intended to vote. When he reached Rosenmeier, he was relieved that the response was one of enthusiastic support. He not only had the support he needed to override the governor's veto; he had broken Senate tradition and established the majority leadership as the guiding force in the Senate.

In 1971, Holmquist's majority was whittled down to one vote. A DFL governor, Wendell Anderson, had been elected, and the House was now led by Speaker Aubrey Dirlam, who also had a narrow majority and factional divisions to contend with. Governor Anderson vetoed the tax bill agreed on by the conference committee, necessitating the long special session. Holmquist and the Senate minority leader, Nicholas Coleman, appointed several senators to negotiate a compromise with the governor and the House. Only the minority caucus was represented from the House, as the House majority leader, Ernest Lindstrom, refused to appoint negotiators. Speaker Dirlam decided to participate, however, in the negotiations on the legislative package. After weeks of meetings, privately in the governor's office and occasionally in public, a compromise was reached that became the Minnesota Miracle — the program to alter the tax and spending system to provide state equalization aid for education and to reduce property taxes by shifting the state toward increased use of the income tax. Holmquist returned to his caucus and told them it was the best that could be done. The package passed the Senate with 37 votes, three more than were needed.

Coleman: The Expansion of the Majority Leader's Power (1973–80)

In 1973, the DFL gained control of the Senate for the first time since Minnesota achieved statehood. With reapportionment of seats on the basis of population, there was a great turnover in membership, with many of the conservative stalwarts having retired or been defeated. Coleman came to the majority leadership with a determination to lead. Like Holmquist, Coleman was energetic and dedicated to the promotion of certain policies. Roger Moe, who was a protégé of Coleman's and his successor as leader, described Coleman as having:

> more political skills than anyone. Ideology was important to him, but he was also a pragmatist. He was quick, a great talker, had a cutting wit. He was masterful at diverting attention from the real issue. With him there was no planning. He was intuitive, he seized timely issues, and authored every controversial bill.

Coleman realized and exercised the ability of the majority leader to speak for the Senate, in much the same way the speaker could represent the House. He even persuaded the Senate to pass a resolution recognizing the office of majority leader. While he carried a heavy personal agenda of social programs, Coleman did not try to impose his own agenda on the liberal/DFL caucus. He accepted personal responsibility for carrying highly controversial civil liberties bills, such as homosexuals' rights, as a means of relieving other senators of the electoral burden of handling such hot potatoes. He also tried to accommodate conservatives in the Senate who disagreed with him by seeking compromises with them.

Basically, Coleman led by force of personality and a keen sense of what was politically possible. He melded the older Senate tradition of forceful personal leadership with an extension of formal power in the majority leader begun by Holmquist. He also broadened the distribution of power by bringing younger members into positions of responsibility in the caucus and in committees, in the process creating strong bonds of loyalty from his young protégés. He was instrumental, for instance, in placing Douglas Johnson on the Tax Committee during his first term. He persuaded Gene Merriam to take a seat on the Judiciary Committee, which he was interested in weaning from its "lawyers-only" tradition (a virtual necessity with the sudden decline in the number of lawyers elected to the Senate). He took Roger Moe under his wing, moved him into the leadership group of the DFL and appointed him to chair the campaign organization committee of the caucus. Linda Berglin was appointed vice-chair of the Rules Committee, where she could gain valuable experience in the legislative process by chairing the committee when Coleman was absent. He further extended his influence by ensuring that all freshmen senators got to carry bills. After Coleman, it seemed unthinkable for the Senate to revert to the pre-Holmquist pattern of informal leadership by a small circle of oligarchs.

Moe: Consolidation and Institutionalization (1981–)

Roger Moe succeeded Coleman in 1981, and the patterns established by

Holmquist and Coleman were institutionalized. The caucus had become far readier to accept, even expect, leadership. In part this may have been a factor of the disappearance from the Senate of strong-willed veterans. The Senate was younger and less experienced. Only three senators had served three full terms when the Senate convened in 1981. Individual senators were more dependent on the leadership for a sense of direction and cues on how to vote than in earlier years. Senators no longer lodged at the same hotels, as more of them brought their families with them to St. Paul for the long session, or commuted from distant home districts by air or highway. Half of the Senate now lived permanently in the metropolitan area and could return home every evening after the day's session was over. Reapportionment and improved transportation undermined the social basis of the old Senate.

Selection of the Committee on Committees had changed from automatic election of the senior members from each congressional district to election of senior members and a freshman senator by the caucus. The majority party members were recommended by Moe. The committee still picks the chairs and members of other committees, but is heavily influenced by the judgment of the majority leader. The leader may have slightly less influence on the selection of the chairs of the Tax and Finance committees, but Moe concluded that overall the selections by the committee are not much different than the choices he would make if he alone were assigned the job. That judgment would seem confirmed by the 1986 decision of the Committee on Committees to transfer Senator Gerald Willet from the chair of the Finance Committee to the Agriculture and Natural Resources Committee. The basic reason for the transfer of this senior senator against his wishes was his disagreement with the leadership on major policy issues.

Under Moe's leadership, more and more of the legislative agenda has come under his control. The steering committee of the caucus, consisting of the officers of the caucus, nominally has the function of guiding the caucus on legislative issues. In fact it meets rarely, especially since Moe established his own set of reliable contacts—his "own people"—to keep him informed of the temper of the caucus. In the modern Senate, the caucus has not been a dynamic body, from which the positions of the majority emerge by a process of discussion and decision; nor has it been a passive group, which Moe can move at will in any direction he chooses. The tradition of senatorial independence means that the majority leader must be respectful of the interests of each of his colleagues, and that the caucus provides an informal set of parameters within which Moe works to establish positions with which most members of the majority can live. It has become his job to formulate and articulate these positions with help from the committee chairs and other key members. The caucus meeting itself has become a forum for informing the members of the position to be staked out by its leader, to test the water on a policy or tactic to be pursued, to vent concerns or dissent, and to combat hardening of factional lines.

Gene Merriam, in assessing the leadership of Coleman and Moe, pointed out that Coleman was a good consensus leader who could recognize and manipulate talent and ability in others. Unlike Moe, Coleman paid no attention to detail, but had a good notion of the general agenda. As a senator, Merriam saw Moe's leadership as loose, informal, and unstructured. The majority leader offers general guidance, but the particular problems should be resolved by the committees.

Douglas Johnson, chair of the Tax Committee, the most politically sensitive of the Senate committees, felt much the same way. Moe, he pointed out, expects his committee to develop the policy position of the majority on taxes, and Johnson and the other Senate conferees to work out the details of any compromise with the House. The majority leader's counsel will generally be followed, however. But, he emphasized, it is personality and not institutionalized power that carries the day. As with the speaker, however, the fact that the majority leader is the only link among the Tax, Finance, and Education Aids committees gives him a great deal of de facto power. Moe is the only person in the Senate who knows how all of the pieces fit into the big picture. In addition, the majority leader is his caucus's most experienced person in negotiating among members of the Senate and in working out deals with the House and the governor. It generally makes sense to other members to rely on their leader's political instincts and judgment.

Institutional Limitations on Senate Leadership

Like his or her counterpart in the House, the Senate majority leader is an officer primarily of the caucus, not of the Senate. But there is an important difference between the two leaders. The House majority leader is not the leader of the majority caucus in the House; the speaker is. While not exercising the power of a speaker, the Senate majority leader can be the speaker's political equal in the governance of the Legislature. Lacking the formal authority to command, the skillful Senate majority leader may nonetheless be able to commit the Senate to a position that either has been negotiated with Senate colleagues or one which the leader senses that they can accept if the political prestige of the office is placed behind it. Although a partisan figure, the Senate culture, being less partisan than that of the House, ironically allows its leader more latitude in fashioning policy positions and putting together a majority (which may include some members of the opposition party) in support of them. In this sense, the Senate majority leader is occasionally more able to represent his chamber than the speaker can his.

There are senators who feel that more formal power in the majority leader is desirable. A leader with powers of appointment and control similar to those of the speaker would be able to move the Senate more expeditiously toward decisions, they argue. Others rejoin that such an arrangement would stifle the Senate's ability to make effective use of both majority and minority members by increasing the political polarization of the Senate. The collective leadership of the Senate is conceded to be slower and more complex than the central control and tight discipline in the House. This occasionally puts Senate leaders at a disadvantage in negotiating with the House. It produces, however, a system that differentiates the Senate from the House in the seriousness of its attention to debate of the issues and in its ability to maintain a high level of mutual trust and legislative courtesy that is conducive to finding effective ways of resolving issues.

The President of the Senate

One of the key differences between the ways in which the House and Senate function is that the presiding officer of the Senate is not the leader of the majority. Until 1973 the lieutenant governor was charged by the constitution with the duty of serving as president of the Senate. The Senate elected its senior member as president pro tempore to preside in the lieutenant governor's absence.

Lieutenant governors only rarely involved themselves in the political affairs of the Senate, but they were available to break a tie vote on an important issue. Since lieutenant governors were elected separately from governors, they did not necessarily work the Senate as emissaries of the governor. A lieutenant governor might indeed be a strong opponent of the governor, as was the case when Lieutenant Governor Karl Rolvaag ran against and defeated Governor Elmer L. Andersen. Thus, when presiding, the lieutenant governor was primarily a facilitator of debate and keeper of the rules of the Senate. Unlike the speaker of the House, it was not the job of the presiding officer to follow the interests of the majority caucus in shaping parliamentary rulings.

The move to eliminate the presiding role from the office came after Lieutenant Governor Rudy Perpich, in 1971, refused to accept the certificate of election of Senator Richard Palmer, whose decision to caucus with the conservatives gave them a one-vote majority. Perpich further ruled that he possessed the power to break ties in matters of organization of the Senate. Conservatives walked out of the Senate and challenged Perpich's actions in court. The state supreme court held that the lieutenant governor had no power to refuse the certificate of election of a member or to prevent a member whose election was contested from voting on the organization of the Senate. The Senate alone was the judge of the qualifications of its members.

The decision resulted in the seating of Palmer and the organization of the Senate by the conservatives. The institutional consequence of the incident was the approval of a constitutional amendment changing the method of election and duties of the lieutenant governor. Since 1972, the lieutenant governor has been paired on the ballot with the governor, in the same manner as the president and vice-president are, so that the two are always of the same political party. The same amendment removed the duty of presiding over the Senate from the responsibilities of the lieutenant governor and provided that the Senate should elect its own president. Under this amendment, the Senate could have chosen to fashion the office in the image of the speakership, or of the strong Senate presidencies of other states, like Massachusetts or Maryland, where the president is the counterpart of the speaker. Such a move, however, would have been too sharp a break with tradition and senatorial aversion to strong formal leadership. The selection of the first president, Alec Olson, set the pattern.

Olson was a highly respected member of the Senate. He had served in the U.S. House of Representatives for two terms in the early sixties, and after being defeated for that office, he was appointed assistant secretary of agriculture in the Johnson administration. He had been elected to the Senate in a special election in 1969 and subsequently reelected. He was not, however, a senior member or a Senate power in his own right. His real interest was in becoming chair of the Tax Committee. When he was denied this position by the Organizing Committee, he decided to seek the presidency as a second choice.

Olson established the tone of the presidency as a facilitator of the business of the Senate. He took the position that the rules of the Senate determined the proper manner of assigning bills, and that he would follow the rules. He recognized that the credibility and influence of the presidency ultimately would rest on its fairness, but that as a practical matter, the majority could set the agenda and determine the outcome. Olson was insistent that the Senate maintain a level of decorum consistent with good debate. In 1976, during a raucous debate over the Metropolitan Stadium tax rebate bill, Olson lost control of the highly emotional situation. Angry at his colleagues' behavior and determined to stress the importance of decorum, he walked out of the Senate and went home for two days before returning to preside over the closing session of the Senate.

This incident underscores both the weakness and strength of the presidency. The president is in no position to control the majority or its behavior, lacking the levers of power available to the speaker of the House. Indeed, the task of maintaining order and fairness may at times frustrate the members of the president's own party. On the other hand, because the office has no direct leadership responsibilities, the president may set a personal and institutional norm of behavior that can have a profound effect on the way in which other members behave and the institution works. As Jack Davies, who served as the third president of the Senate, put it: "The rules are to protect the minority. . . . the majority can do whatever it wants when it wants. . . . the presiding officer rules by precedent and political tides." In other words, the president cannot prevent the majority from having its way, even if its way is less respectful of Senate traditions than the presiding officer would like; but he or she is not powerless to influence the process and the result through the force of personality and the use of the rules. "The president," said Olson, "has no power if the majority realizes its own power. Ultimately, he only helps the body to conduct its business."

The president is chosen in fact by the steering committee of his or her caucus and can be removed by the caucus if the chair is used to obstruct the majority program. As a member of the leadership circle of the majority party, the presiding officer is expected to let the majority win, but, as an officer of the whole Senate, require that it win fairly.

In 1976 when the office of lieutenant governor became vacant due to Rudy Perpich's succession to the governorship, Alec Olson automatically became lieutenant governor. Edward Gearty, the second person to become president of the Senate, was a faithful member of the Senate leadership group headed by Majority Leader Coleman, who approached Gearty to suggest he seek the job. Gearty at first urged Coleman to seek it himself, thinking that it made sense to convert the presidency into a position comparable to that of speaker of the House, where Gearty had served for eight years before coming to the Senate in 1970. Coleman, however, felt that the Senate was "not ready" for that kind of consolidation of power. Gearty accepted the position. "I enjoyed it," he said, "but not as much as chairing the Government Operations Committee," which he had to relinquish in favor of the Committee on Elections and Ethics, which Senate presidents have since chaired.

Gearty maintained Olson's regard for the deliberative functions of the Senate as opposed to the high-speed action characteristic of floor debate in the House. His pacing of Senate consideration of bills occasionally irritated House leaders and the press, but Gearty remained unimpressed. "We want to look at the process, the functioning of government. In that respect the legislative process does not happen fast," he told a reporter in 1976.

Gearty's and Coleman's decisions not to seek reelection in 1980 meant a complete change in the leadership and presidency of the Senate in 1981. Roger Moe became majority leader, and Jack Davies won the DFL caucus's support for the presidency after a 5-4 vote in the steering committee of the DFL caucus. Davies, a veteran of 22 years and the most senior senator, had a reputation as a maverick but an effective member. He had been chair of the Judiciary Committee and the author of important legislation, most notably, the no-fault automobile insurance law. A law professor and author of a book on the law of legislation, Davies was an extraordinarily able parliamentarian. Unlike Gearty, however, he was not really a part of the leadership of the Senate, and performed a more neutral role in the office. He clearly established the authority of the president in matters of procedure, and emphasized the importance of a standard of fairness. He also set a high standard in the Senate for decorum and grammar, about which he was meticulous himself and demanding of his colleagues.

But even Davies acknowledged that the independence of the president is limited by the determination of the majority to prevail. He pointed out that the president is in no position, for example, to rule unilaterally that some of the provisions in a "garbage bill" are nongermane if the majority wants them to remain.

The president will be overruled, and a precedent will be set for the acceptability of such measures. Silence may be more in the long-term interest of protecting the principle at stake so that it may be used at a more propitious time to uphold a challenge from the floor to the germaneness of an amendment.

Like Jack Davies, Jerome Hughes, who became president in 1983, was the dean of the Senate in years of service. Representing the district adjoining Coleman's and long a friend of the late majority leader, Hughes served as chair of the Education Committee until he was elected president. Hughes was the last link to the Senate as it existed prior to the Coleman era, as he was elected in 1966 and served with Rosenmeier, Sinclair, and Holmquist. While a loyal member of the DFL caucus, Hughes as president has been a strong advocate of the independent tradition of the Senate and of the importance of the maintenance of a high standard of fairness in the conduct of the presiding officer. Hughes argues that the less partisan role of the president contributes to more deliberative and thoughtful debate and allows members of both parties to contribute fully to the development of public policy. He has evinced a strong scholarly interest in the Legislature and taken seriously the duties of the Senate president as chair (rotating with the speaker) of the Legislative Coordinating Commission, which manages the joint staff agencies of the Legislature.

The president of the Senate holds a position second in line of succession to the governorship, but far less powerful in state affairs than either speaker of the House or majority leader of the Senate. Although chosen in fact by the majority caucus and part of its leadership group, the presidency is not regarded by the members or incumbent as an instrument of majority power in the way in which the speaker of the House is seen. Still, the president is not a completely "neutered" presiding officer as is the speaker of the British House of Commons, who resigns party membership when the chair is assumed.

The tradition of impartiality established by the four who have held the presidency, and the lieutenant governors who preceded them, however, has been an important factor in establishing the parliamentary authority of the office. A challenge to a ruling by the president is extremely rare; the idea of doing so is virtually anathema to the members. Rosenmeier could recall only one instance in his entire service when the president was overruled by the Senate:

> Sandy Keith was the presiding officer as lieutenant governor and he
> made a ruling in favor of the minority leader. . . . they always called it
> "leader" on the minority side, that's because they had no Rules
> Committee Chairman. . . . well, we were shocked. At that time no one
> in memory could ever recall an appeal from the rule of the chair, but we
> got a recess, a quick meeting with a few of us. . . . the question was
> whether we could tolerate that kind of a violation of the rules from the
> chair. . . . none of us knew how to appeal. . . . nobody ever heard of it
> before. I was designated to work out a procedure so we got back in

again and all I could think of was, I said "I appeal the ruling of the chair." . . . and we overruled him, but that's the only time it ever happened I guess.

Such action is no more common today.

The relationship between the president and the majority leader is a subtle one. The president is a member of the Rules Committee and privy to the deliberations of the leadership on strategy. Although limited as an instrument of the leadership in steering the legislative process, the president can often exercise a considerable amount of personal persuasion on colleagues by virtue of the office and long legislative experience. Maintaining a good working relationship without intruding into the responsibilities of the majority leader is an important part of the relationship. At the same time, the majority leader must often act indirectly through the president rather than acting directly. The potential for conflict between the two has been avoided thus far largely as a result of the ability of those who held the positions to develop a working relationship.

Both those who have held the office and others disagreed on whether the presidency should be strengthened or consolidated with the majority leader. Gearty flatly stated that the president should have more power. Senator Douglas Johnson agreed. He argued that the powers of the majority leader should be increased by incorporating within them the presidency of the Senate. A system more like that of the House would, he felt, make the system work better. With more power, including the power to appoint committees, the leader would have an easier time in selling programs and unified positions on them to the caucus.

Majority Leader Roger Moe pointed out that it was useful to a leader to have the implied threat that action could be taken against members who did not support the leadership position. Now, he laments, "I hold hands, cajole, discuss. . . . With more authority I could get more done and have more discipline."

Olson strongly disagreed. He felt that the combining of the offices would destroy the delicate balance that should be maintained between the role of the party leader and that of the presiding officer. In commenting on Gearty's plea to Coleman to fuse the two positions, he said, "Coleman wanted more power and did not like sharing it. He wanted no interference." Davies and Hughes appeared to agree with Olson that combining the offices would ultimately change for the worse the traditional independence of senators and the more deliberative nature of Senate debate. Hughes, particularly, valued the independence of the Senate and the more stately processes that nurture the development of consensus through the entire session. Senator Merriam noted with favor the diffusion of power in the Senate, and Senator Linda Berglin felt that the Senate, because of the way it was structured politically, operated more formally than the House but functioned more democratically.

In many respects, effective leadership in the Senate requires more subtle exercise of political skills than does leadership of the House. The successful Senate leader does not even appear to command, but must persuade. Power is shared, not only with committee chairs, who have greater autonomy in the Senate than in the House, but with the president of the Senate.

The Senate's Committees

The fact that committee chairs and members are formally appointed by the Committee on Committees rather than by the majority leader tends to give both the chair and the members greater autonomy. The process is less centralized and more consultative than the selection process in the House. Seniority, which was rigidly followed during the era of conservative hegemony in the Senate, remains an important factor in the assignment of chairs and memberships, but it is no longer the sole rule. The majority leader does not make the appointments, but is a potent force in the selection process. The removal of Senator Willet from the chair of the Finance Committee in 1987 reflects a major difference in the way in which the Senate operated in 1987 compared with 1963. Such action would have been unthinkable in those days. But even though power has become more centralized than in the past, Senate committee chairs, once installed, remain more powerful than their House counterparts, and within the Senate, are treated with respect and deference by their colleagues.

The power of committee chairs is reflected in several ways. Through control of their own domains and through the Rules Committee, they share with the majority leader responsibility for running the Senate. The financial committee chairs, in particular, have great leeway in scheduling consideration of bills and they figure prominently in the development of the leadership's strategy for dealing with the governor and the House, as well as management of Senate consideration of budget and financial issues. The chairs are usually the chief negotiators for the Senate in conferences with the House. They will also normally be consulted and participate in negotiations with the governor on budget and tax issues, especially during the final days of a session when a compromise between the two houses and with the governor must be hammered out.

Their power over tax and spending legislation ensures them considerable deference by colleagues, not only in their management of measures reported by their committees, but often in other matters as well. Many bills that are originally referred to other committees must also be reviewed by the financial committees before they can come to the floor of the Senate. This gives the chairs of these committees additional clout over a wide range of legislation and a respectful hearing when they ask consideration of bills or amendments dear to their own districts or other interests.

The chairs of the Tax and Finance committees do not operate totally independent of the majority leader, but they are not the leader's lackeys. Traditionally, the senators heading these committees have operated at the center of the Senate oligarchy. Their views have been given great weight by the majority leader, and each has been a major spokesperson for the Senate in handling of tax and spending legislation. Their power in the Senate derives from their positions and the expertise that they gain as managers of the big money bills. In a sense, they control access to the treasury by other members of the Senate. Their judgment or preferences are likely to be accepted by others on the committee even if they are regarded as "wrong."

This power is subject to occasional abuse, as when Tax Committee Chair Johnson lobbied colleagues in the 1987 session to support legislation that would have benefited a firm that proposed to build a plant on the Iron Range. After he had managed the passage of the bill, it was discovered that the firm was under investigation for securities fraud—a fact known to Johnson and the majority leader, who apologized to the Senate for not disclosing the investigation. The bill was recalled from the House and buried. It is fair to say that the bill was passed by the Senate almost solely because Johnson was one of its sponsors, and few senators, even those with serious doubts about the firm and the bill, wished to antagonize so powerful a committee chair.

Because senators must serve on several committees, they do not become as specialized in their knowledge of legislation as members of the House. On the other hand, longer service allows for greater experience in dealing with legislative issues and procedures, and produces a number of senators who are comfortable participating in almost any area of substantive policy, whether they have personally worked on the subject before or not.

Senate committees tend to be less partisan than House committees. Minority members are accepted for their expertise and ideas, and may make substantial contributions to the committee process. A minority member may occasionally head a subcommittee or be accepted as the author of important measures or amendments. While there may be clear partisan differences over critical legislation, and a certain amount of partisan sparring is accepted as part of the game, committee members are generally respected for what they have to offer, without too much concern for whether they are members of the majority or minority caucus.

Committees in the Senate also make somewhat more extensive use of staff than do House committees. Committee staff, however, are regarded by senators even less well than by their House colleagues. Thirty-three percent of the senators serving during the period from 1981 to 1985 rated their committee staffs inadequate (compared with only 15 percent in the House). Among Senate leaders from the majority party (DFL), including committee chairs, 41 percent thought committee staffs were less than adequate (Backstrom, 1986). This is a curious finding, since the senators who chair committees have considerable discretion in the employment of committee staff and generally express high regard for individual staff members in interviews. The finding may reflect on hiring practices, on committee management by the chair, or on the degree to which senators with long experience as heads of committees rely on their own knowledge rather than that of staff. It may also reflect the problems that arise when data available for analysis cannot be disaggregated for more detailed analysis. The same survey, for instance, shows that more than half of the Senate leaders who responded thought that the greatest needs for additional staff were in computer and data processing assistance and in development of an independent staff capacity in the Legislature to analyze the budget. An even 50 percent of the Senate leaders thought that more scientific and technical experts were needed on the staff. These are substantial deficiencies, which could lead senators who have great respect for existing staff as individuals to conclude that their overall committee staff resources are inadequate.

Pluralism and Persuasion

Over the past 25 years, Senate leadership has evolved from a process of articulating a shared political culture to one of mediating among factional interests. In the Rosenmeier era, the senator from Little Falls and his colleagues provided a collective leadership based on widely shared values about government and the legislative process. Government was recognized as having a positive, but limited role to play in dealing with public problems. The Legislature was regarded as a place where good citizens, steeped in these values, assembled to meet clear needs after taking counsel together. The Senate, in particular, was a council of equals whose job it was to see that policy was both wise and well crafted. Policy was regarded as better if it had broad support from members of the Senate and reflected conservative values. This result could be achieved more readily if division of the Senate into hardened caucuses was avoided, and if no senator or group set itself up as leader of the rest. The only organization needed was a means of securing the committee system in the right hands, so the process could work to produce legislation consistent with these values.

As the Senate was reapportioned, and the leaders of this era left it through defeat, retirement, and death, and as new members arrived from the Twin Cities and their suburbs, the old consensus came under strain. While many of the traditions of the Senate remained intact, the impact of new interests eager to be satisfied and the requirement that senators be elected from a ballot that showed their party affiliation necessitated changes in the way in which the Senate was led. These changes were presaged by Stanley Holmquist, who, even prior to party designation, began to turn the caucus into an instrument of leadership.

The majority leader under Nicholas Coleman and Roger Moe has gradually become a near equal to the speaker in legislative influence. The method of operation is different, however, depending more on persuasion and mediation skills among caucus factions rather than command of the process and control of appointments. As has happened with the House leadership, the use of the caucus to raise campaign funds from political action committees has enhanced the influence of the leadership over newer senators and those with more competitive districts. As in the House, Senate leadership has become a full-time occupation for the majority leader and a few other major leaders. The Senate presidency now takes over half the time of Senator Hughes.

In spite of all the changes that have occurred over the last generation, leadership in the Senate remains more dispersed than in the House. The caucus is weaker as an instrument of leadership. Consequently, discussion of most issues in the Senate is less partisan in tone than in the House. Perhaps most important, there is a culture of collegiality. These factors in combination produce a process that places greater emphasis on consensus, even though it may be orchestrated by an oligarchy of leaders and committee chairs. Minority members are not relegated to ineffective opposition, as in the House, but are consulted, and their talents and ideas are used in the deliberative process.

Debate in the Senate tends to be more orderly and deliberative than in the House. Because the presiding officer is not viewed as the leader of the majority party, there is almost no emphasis on procedural skirmishes and challenges to authority of the president.

The diffusion of power and consensus politics make it harder to affix clear responsibility to the majority in the Senate than in the House. The tendency to accommodate the minority caucus or individual senators, combined with the other factors, means that the Senate does in fact give legislation a different look than it receives in the House. The difference is less in ideological or interest-group perspective than in method of consideration. While the House tends to draw the differences between the parties in stark terms, the Senate is more likely to examine the merits of an issue and to try to find a way to bridge the differences between majority and minority or factional views.

The experience of senators, compared with members of the House, is another important factor in understanding the differences in the operation of the two chambers. Four-year terms tend to make them more patient in dealing with policy issues. The lower rate of turnover and longer tenure changes the perspective of the body, making it less susceptible to demands for immediate action, whether from the governor, colleagues, or external interest groups.

6

The Third House:
Conference Committees

Constitutionally, the Legislature consists of two separate houses, both of which must enact legislation in the same form for it to become law. For that to happen, an extraconstitutional institution had to be created to reconcile the inevitable differences that arise not only because the House and Senate are composed of different people, but also because they approach their legislative tasks in different ways. Although the steps in the process tend to parallel each other, the results often diverge in significant ways. The conference committee, made up of an equal number of members from each house, is the mechanism legislatures use to resolve differences between the houses that cannot be settled through informal consultation between the sponsors of legislation.

The legislative procedures of each house are not designed for speed but for deliberation. Getting a bill through either the House or Senate presents its author with a considerable challenge. In Minnesota, for example, only about 10 to 15 percent of the bills that are introduced in a session are enacted into law.

The culture of each house shapes its response to a legislative issue. In 1985, for example, similar witnesses testified before the House and Senate committees on the farm crisis, yet the Senate bill emphasized debt restructuring and authorized a foreclosure moratorium, while the House bill rejected that approach and provided instead for an interest buy-down program. The Agriculture committees of the House and Senate responded to different interests and pursued different agendas. Even when both houses are controlled by the same party, the parallel processes produce divergent results (Gross, 1982).

An identical bill introduced in both houses must hurdle unique obstacles in each chamber. It may face a hostile committee chair in one house and a friendly one in the other. Senate and House sponsors may be quite different in their interest, zeal, and skill in persuading colleagues to support particular provisions. Interest groups may have the ear of key members of one house, but not of the other.

The attitude of the one house toward a bill, if known, may be a factor that affects what the other does. One house may, for example, give the bill only a cursory review if it is known that the other house examined it thoroughly. Knowledge that there are fundamental differences between the houses on a bill may lead to a stratagem of confrontation if its managers feel that they will have to demand a lot in conference in order to achieve a compromise they and their house can accept. Confrontations may be exacerbated when the houses are controlled by opposing parties and the bill in question has important symbolic value for electoral politics. Knowledge that the second house will almost surely kill a bill can lead to irresponsible behavior by the first house. Members can grandstand and vote for measures they would not support if there were a real prospect they would become law. In other cases, if a bill is much desired by one house, the other may make it a bargaining chip for something more important to it.

Members constantly look over their shoulders to watch the other house. An action in one house can reverberate through the other, changing the way it looks at an issue. A bill's sponsor must balance the actions that have to be taken to gain passage in that house with the need for a bill capable of passing both houses. Typically, a representative cooperates with a senator, and each guides the bill through his or her respective house. Networks of cooperation exist between the houses, and informal discussions coordinate action.

A bicameral legislature, by definition, promotes a form of deliberation (Page, 1978). Every bill that passes in one chamber has the opportunity to be considered twice. But the fact that an identical bill must pass both houses places great stress on legislatures like Minnesota's, where there are constitutional limits on the length of sessions. Ironically, this sometimes tends to produce less scrutiny of legislation rather than to lengthen or broaden the deliberative process. Considerable pressure builds for early action in one house to allow enough time for the other to consider it. Important, controversial, and complex bills must be considered simultaneously by each house rather than sequentially to meet deadlines for committee bills and for final adjournment of the Legislature. Even with parallel action on companion bills, major legislation rarely clears both houses before the final three or four weeks of the session. Some cannot be scheduled for floor action in one of the houses until the final week. This, in turn, means that conference committees must reach compromises during the hectic end-of-session rush.

Fortunately, the House and Senate versions of many bills are easily reconciled. Most bills do not require extensive debate or engender opposition. When the language or basic intent of House and Senate bills are similar, one can often be substituted for the other. Local issues may be settled by the members whose districts are involved, and the result is readily accepted by each house. Of the 309 acts signed into law after the 1985 regular session, only 48 were the products of conferences. These were, however, the most important, complex, and controversial measures.

At the beginning of a session, the leadership of both houses meets informally. They discuss the coming session in general terms, and have been known to set budget guidelines and agree on bills that deserve prompt attention. This type of meeting continues intermittently through the session and is an unofficial predecessor to the conference process. Meetings such as these set the tone for the conference committees to come. If deals are struck and adhered to in passing the bills in each house, the conference process will go relatively smoothly.

Conference committees are the necessary, formally empowered continuation of informal discussions that seek to bridge the gap between houses. Governed by Joint Rules adopted by both houses, no bill can be reported by a conference unless a majority of the members from each house assent to it. Once reported, a conference bill may not be amended by either house. It must be accepted, rejected, or recommitted to the conference.

Once the major bills reach conference, a shift in the focus of the Legislature occurs. The leadership of the House and Senate, rather than concentrating on the politics of passage in their respective chambers, shift their efforts toward an emphasis on the politics of interhouse compromise. The Legislature turns from a parallel process that duplicates efforts and produces divergent results to one that places high value on reconciliation of differences.

The Rise of the Conference in Minnesota

In the Minnesota Legislature, as in other bicameral legislatures, a conference committee is appointed by the leadership in the House and Senate to reconcile differing versions of a bill. Under the Legislature's rules, three or five members of each house are appointed to meet and reach a compromise that can be presented to both houses for final passage. The compromise might necessitate only minor changes in language, reconciliation of a single section, or sweeping revision of an entire bill.

In the last 20 years, conference committees have become the standard way the Legislature arrives at agreement and closes each session. In many respects they are the dominant policy bodies of the Minnesota Legislature: In 1963, as Table 3 shows, 19 conferences were held. The number roughly doubled from 59 in the 1971–72 session to 122 in 1973–74. It seems reasonable to suggest that the introduction of the flexible session and the new rules requiring open meetings contributed to the sudden ballooning of conferences. By the 1977–78 session, the number of conferences had grown to 148. This eightfold increase in conference committees has become the pattern, and in each biennium since 1978 at least 100 conferences have been held. The first session of the 74th Legislature, in 1985, held 76 conferences by the time the regular session ended on May 20. Another 38 were held in 1986. In the 1987–88 session there were 157 conferences, setting a new record.

Table 3. Use of Conference Committees in Minnesota

Session	Years	Number of Conferences
63d	1963	19
64th	1965	36
65th	1967	53
66th	1969	80
67th	1971	59
68th	1973–74	122
69th	1975–76	122
70th	1977–78	148
71st	1979–80	109
72d	1981–82	134
73d	1983–84	134
74th	1985–86	114
75th	1987–88	157

The Minnesota Legislature allows informal conferences to meet when the Legislature itself is not in session, and several of these conferences met in the interim between the regular session and the special session convened on June 19, 1985, and again before the special session on April 2, 1986. In addition, at least 3 unofficial conferences were appointed during the 1985–86 interim.

Membership and Selection of Conferees

Conferees are named by the speaker of the House and the Committee on Committees in the Senate. The Committee on Committees is headed by the Senate majority leader, and only one of the five members, the minority leader, represents the minority caucus.

Those frequently named to conferences are the authors and coauthors of bills, the chairs of standing committees, those with expertise or interest in the issue, and those able to represent the body or caucus most capably. But no member serves on a conference by right. Each of these conferees comes to the position through the leadership, which must recognize a member's qualities for the post. Some members are perennial conferees on certain committees, others must scramble to be named to one committee or another.

Conference committee membership thus is an index of a member's power, expertise, and ties to the leadership. It augments one's prestige as it is a form of recognition of a member's legislative ability. It is a badge of power because a conferee is in position to provide benefits for one's own legislative interests and those of friends.

In 1985, 82 percent of all legislators served on at least 1 conference. In the Senate, 90 percent were on at least 1 conference. In the House 77 percent were on one or more conference committees. The House excluded 23 percent of its members from serving on a conference, and the Senate excluded 8 percent. The larger House provides fewer opportunities for a member to serve on conference committees, and each member served on an average of only 1.94 conferences, as opposed to an average of 3.88 conferences for each senator.

Serving as cochair of 1 key conference is more important than mere membership on several less significant ones. Leaders in both houses seldom serve on many committees, and it is typical that the chair of an omnibus conference such as tax, education aids, state agencies, or human services is on only a small number of conferences.

In 1985, 16 representatives served in 5 or more conferences. In the Senate, 18 members served in between 5 and 9 conferences, and 5 members served in 10 or more. It is clear that these members—13 percent of the representatives and 42 percent of the senators—had more influence on legislation during the final days of the session than their fellow members who did not serve on many important conferences.

Conference committee appointments are weighted heavily in favor of the majority parties in the House and Senate. Each house selected 260 conferees in the 1985 session. The Republican House leaders named 182 Republicans and 78 Democrats, a 70 percent majority for Republican members. The Democratic Senate named 190 DFL members to conference and 70 IR members, a 74 percent majority for the Democrats. In the Senate, minority members were on roughly the same number of conferences as the average member. In the House, however, minority members served on an average of 1 conference each, roughly half that of the average member.

While the party in control of a house uses its power to dominate conference committees, minority members usually gain a seat on most conferences through appointment by the speaker and majority leader. The House in 1985 named a minority member to 90 percent and the Senate had a minority member on 86 percent of all conferences. One significant exception was the omnibus tax conference committee, which contained no minority members from either house.

To some extent the ability of the majority leaders to appoint minority conferees is constrained by legislative courtesy and the undeniable expertise of some minority members in the matter at hand. As a general rule, a minority member will not be appointed if he or she voted against the bill when it was before the house. Even within that constraint, on crucial conferences the leader can appoint a minority member more to his or her liking than to the liking of the minority leader. And if any minority member is appointed, it is clear that the favor came from the leader of the majority, not the minority leader. It is not unknown for a house to name a minority party member (who voted with the majority) to embarrass the conferees from his or her party from the other house who took an opposing view.

The increase in the number of conferences over the last 20 years has allowed more members, including more members of minority parties, to take part in the conference process.

Significance of the Conference in the Legislative Process

Conferences vary in size, importance, duration, and result. There were 60 conferences with three members per house in 1985, and 16 with five members per house. Topics ranged from the attempted reconciliation of omnibus bills concerning taxes, education, transportation, and state agencies, to bills concerned with trail land conveyances, school bus book racks, and coroner removal of pituitary glands. A conference may require only a negligible amount of time to report a compromise, or may take days, weeks, and even months, as was the case in the 1971 special session.

During the 1985 regular session, 48 laws resulted from conference reports, representing 63 percent of all conferences. Several of the remaining conference reports were enacted during the special session.

With very few exceptions, major legislation, and especially tax and spending legislation, is given its ultimate shape in the conference. For many policies, what happens in conference is more important than what happens in either house. Aware of this fact, both lobbyists and some members have in recent years waited to advance proposals until bills reached conference. Then they have sought to have a conferee insert them in the final report. Several important pieces of legislation, including the establishment of the community college system, were added to other bills in the conference committee. This practice has been justified as occasionally necessary to prevent important, but highly controversial, legislation from being killed or weakened by the regular legislative processes. But it has also been widely condemned as an abuse of the conferences and a needless circumvention of both good legislative practice and the Minnesota Constitution's single-subject rule.

The Environment for Legislative Collective Bargaining

The conference is where two previously separated legislative and representative streams converge. The protocol and procedure of conferences are different from those of standing legislative committees. Traditionally, conferees from the House and Senate sit on opposite sides of the committee table. The chair rotates between a member of the House and a member of the Senate, with the house in which the bill originated holding the chair first. Rotation may be daily, hourly, or by meeting.

Conferees bargain as teams, representing the interests of their houses. Each side has its own staff, its own resources, mentors, leadership, and mandate. One side often accepts research or legal advice form the other house's staff, preferring to debate the substantive differences. There have been, however, significant differences of opinion either caused or buttressed by separate staffs.

The bicameral system also produces conferees who have significantly different sources for their mandates. House districts are smaller, and House members more numerous, requiring more extensive coalition building. Senate conferees have a broader political base, coming form larger districts and a smaller party caucus. As a result, interests and strategies are different, and House and Senate conferees may feel the weight of public opinion or of their colleagues in different ways.

Conferences are concentrated during the last three weeks of the legislative session when more bills come to the floor than at any other time. This occurs because major, complex legislation usually takes a long time to work its way through each house. Unlike regular committees, conferences are allowed to meet while the House and Senate are in session. This generates severe problems in scheduling conferences and in conducting them, as conferees of either house may be summoned to the floor by their leaders to participate in a close or important vote. Senators, since they generally serve on more conferences than their House counterparts, may have more difficult scheduling problems. If the conferees can hammer out an agreement in an hour in one of the smaller meeting rooms, however, no scheduling conflicts occur. More complicated bills require longer conferences, which must fit into the rush of activity in both houses. With all these conflicting schedules, the result is a process that moves by fits and starts. The 1985 conference on taxes, for example, was constantly interrupted so that members of one house or the other could answer a call to vote. Required to vote, senators often had to leave the conferences for as little as 5 or as long as 15 fifteen minutes.

The momentum of a conference may be lost through these intermittent intrusions of other concerns, such as the need of a conferee to attend a committee meeting or a caucus or to participate in debate on a bill in which he or she has a strong interest. Members of a conference may have to switch roles at a moment's notice, one minute debating broad policy on the floor and the next discussing technical differences in language in a conference room.

The activities and positions of the full houses also intrude in a larger sense. If the House passed its version by a substantial majority, or if the majority seems to be adamant in its position on a contested provision, this affects the latitude of conferees in agreeing to a compromise. Conferences are not separate events apart from the momentum of the Legislature as a whole. Rather, they tend to reflect the tone of the session. Thus, the House leadership in 1985 carried its banner for large tax cuts into the conference committee and used it as a forum to confront the DFL senators and governor with the House's adamant posture for a billion-dollar cut.

Because the houses are still conducting business while the conferences meet, conferees must be aware of simultaneous activity elsewhere. During a 1985 conference on farm relief measures, for example, one senator was arguing for a voluntary mortgage foreclosure moratorium in conference while his separate mandatory foreclosure moratorium bill was being debated before the full House. House conferees had to combat one form of the measure in conference and another form on the House floor.

Legislators are sensitive to the circumstances that brought them to office and to public opinions that may influence imminent elections. Even when representatives and senators are elected in the same year, variations in district size and diversity can produce conflicting perceptions of Minnesota public opinion. House and Senate conferees may come from different geographic regions and weigh issues differently as a result. House members must face the voters every two years and the midterm elections can bring in a House that feels it has a significantly different mandate from that of the holdover Senate. In 1985, the change of party control in the House highlighted the "mandate" problem. Having been elected more recently than senators, the House majority claimed a fresher mandate from the electorate and used this perception as a reason to stand fast and demand concessions from the Senate. The two-year term for representatives tends to produce a greater awareness of public opinion in the House and a higher and constant level of apprehension about facing the electorate in an upcoming election

Different lengths of terms are only one way the politics of each house bears on the conference committees. The Minnesota House uses a more rigid set of rules than does the Senate. The Senate fosters a more formal atmosphere, but the House is far more partisan. Lobbyists and interest groups, therefore, use different approaches in crafting legislation in each house. In the House, a major bill is likely to be the product of compromise in the majority caucus, but then to be rammed through with little concern for minority views. The key problem is to gain support from the caucus or the committee members of the majority party. The companion bill in the Senate may be a product of compromise among interested senators, regardless of party. Gaining support from senators regarded by their colleagues as the experts on the subject is important.

Conferees may be bound by deals struck earlier in order to secure passage in their house. The margin by which the bill passed the house may also be a factor. Conferees working from a large majority often feel compelled to insist on their position if the bill had only a bare majority in the other house.

The wide variety of forces that brings each house to a conference table produces interests on each side in both the substance of the bill and in the personal political value of managing its enactment. The reputation of members can be enhanced or damaged by what they gain or lose for their house in conferences. Being named to a conference committee is itself a recognition of leadership capacity. Bringing home the bacon confirms it and builds capital for future use in legislative battles.

While conferences are an integral part of the legislative process and conditioned by the politics of bicameralism, they also are a distinct stage in the legislative process, with separate dynamics. Much of the research on conference committees tends to focus on which house prevails most frequently (Fenno, 1966; Vogler, 1970; 1971; Strom and Rundquist, 1977). The conference is seen as a game or contest; and indeed, in the context of a particular session of the Legislature, a conference has some of the characteristics of a game or a set piece in conflict resolution.

To the extent that legislative politics is a game, each side is interested in winning — or at least in not losing. Rather than concentrating on which house seems to win, however, it is more important to understand how the conference works. The emphasis on winners and losers treats the conference as a zero-sum game, which it rarely is. A successful conference is one in which both houses win things important to their members. It is more important for an understanding of democratic government to know just what goes on in the conference process, for it has become, for all practical purposes, a third house of the Minnesota Legislature.

The Typical Conference

The legislative session can be broken into three major periods. The first several weeks are given over to introduction of bills, testimony, and preliminary debate on the issues of the day. The pace is almost leisurely. The Legislature is looking outward and is concerned with policy proposals and hearing from organized groups and the public at large.

As the session continues, coalition building and decision making assume greater importance, and information gathering narrows. Committee activity moves from hearings to work sessions to "mark up" bills and amendments. As deadlines for bill introductions and committee reports approach, the pace of the session intensifies, and the time spent in committee sessions and on floor debate grows longer. Interest-group pressure becomes intense and visible during this period when each house is shaping major legislation.

The appointment of conference committees marks the third phase, and a final turning inward of the Legislature. Small groups of conferees (usually in close contact with the leadership) supported by research staffs, the relevant state agencies, and self-selected lobbyists, meet to hammer out final versions of major bills. This stage of the process is marked by a chaotic schedule of conference committee meetings interspersed with long, contentious, sometimes raucous debates on the floor of each house as the leadership of the Legislature drives headlong for adjournment. The leadership has its greatest leverage on legislation during the conference phase, where debate is curtailed and a few trusted members shape the final content of the most important bills (Rosenthal, 1981).

Few rules limit conference committee activity. The Joint Rules outline the procedures for moving bills into and out of conference committees. The actual process of a conference is described only very generally:

> [At] the agreed upon hour the Conference Committee shall meet. The members from each house shall state to the members from the other house, orally or in writing, the reason for their respective positions. The members shall confer thereon and shall report to their respective houses the agreement they have reached, or if none, the fact of a disagreement. (Joint Rule 2.06)

Great latitude is left as to exactly how meetings shall be conducted and staffed, proceedings recorded, and issues debated. Yet, even clearly stated rules are interpreted within the discretion of the conferees. The joint rule on conferences requires that "all Conference Committees shall be open to the Public" (Joint Rule 2.06). From one point of view, this rule is satisfied if a particular conference committee meets at least once in public session.

It is clear that nothing in the rules and very little in the literature outlines the actual processes that conferences follow. When rules do not prescribe, however, custom and usage tend to provide the ways conferences go about their business.

The Preliminaries

After the house in which a bill originated refuses to accept the other's version or amendments, a conference is requested and the leadership names its conferees. A day or so usually passes before the other house officially names its conferees. At times, however, conferees for major bills are known well in advance of their actual appointment. Informal meetings may be held among the conferees of each house before they have been officially appointed. In the 1985 session, such a group met in public in an unofficial meeting, resolved the differences between the houses, and then reconvened when the conference was officially named to ratify the earlier decisions. The conferees are prepared by their leadership with a strategy and a tentative list of key issues and possible compromise points. Informal meetings between the conferees may explore the possibility of an easy compromise.

Informal meetings are often all that is necessary to reach a compromise on an issue. A brief public meeting then follows, a compromise is announced, and the conference committee report is sent to each house for final passage. One house might simply recede from its position on a point, clearing the way for final passage. In these instances, the conference is usually the first serious attempt to compare two essentially similar bills, and can quickly clear up minor differences. On larger matters, a more lengthy conference follows the early, informal meetings. These early meetings allow each side to be prepared, and permit each house to check out the other's positions and degree of commitment to them.

When each house has named its conferees, the formal committee meetings can begin. Major conferences dealing with taxes, appropriations, or education are very different from conferences dealing with one narrow policy or program. The negotiations are more complex, the leaders and the governor often are deeply involved in the strategy of the conference and in the development of compromise formulas and proposals. Lobbyist and media attention are more intense, as the conferees are pursued, interviewed, and buttonholed.

Public Meetings, Private Negotiations

Once each house has appointed its conferees, the House and Senate cochairs agree on a meeting time, which is posted on bulletin boards outside of the Senate and House Index offices. Often, a handwritten sign will be posted on the door of a committee room taken over by a particular conference. A conference that meets daily will usually set a time for the next meeting at the end of that day's meeting. Conference meeting times are typically haphazardly posted, and very little systematic advertising is done. Often, the only way to be sure when a conference will meet is to call the chief author of the bill before the conference. If the chief author does not know when the meeting will convene that afternoon, the caller must keep calling until a time is known. Some conferences are so poorly advertised that short of camping out at the Capitol, it is impossible for an observer to keep apprised of all meeting times.

Conference committee meetings are sandwiched in between important floor actions, meals, private meetings, and brief periods of sleep. Meetings may occur late at night, only to be followed by another meeting early the following morning. Public meetings are held at and advertised for the convenience of conferees. The haphazard posting system and the penchant for holding meetings at unusual times shut out all but the most dedicated observers.

Public meetings are held in meeting rooms at the Capitol and State Office Building. Tables occupy the center of each room, and are ringed with seats for staff and audience, an arrangement that tends to encourage partisan behavior (Patterson, 1972). Microphones are available if conferees want to speak to the entire room, but are usually ignored in favor of quietly speaking directly to the members on the other side of the table. Rooms are equipped with telephones to allow members to be contacted if they are needed for a floor vote. Lights can be dimmed for regular meetings or raised to accommodate television cameras.

House and Senate conferees are staffed by their respective houses. A conferee can call on the staff from his house, committee, or caucus. Research staffs provide members with comparisons between House and Senate bills, section by section. In addition, conferees can ask relevant state agencies for information on technical points and on the position of the agency or the governor. Occasionally, committee members may ask an interest-group representative for information. In most meetings the conference has four separate sources of information available to it: the state agency, the House staff, Senate staff, and lobbyists. Where these sources differ on facts or in opinions, the conflict between the legislators representing each house may be exacerbated. During the 1985 tax conference, for instance, the House conferees disputed the validity of Department of Finance data. In that conference and others, the separate legislative staffs were often asked to prepare quick reports to buttress the position of the conferees. The availability of separate staff reinforced the strategy of confrontation pursued by the conferees.

The public deliberations of a conference committee vary in intensity from perfunctory technical discussions about the language of a bill to shouting and political acrimony. Conferences usually begin with a reading by staff members of each provision on which the houses disagree. As the staff reads the provisions, conferees comment, ask questions, and probe each other to determine how strongly positions are held. Quick agreements can often be reached on minor issues or technical differences in the bills, and the possibility of larger compromises can be indicated, but usually this stage is only a preliminary skirmish. Major differences that are politically crucial in the section-by-section review may result in a pause while senators and representatives indulge in political posturing. If each side envisions a different impact for an unemployment program, for example, the conferees interrupt the slow detailed comparison of sections to give the issue the political attention it deserves.

A tension exists between the two primary activities of the public meetings. Technical consideration of concrete provisions and broad political statements do not fit easily into the same meeting. Both, however, are important in producing the compromises that ultimately must be struck. When issues can be reduced to technical points, the conferees can turn their attention to a search for language that either achieves a mutual objective that was worded poorly in one or both versions, or to devise language that is sufficiently ambiguous in meaning or effect to satisfy both houses.

Venting of political opinions may also be a preliminary step in resolving an issue. It can offer clues about the basis for future compromise. A conferee may want to let the world know where he or she stands, but also to point out that the need to compromise is reluctantly accepted in order to achieve some progress or to prevent a greater calamity.

Neither political speech making nor technical fine tuning by itself produces the major compromises necessary to finish conference work. The 1985 session conferences on minor bills often used a strategy of first cleaning away the small details and then focusing the conference's attention on the central issues in dispute. Larger conferences, however, waited for their cues on major compromises from the leaders, who were slow in providing them. In both cases, the critical compromises themselves were not worked out in the public meetings, where very little actual bargaining occurred. Political speeches, argument over the meanings of facts and figures, and the reconciliation of small details filled the time at public meetings.

A conference committee frequently conducts its most serious business in private sessions among members, sometimes between only the chairs, and sometimes involving others, such as the leaders of each house or representatives of the governor.

A little reflection suggests why so few important compromises are reached in public. Unlike debate in a house committee or on the floor, where a member can lose a point while defending it with vigor, a good-faith negotiation session requires a person to concede that an adversary is correct, that the point doesn't matter all that much, that one is willing to trade a concession on one issue for support on another, or that a concession is required to get something passed. This is not the kind of talk on which political careers are usually founded. Negotiation is far more ambiguous in both practice and perception than advocacy.

Therefore, much of the actual bargaining occurs in private meetings. The pressures brought to bear on members in public meetings also make private meetings more attractive than bargaining in public. The messy spectacle of bargaining is shielded from the public eye. Compromises are not necessarily produced through statesmanlike behavior, although the end products are at times worthy of the finest statesmen. Conferees are concerned that, in public, bargaining would be seen out of the context that makes it necessary and desirable. Private meetings allow face-saving compromises, and this is a major function of the conference process, as it is of any earnest effort at conflict resolution (Fisher and Urey).

Discussions are also conducted in private because the leader of each house and the governor need access to the conference. Private meetings allow the leadership and the governor to act without the embarrassment of exposing conferees as secondary actors and without appearing to manipulate the process.

Finally, holding private meetings allows an issue to be settled without floating too many trial balloons. A public bargaining process might expose fragile pieces of the eventual compromise to attack by legislative opponents, lobbyists, or the media and allow mobilization of opposition before all of the pieces are firmly in place. Private meetings allow the final compromises to be announced en toto, as an accomplished fact. This leads to the event of interest in any major conference: *the announcement.*

During the course of a conference, the results of the private discussions are bled into the public meetings through a series of announcements. The existence of private meetings are themselves the subject of sheepish announcements. The chairs will announce that the next public meeting will take place after a meeting with leaders, or a conference chair's secretary will tell a caller that the conference is meeting privately that day. When results finally come, the public meetings tend to take the form of briefings for the public and media concerning a final version of the bill that all have agreed to support. Instead of providing a forum for public debate and negotiation, the public conference meeting is often chiefly a place to announce the contents of a package that has been put together in private.

Before the conferees sign the final conference report, they will have presented and defended the positions of their houses, dealt with tiny details and boring technicalities, heard hasty expert and curbstone advice on the effect of their decisions, and perhaps have seen themselves on television or read their statements in the newspapers. The process contains room for public posturing and for detailed work, but generally reserves the toughest negotiations to the private arena.

The conference report itself consists simply of a revised bill. Separate reports identifying changes made in the conference are not provided to other members or to the public. A staff summary may occasionally be available, but there is no document comparable to a congressional conference report. Members must wade through the bill itself to see what has actually been done, although the Joint Rules were amended in 1987 to require the bill's manager to explain the changes from the bill as it was last before the body (Joint Rule 2.06). The rules also require that, except for the last few days of a session (when the most important conference reports are usually completed), conference reports be printed and available to members for at least 12 hours before action is taken on them. Even when this rule is honored, it may be difficult for any but a few members other than the bill's manager to know what changes have been made and whether they were a result of genuine compromise in the conference, or if new, extraneous matter has been inserted by a conferee with the mutual consent of other members of the conference. And time may not allow for a full disclosure of the changes in the rush to adjournment. It is possible, indeed likely in the case of voluminous bills, that no one, including the bill's manager, knows about every change that has been made.

Roles and Dynamics of the Conferees

Only a concurrent agreement by a majority of the conferees from each house can produce a conference report for final passage. Members are named by their leadership because of their interest and expertise in the bill and their ability to represent the house and caucus. Conferees do not work in a vacuum. A variety of other actors make their views known during conference and try to influence the process. The conferees are essential to the process, but as we have seen, they are not always the most important actors in it.

If there is a sharp division between the houses on a particular issue, the rotating chair allows each house's delegation to practice its political stagecraft. The

1985 tax conference was deeply divided over the size of the tax cut to be made. Conferees alternately walked out when the other body held the chair and presented partisan interpretations of issues when their side occupied it.

Each house's members take the turns in presenting their position and in leading the bargaining process. When the cochair from the House holds the gavel, the powers of recognizing speakers and adjourning the meeting are available to be exercised. The Senate cochair must wait until the next meeting to exercise these powers, and in the meantime leads the Senate's conferees in the discussions.

The other conferees may fill a variety of supporting roles. One member may be responsible for making a political attack on the positions of the other house or on the governor, if of a different party. Such a member may also serve as the "bad guy" on the negotiating team, taking a hard line against compromises to sustain as much as possible of his/her house's position on politically sensitive issues. This member may work as the enforcer for the leadership, to convince the other side that they will have to make major concessions if they want an agreement and to prevent easy concessions by colleagues.

Often members are assigned to a conference because of their expertise in some aspect of the larger bill. In one 1985 conference, a member suggested that a subcommittee of the conference be created to allow the House and Senate expert members to work out a compromise on an issue they were placed on the conference to handle. Members of a conference committee fill these roles according to their talents and the strategy of the leaders who appointed them.

The leaders of each house are de facto participants in each conference. They set the strategies that guide the conferees in particular conferences and meetings, and the overall strategy that all conferees will follow. The speaker and majority leader meet with and encourage the conferees they appoint, and can exercise a voice in the decisions they make. Many of the short breaks in conferences allow the conferees to check with their leaders, in order to ensure that any potential change will be acceptable and capable of passage in the whole house. Major conferences often require long recesses to provide time for full-scale strategy meetings between a house's leaders and its conferees.

Conferees are accorded varying degrees of latitude. Conferences on minor matters are entrusted completely to the conferees. More complex and central matters are watched closely by the leaders. Two basic types of conferences can be identified based on behavior of conferees. In most conferences the conferees serve as trustees. In the few important conferences they act more like agents. In a "trustee" conference, the conferees have a mandate to act in the interests of their respective houses to secure the best bill they can, consistent with the views of the house as represented by its version of the bill. They receive little direction from their party leaders and have wide latitude within which to reach agreement. Trustee conferences tend to handle less controversial and partisan bills, although they may deal with important subjects. In "agency" conferences, on the other hand, conferees operate more as agents of their house leaders, their discretion is more limited, and any agreement must be ratified by the leaders before it can be finally accepted.

Major policy issues are directly the concerns of the leaders of each house, and for all practical purposes the speaker, majority leader, and governor are the key conferees. Conference chairs act as lieutenants to the leadership. They may propose or even make the deals that are critical to resolving the differences between the houses, but no deal is final until accepted by the leaders. Before each major session of a conference gets under way, the chairs usually meet with the leadership while the other conferees mill about, waiting. Rosenthal (1981) understated it when he noted that the conference was where the leadership has their greatest leverage. In Minnesota, conferences have at times been entirely orchestrated by the leadership, with the tacit consent of caucuses.

The centralization of authority in the hands of the leadership goes even further. In the 1985 session, appropriations conferences awaited the results of the tax conference, since spending levels depended on final revenue estimates. The tax conference awaited a compromise among the leaders and the governor. These major conferences were reduced to satellites revolving around the central actors: the majority leader, the speaker, and the governor. The governor came directly before the tax conference to announce his compromise proposal, which incorporated earlier offers from both the speaker and the majority leader. The resulting compromise then rippled through the other money conference committees, setting the framework for their decisions.

Besides the leaders and members, many other actors have an impact on conferences. Chief among these is the media, especially television. The arrival of a camera crew at a conference changes the tone of the meeting in progress. The room lights are turned up, usually followed by an escalation in rhetoric. Conferees who have been mumbling under their breath across the table turn toward the camera and speak into the table microphone, which they have until now ignored. Discussion quickly leaves the subsection at hand, and political speech making breaks out. This leads to face-to-face argument. The camera captures a few minutes of film, the lights go down, and the conference discovers that the exchange for the benefit of cameras may inhibit an easy return to the discussions of subsections.

Political speech making aims to sway public opinion. It is not addressed to the conference as such. As a negotiating tactic, its object is to encourage public or lobbyist pressure on the leaders of the other house to concede a point. When Senate members walked out of the 1985 tax conference on several occasions, they did so hoping the public would see the House conferees as unwilling to bargain in good faith and as inept legislative tacticians. The aim was to put pressure on the House leadership to be more "reasonable." The media, in this instance, was used to carry a message to the other side. In other cases, the TV crew triggers oratorical outbursts simply by arriving; but the accusations, speeches, and shouting may be used in an effort to shift the weight of public opinion in order to pressure conferees of the other house to come around to the speaker's position.

The audience at a conference committee meeting is usually made up of those with some stake in the bill. State agency heads or their representatives are almost always in attendance to answer questions and to make sure that the department's interests are protected as much as possible. The concentration of matters in conferences and the hands of the leadership has not escaped the notice of lobbyists. Their regular attendance at conferences is routine. They know that contacting one or two members at this stage can have more effect than contacting dozens earlier in the process. Public-interest activists have not yet fully discovered the conference. A rally of 300 people shouting about taxes at the House doors disbanded without ever walking down the two flights of stairs to where the tax conference was meeting. Audiences are nonexistent for small or short conferences, but may range up to 250 people for major conferences. Until 1988, conferences were not recorded, either on tape or in writing, and conferees often prefer to speak so quietly that the little the audience could hear and remember was the only record of a conference's deliberations.

Ultimately, the conferees do not pay much attention to anyone but themselves and their legislative leaders. The pressure is on for some sort of compromise, and confining the discussions to themselves, shutting out all but the most persistent lobbyists or colleagues, facilitates reaching an agreement. Thus, the number of principal actors in the typical conference is small. The chairs and one or two conferees from each house make the final, crucial decisions. Of course, these members must still sell the decision to their caucuses and houses; although this is not difficult if the decisions are endorsed by the leaders, and the deadline for adjournment of the session is too near to permit another round of negotiations to take place. The decision power over much of state policy rests effectively in the cochairs of conferences and the leaders. The bicameral system masks this fact by prolonging preliminary stages of legislative consideration and allowing many members to have a say in these early stages. But the necessity for conferences means that the leadership will eventually exercise its power.

Problems in the Conference Process

There are two central problems with conference committees as they have evolved in Minnesota. The first is lack of time for them to work as effective instruments of public negotiation and compromise between the houses. The second is the abuse of the conference powers by inserting new material in conference committee reports—the garbage bill syndrome.

The Pressure for Decision and Private Meetings

The big bills of a session rarely reach the conference stage before the final weeks, or even days, of a session. Although differences may be deep, both houses feel compelled to reach agreement to pass *something*. In the case of money bills, agreement is necessary for the state to continue to function after the end of the fiscal year. This pressure for decision virtually requires private meetings to do the real work, rendering public meetings empty of significance, except for posturing, technical compromises, and announcements of the real deals made off-the-record. Meetings must be chaotically sandwiched between other legislative business. Records of public conference discussions and decisions are not kept, and if kept, would omit the more significant negotiations that are carried out off-the-record.

During the final days of the session the drama of activity on the floor of each house masks the importance of conference committees as a separate stage in the legislative process. Conference committees are not given the care, planning, staffing, and attention their importance warrants. The result is a rush for compromise that erodes public norms calling for open meetings, debate, and public scrutiny of the decision-making process. At the same time it is probable that without the pressure of impending adjournment and the ability to meet privately to hammer out final agreements, legislative sessions would be substantially prolonged. Some members who served in the days when conferences were all held behind closed doors feel strongly that the conference, as a negotiation between the two houses, should not be held in public and that it should be confined strictly to reaching agreement on matters in dispute.

The need to compromise quickly and the inability to give attention to conferences as a separate stage of the legislative process results in a reliance on the leaders and further centralization of their power. A compromise gained by the leaders of each house has fewer hurdles to jump than one reached independently by conferees after due deliberation. With an adjournment deadline bearing down on them, leaders cannot always wait for conferees to reach agreement on major issues. They are forced to enter the process as bargaining elites, weakening the integrity of the conference as the decision maker. Once leaders become the central brokers, no major deal can be sealed without them. Key conferences can be reduced to marking time to await the "word" from the leaders.

When the conference reports come to the floor, after hectic days and nights of hammering out compromises, few members are fully aware of the provisions they include. Even conferees and the leaders may not have read the final language of the entire bill. In 1987, for example, a conference report created a new seat on the court of appeals. Speaker Norton was unaware of the provision when it passed the House as part of the conference report. He discovered it after the bill had been signed. The pain of this oversight was assuaged, however, when the governor appointed him to the new judgeship.

Huge masses of bills come across a member's desk, and little time is available for reading them. Conference reports are summarized on the floor by the chair from each house and usually passed quickly. The 1987 Joint Rules make the manager of a conference report responsible for explaining how the report differs from the version passed by that house. This may be done orally or in writing. The latter is almost never the method used.

As time runs out the leadership is almost compelled to rely on private meetings to conclude the business at hand. Leaders shuttle among meetings with conferees, each other, and the governor. They must also spend time on the floor to provide cues to members on how to vote and to enforce discipline, which almost always begins to fray under the pressure of end-of-session politics and exhaustion. Their schedules are changed instantly and frequently. Meetings often must be arranged at the last minute. The telephone may have to serve as a substitute for a face-to-face meeting. A single meeting may have to deal with issues that are before several conferences. Under the circumstances, it is not remarkable that private meetings occur.

For the official conferees, however, explaining the lack of substance in public meetings can be an embarrassing obligation. Conferees are often careful during early meetings to call private meetings to the public's attention. In the 1985 farm policy conference, for example, the chair was careful to mention several times that private meetings had gone on all week. At one public meeting that was delayed due to a private meeting between leaders and the chairs of the conference, one of the waiting conferees was heard to suggest that they begin the meeting so as not to waste the time of those who were there. Another member asked, "What would we have to talk about?" Eventually, the existence of private meetings is winked at and conferees become less abashed at having to brief those attending the public meeting on compromises agreed to or proposed elsewhere. Circumventing the public-meetings rule becomes a routine matter.

In part, the proliferation of conferences is a palliative for the centralization of power in the hands of a few legislators that occurs at the end of each session. If only 19 conferences had been held in 1985, as was the case in 1963, the degree to which power was concentrated would have been starkly revealed and far less acceptable than a generation ago. Without conferences on minor bills, there would be little for most members to do but wait for the elites serving on the important conferences to bring back reports for them to ratify. Arranging conferences on minor bills, instead of having the sponsors from each house work out the differences informally, gives the illusion of the dispersal of power and fills an institutional need for meaningful activity. But the proliferation of conferences does not provide more time to deal with the major business still before the session. If anything, it makes the closing days even more hectic and dissipates time and resources the leadership needs to devote to critical issues.

When difficult issues such as tax policy reach the conference stage of the legislative process, there may be little institutional resilience left to facilitate compromise. It is bad enough when the House and Senate have taken polar positions on the political issues involved. The problem is compounded when the subject is also technically complicated and not only must there be an agreement, but the agreement must work. In the 1985 tax conference, the leadership became so involved in the process that each potential compromise was a political problem for both houses. There simply was not enough time left in the session to work out a political agreement, resolve the technical details, and formulate public positions on the result. The special session of 1985 was the consequence of a centralized and weakened conference process that did not have the time, energy, or power to resolve a politicized issue.

After the May 20 adjournment of the Legislature, the 1985 conferences continued to meet and work on compromises without the distractions of the regular session and the rush of bills to the floor. Only the key conferences met. These meetings occurred despite a rule automatically disbanding conference committees when a session ends. With a great deal more time to devote to each conference and no interruptions from other legislative business, conferees were able to deal with detailed but important provisions with a greater thoroughness and under less pressure than would have been possible during the session. The leaders retained the dominant role in reaching the compromises on major provisions, but they were able to relax and work out better compromises without imminent adjournment hanging over them. The conferences were given the time to work, as the governor refused to call a special session until the houses were in agreement. In the month between the regular and special sessions, the major conferences acted as a separate stage of the bicameral process. Compromises were introduced in the special session as new bills and were passed into law in one day with a minimum of debate and no amendments, as if they were true conference reports.

In 1986, the impasse over budget policy between the House and Senate precipitated another breakdown in the conference process. Speaker Jennings used the impasse as a reason to adjourn the House abruptly sine die, forcing the governor to cut programs to stay within the revenue estimates for the biennium and to call another special session to complete action on a number of bills that were stranded when the House went home. As in the previous year, conferees used the few days between sessions to finish their work unofficially.

Christmas Trees and Garbage

As in many other states, the Minnesota Constitution contains a "single-subject" clause (Art. IV, Sec. 17). This provision requires that a law may not contain more than one subject, which shall be expressed in its title. The courts in some of the states with similar provisions in their constitutions construe the single-subject rule strictly, and will void statutes that incorporate two or more unrelated subjects (Dunn, 1958). Minnesota courts have taken a liberal interpretation of the single-subject rule, since the late 19th century, when the Minnesota supreme court held:

> All that is necessary is that the Act should embrace some general subject; and by this is meant, merely, that all matters treated of should fall under some one general idea, be so connected or related to each other, either logically or in popular understanding, as to be parts of, or germane to, one general subject. . . . All that is required is that the act should not include legislation so incongruous that it could not, by any fair intendment, be considered germane to one general subject. . . . ''
> (*Johnson v. Harrison*, 47 Minn 575, 577, 578 (1891))

The courts have approved, for example, the inclusion of a constitutional amendment in an omnibus bill containing related matter (*Wass v. Anderson*, 312 Minn 394 (1977)), holding that:

> [t]o constitute duplicity, an act must embrace two or more dissimilar and discordant subjects that beyond fair intendment can be considered as having any legitimate connection with or relation to each other. (312 Minn 394, 252, N.W. 2d 131, 136).

Based on this ''stretch it to fit'' philosophy, the Court of Appeals found, in 1984, that the single-subject rule was not violated when the Legislature inserted the implied consent law (covering tests of motor vehicle operators for intoxication) into a bill that ostensibly dealt with contracts between cohabiting individuals. The court observed, in a classic judicial deadpan:

> The purpose of the [single-subject rule] is to prevent deception as to the nature and subject of legislative enactments. . . . The restriction must be liberally construed. A strict adherence to its letter would seriously interfere with the practical business of legislation, and would frequently nullify laws not repugnant to its spirit or meaning. . . . although it would have been better practice for the legislature to break Chapter 553 into two separate acts, its provisions are marginally related in that they both deal with admissibility of documentary evidence. (*Bernstein v. Commissioner of Public Safety*, 351 N.W. 2d 24, 25 (Minn. App. 1984))

In essence, this judicial willingness to accept garbage bills means that for all practical purposes in Minnesota, a single subject is whatever is contained in a single bill.

In the absence of judicial enforcement of the single-subject rule, the Legislature has developed a practice of producing not only omnibus bills that deal with many aspects of a broad policy area like taxes, appropriations, or regulation of particular industries or activities, but other bills that embrace a wide range of quite unrelated matters. The bill establishing the no-fault insurance system of the state, for example, was attached to an unrelated bill.

Some bills, particularly appropriations measures, often serve as vehicles for unrelated substantive legislation sought by a large number of members. These usually minor pet projects and amendments are collected in a few bills and become known as "Christmas tree" bills because they offer something for almost everyone in the Legislature. Each house hangs its own ornaments on its version of the bill, and the practice is for the conferees to accept all of the amendments that are not in direct conflict with each other. Although it will rarely disturb these provisions, the conference may add a few touches of its own that may be desired by conferees or by the leadership.

A garbage bill is distinguished from a Christmas tree bill primarily by the fact that, in the case of the latter, most of the stuff is "front loaded," that is, it is usually added to the bill as it goes through the regular process in each house. The ornaments are simply nongermane amendments that are not stricken through enforcement of the rules of either house. Garbage, in contrast, is legislative refuse that has been rejected or at least not picked up by one or both houses. It is material that was not in either the House or Senate version of the bill. It is "back loaded" at the end of the process, and there is no opportunity to strike it from the bill without killing the entire package.

While Christmas trees are grown in both houses, garbage bills are produced only by conference committees. The garbage inserted into a bill may consist of measures that were defeated in one or both houses, as amendments to the bill in conference or as separate bills; unrelated bills that were passed by one house but not the other; matters that may have been considered by a committee in one or both houses, but could not reach the floor in time for action; or entirely new ideas that were not considered by either house through its regular committee or floor processes. These items are often not the products of compromise over a section of the bill on which the houses differ, but simple logrolling among members of the conference. They rarely can pass a laugh test for germaneness. In some cases conference bills have been amended to add whole titles that are not remotely related to the subject of the bills sent to conference.

House Rule 6.11 limits the compromises coming out of conference to subject matter contained in either the House or Senate versions of the bill sent to conference or like subject matter in a bill passed by the House. The rule thus allows the conference to revive a related bill that passed the House but was defeated in the Senate, a situation that normally would not provide a basis for a conference. While this circumvents the basic presumptions about the way a bicameral system works, the practice is less odious than the inclusion of items that were passed by neither house, or items that, while passed by one body, are not logically related in any way to the bill in conference.

Conferees and leaders systematically ignored even the lax House rule for years, justifying their actions as a means of building support for other important aspects of the conference report, or as necessary to secure enactment of needed legislation that for some reason had not quite made it through one or both houses in any form. The leadership easily can ignore the germaneness rules, as it is its responsibility to enforce them. Once the deal is made to incorporate an irrelevant provision in a bill, the leadership of both houses is committed to defending it against any procedural challenge, thus invoking caucus discipline, if necessary, to sustain open violation of the rules.

In the 1985 session, the House's Republican leadership vowed to hold strictly to the House rule. To an extent, they were successful in limiting one form of abuse, the retention of only the title of a bill, substituting entirely new material for its original content. They were less successful in preventing other nongermane additions. In fact, the House conferees joined senators in stuffing conference reports with measures that otherwise would have failed to reach conference at all, much less the governor.

It is difficult to obtain a full assessment of the extent of the use of garbage bills without detailed content analysis of every conference report. The most common legislative garbage cans are the appropriations bills. Because they must pass for the state to remain in business and because almost every member has an interest in seeing some agency or project funded, it is a convenient place for the leadership, lobbyists, and members with a friend on the conference to stow things that otherwise would not make it through the legislative mill in that session.

A detailed content analysis of the 1985 Appropriations Act was conducted to develop an example of a bill moderately loaded with garbage. The 1985 act reputedly contained less garbage than the 1984 act, which set the standard for such bills. The 1985 act was the product of a Legislature in which the two houses were controlled by opposing parties. The House leadership's announcement that it would enforce the germaneness rule to prevent garbage bills from being enacted makes it fair game for analysis.

The 1985 Appropriations Act contained 323 sections. Of these, only 112, about one-third, were actually related to appropriations. Table 4 identifies the origins of the 211 unrelated sections. Over half were included in both the House and Senate versions of the bill when they left their respective chambers. Fifteen nongermane sections were unique to the House bill and 26 were found only in the Senate version. The conference accepted all of these sections as part of its final report, confirming the observation that neither house likes to knock the other's ornaments off the Christmas tree. The conferees negotiated over 13 nongermane sections on which the houses differed. The House prevailed on one of these sections and the Senate on 7 of them. The conferees struck a compromise on 4 sections, and 1 was apparently dropped from the report.

Table 4. Analysis of 1985 Omnibus Appropriations Act

Sections related to appropriations	112
Sections unrelated to appropriations	211
	323
Breakdown of sections unrelated to appropriations	
Common to both versions	122
In House version only	15
In Senate version only	26
Created in conference	31
Amended in conference	5
Different version in each house	
House version accepted	1
Senate version accepted	7
Compromise	4

Thirty-six new provisions, which had not been passed by either house, were added in conference. These provisions were not a product of compromise over appropriations contained in the bill. They included items that had not been considered by either house, such as establishment of community dispute resolution guidelines and a new requirement that employers produce information on earnings. New sections that had been considered in both houses, but did not reach the conference stage independently and were not germane to appropriations, created a Legislative Commission on Economic Development Strategy, amended the process for federal housing assistance support, and created a statewide agency for affirmative action. Additions that could be traced to only one house gave the Minnesota Pollution Control Agency authority over underground storage tanks, created the Governor's Nuclear Waste Council, and amended the safety regulations for abandoned mines.

Interestingly, the bill was virtually free of riders in the appropriations sections, a common problem with appropriations in Congress and many states. A rider is language in a money bill that changes the substantive law governing the area for which the appropriation is made. Only 10 of the 189 line items in the bill contained riders.

The continuing use of garbage bills has prompted severe criticism from the media, citizen organizations, and members of the Legislature themselves. In 1986, the Minnesota Supreme Court was confronted with a case that raised the issue of whether such an act, which contained a section transferring duties of the state treasurer, an independently elected constitutional officer, to other agencies of state government, violated the single-subject rule. The court avoided that issue by deciding that the section was void under the separation of powers doctrine as applied in Minnesota (*Minnesota ex rel. Mattson v. Kiedrowski*, 391 N.W. 2d 777 (1986)). A concurring opinion signed by two members of the court, however, warned that if the Legislature did not correct the practice of enacting garbage bills, the court might have little option, if presented with a case that had no alternative grounds for decision, but to enforce the single-subject rule and declare such statutes void (391 N.W. 2d 777, 783–85).

The opinion pointed out that modern demands on legislatures could justify the reasonable use of omnibus bills to enable legislators to take a comprehensive look at a major area of public policy, but that this should not open the door to a flagrant violation of the concept that a bill should deal with only one subject. Justice Yetka pointed out that the policy rationale behind the rule has two important aspects. The first is to give the public proper notice of what is in a bill, so people can know if they may be affected by it. This purpose is frustrated by bills that deal with many subjects, especially if the additional subjects are inserted so late in the process that they cannot be considered in the regular process or even amended on the floor of either house. The second rationale for the rule is that it gives members of the Legislature the opportunity to deliberate on the matter on which they are expected to vote. Insertion of extraneous matter into conference reports clearly circumvents the deliberative functions of the Legislature (391 N.W. 2d 777, 783–85).

Following the 1986 elections, leaders of both parties responded to criticism of the conference process from the court, colleagues, and others. They pledged to police conferences more closely and to restrain the use of garbage bills. The Joint Rules were amended to require that provisions of a conference report be germane to the bill or amendment submitted to the conference. A provision was defined as not germane if "it relates to a substantially different subject or is intended to accomplish a substantially different purpose . . . " from the bill referred to the committee (Joint Rule 2.06).

While the rule was not perfectly enforced, there were far fewer complaints about garbage bills after the 1987 session than in prior years. The key appeared to be in the resolve of the House and Senate leadership and the chairs of the major conferences to limit the practice. There is, of course, some chance that the loading will occur in each house, since the House Rules accept as germane to a conference report any matter that was in the House version of the bill (House Rule 6.11). While there is no comparable Senate rule, one should expect each house to honor the evasions of the other.

There is wide agreement in the Legislature that the conference process has been abused and should be reformed. In a survey of members serving between 1981 and 1985, 70 percent of the respondents favored prohibiting insertion of new material in conference reports (Backstrom, 1986). As Table 5 shows, 86 percent of these members and former members felt that conference reports were available too late for intelligent reaction and that extraneous materials passed by neither house should not be permitted in them. Nearly three-fourths of these members agreed that the conference process tends to concentrate power too much in the hands of a few legislators, and two-thirds felt that the conference process is too secret.

Table 5. Legislators' Attitudes Toward Conference Committees

Position	Percent Agreeing						
	Both Houses	House			Senate		
		IR	DFL	Leaders	IR	DFL	Leaders
Reports too late for intelligent reaction	86	86	100	79	94	70	82
Extraneous material passed by neither house should not be permitted	86	95	72	97	94	81	81
Conference committees give too few members too much power over final content of legislation	74	81	72	79	100	67	73
Decisions are made too secretly	65	65	67	64	94	62	71
Many good provisions could never get enacted if they weren't included in conference reports	43	38	62	39	31	59	64
Lobbyists too powerful in getting their provisions into reports	56	46	74	46	69	41	45
Governors have too much influence on reports	23	29	23	24	50	4	5

Source: Backstrom, 1987:36–37

The major defense of the garbage bill syndrome is that it allows enactment of legislation that is in the public interest, but that would otherwise be sidetracked by special interest opposition because it is too controversial, or conversely, that the garbage is generally harmless or useful legislation that just did not have enough time to make it through the regular process. The use of multisubject garbage bills also allows the leadership to wrap important measures that might get "nibbled to death" or defeated on their own into bills that few members dare vote against because they also contain things in which they are deeply interested.

These arguments seem not to be accepted by most members of the Legislature. The survey reported that 57 percent disagreed with the assertion that such measures could not pass on their own merits if separately presented to the Legislature. They would appear to agree with William Dosland's view that garbage bills undermine the process; that if a bill cannot withstand the scrutiny of the regular legislative process, it should not be enacted.

In spite of their concerns about the conference process, legislators did not perceive lobbyists as being too powerful in getting their desired provisions tucked into conference reports. And only one-fourth of the legislators felt that the governor had too much influence over conferences.

It is clear from the survey that minority members are more concerned about the abuse of the conference process than members of the majority party. The survey was conducted in 1985, when each party controlled one house. Regardless of party, members were overwhelmingly in favor of wider participation in conferences and less secrecy.

The leadership of both houses have acknowledged that garbage bills undermine the integrity of the Legislature. They uniformly opposed, however, the idea that the courts should enforce the single-subject rule by voiding such laws. They argued instead for self-enforcement by the leadership and the presiding officers of each house, reinforced by the cochairs of conferences. They pointed out that tax conferences incorporate less garbage than other conferences, although even they have had a recent tendency to add extraneous matter. The 1987 session does indicate that the leadership can curtail the practice, if not stop it entirely.

Leaders are undoubtedly correct when they argue that conferees need a considerable amount of latitude in their efforts to reach compromises satisfactory to both houses. It seems reasonable, however, to limit that latitude to the world in which they are supposed to be working. This allows them to craft new language, so long as it addresses the issue in dispute. The conference process presumes that the final bill will contain measures previously enacted by only one of the chambers, but it seems fair to suppose that those measures should be relevant to the purpose of the bill. In that respect, it would be appropriate for conferees to object to provisions that are not relevant to the subject of the bill, even if they have been passed by the other house, or their own.

Options for Reform

The objective of the conference stage of the legislative process is to permit compromise and reconciliation of the heretofore separate deliberations of the two houses. It is not to provide an unrestrained opportunity for last-minute logrolling. It may be too much to expect, however, that so long as the courts will tolerate it, the opportunity will be resisted to slip through that one little provision dear to the heart of a conferee, a leader, the governor, or a skilled lobbyist.

The South Dakota Supreme Court has recently pointed out that the three purposes of the single-subject rule are to:

(1) prevent combining into one bill diverse measures which have no common basis except, perhaps their separate inability to receive a favorable vote on their merits; (2) prevent the unintentional and unknowing passage of provisions in a bill of which the title gives no information; and (3) fairly appraise the public of matters which are contained in the various bills and to prevent fraud or deception of the public as to matters being considered by the legislature. (*Kanaly v. State*, 387 N.W.2d 819, 827 (S.D. S.Ct. 1985))

Even with the "reforms" of the 1987 session, the Minnesota Legislature has perfected the avoidance of all three purposes. While there appear to be historical reasons for the flourishing of garbage bills in Minnesota (one leader traced it to the "Revisor's Bill," which provided for the correction of grammatical and other technical errors in other bills), there are no plausible excuses for the excess to which it has advanced. There are measures that could be taken to end the abuse of the conference process.

The most drastic remedy would be unicameralism. A one-house legislature has no need for conferences, as the entire process is contained in the single chamber. To the objection that a unicameral legislature loses the check of a second house on the first, it could be answered that in Minnesota that has not been a significant check, since two-thirds of all bills originating in one house are assented to almost automatically by the other (Grau and Olsen, 1986). Further, the garbage bill syndrome in Minnesota has produced a process that effectively denies either house the opportunity to deliberate on a great deal of important legislation. This not only undermines the integrity of the legislative process, it has led to the concentration of legislative power in the hands of a few leaders from each house, frustrating both the deliberative and representational functions of the Legislature. In addition, the widespread evasion of the state constitution's command with respect to the form of laws and the Legislature's own rules governing germaneness have seriously undermined the legitimacy of much of the law that the Legislature writes. The unicameralist argument would suggest that the state would be better off to take George Norris's advice and store hay in the second chamber than to continue a charade of checks and balances that mocks open, democratic processes to which the state claims a commitment.

Absent a unicameral legislature, the Minnesota Supreme Court could decide, in an appropriate case, that the single-subject rule has teeth and strike down garbage and Christmas tree bills. This would probably stop the practice. The court need not take a literal or unreasonably strict approach to remedy the major problems. Omnibus laws that deal with a common policy area are reasonably in compliance with the single-subject rule. Simply striking provisions that have no plausible connection to the main bill would end the worst abuses. While court action may be viewed as intrusion by the judiciary into the functions of the legislature, the rule is well settled in many if not most states, and it is the function of the courts to interpret the constitution. The constitutional and policy rationale for enforcement of the single-subject rule is clear, and the need for it is obvious. Legislative leaders, even with the best of intentions, seem unable to bring the system fully under control. The prevalence of the practice over so many years has virtually created an expectation that "all of the important decisions will be made in conference," and too many members and lobbyists wait for the conference to begin their serious work, rather than conclude it.

If unicameralism seems too radical a departure from tradition, and the court shrinks from reading the constitution to prohibit creative conferencing, there are actions the Legislature itself could take to correct the abuses. The most important would be to require a written analysis to accompany each conference report, identifying the changes made in conference and their origins. Such an annotation to the bill could indicate whether the language of a section came from the Senate or House versions of the bill, or if new language has been added to compromise the differences. New language that does not compromise differences or does not otherwise relate to the bill could also be identified. The technology exists to provide this analysis as fast as the final version of the bill can be prepared.

If such a report were combined with germaneness rules that prohibit amendments that are unrelated to the subject of the bill, and if points of order on germaneness were honored by the presiding officers, both Christmas trees and garbage bills would soon become historical curiosities. Achieving this would probably require a high degree of cooperation between the caucuses to avoid frivolous challenges to bills on germaneness grounds and strong enforcement of legitimate challenges by the presiding officers. While cooperating, the minority has a special obligation to object to nongermane amendments, both in conference and on the floor, and the presiding officer has an obligation to rule fairly on the motion to strike. Such a rule can probably work well in the regular consideration of bills. The acid test is enforcement of the rule when it is used to challenge a conference report. A successful challenge will kill the bill or, if there is enough time, send it back to conference. Basically, the only safe approach, when there is an expectation that the rule will be enforced, is to keep the bill clean.

Such rules and their enforcement could return the conference to its historic function of reconciling differences on bills that deal with the same subject. While this does not cure all of the problems with conferences, it deals with the most serious concerns. Conferences might still conduct some negotiations in private and in conjunction with the leadership and the governor. And they are likely to have their work compressed into the last few weeks of the session. The experience of the last few years strongly suggests that conferences cannot always finish their work in time to meet a deadline established several months earlier. The compression of time and political interests can produce either stalemate or poorly crafted legislation, or both. One way of remedying this problem would be to allow the Legislature, when it is clear that additional time is needed, to recess for up to 30 days while the conference committees complete their work. Such a provision has several advantages. It avoids the subterfuge of informal conference committees meeting between a regular and special session as occurred in both 1985 and 1986. It allows the legislative leadership to assess the situation and to pace the work at the close of a session in a rational manner, rather than be compelled to race for adjournment even if the result is half-baked compromises. It gives conferences the time they need to work through complicated legislation with adequate consultation with the leadership and staff, and to report in time for members to read their reports before having to vote on them. By recognizing the conference process and keeping it as public as possible, instead of driving it underground, such a remedy also allows for better public scrutiny of both the process and the products. Finally, it puts the Legislature itself, instead of the clock, in control of policymaking.

The objection that anything that prolongs a legislative session will lead to dilatory tactics and that the Legislature will simply take up the time allotted it does not seem well placed. The proposal would not allow new legislation to be introduced, or any business other than conferences to be conducted during the recess. At worst, it would legitimatize an awkward but necessary process of providing adequate consideration of important legislation and avoid cleanup special sessions.

An alternative to cleaning up the conference process would be to follow the example of some other states and limit its use to a very few bills. A recent comparative study of how bicameral state legislatures reconcile interhouse differences found that only 12 states rely primarily on the conference to resolve disputed language between the two houses. In 28 states, differences are reconciled through the informal consultation of the leadership from each house. This, of course, could extend the powers of the leaders. Unless accompanied by a very strict enforcement of germaneness or single-subject rules, such power could easily be abused even more freely than through the use of conference committees. Four states combine conferences and leadership consultation, and 5 use other informal methods, such as deference by one of the chambers to the other, or they make fairly extensive use of joint committees to prepare legislation for both bodies so that the initial differences are minimized (Mather and Abney, 1981; Longley, 1986).

Finally, assuming that Minnesota continues to use conference committees, the Joint Rules should require that the minority in each house be represented on each conference. This should mean that the minority member(s) should be chosen by the minority leaders. It seems fundamentally unfair to have minority members of committees, conferences included, chosen by the leaders of the majority party.

While it is true that the function of the conference is to reconcile differences between the houses, and a case can be made that no minority member should serve who cannot support the position of one's house, there is no doubt that the majority members can control the agreement if they are united. It is no less important to hold the majority accountable for its performance in conference than in its house itself. Part of the function of the minority party is to perform that task, and to ensure that the final position accepted by the conferees is not only consistent with the mandate they have from the house, but that it is responsible policy in a broader context. The presence of a bona fide minority member should be some protection against garbage bills and other abuses to which the conference is too frequently prone.

So long as there are bicameral legislatures there will be conferences. So long as there are conferences, there will be pressure to hasten to agreement and temptations to rework legislation to incorporate items on the agendas of the conferees and the leadership that could not be otherwise accomplished. Conferences are the legislative oligarchy at work. The task of constitutional and public policy is to hold them accountable to the respective houses, and to the public, for the quality, fairness, and integrity of what they do. That can be done best if the conferees have the time and resources to accomplish their centrally important jobs, if they operate under reasonable public scrutiny, and in an atmosphere that is conducive to serious negotiations in limited spheres.

7

The Legislature at Work: Making Policy

A state legislature comes as close as any institution of representative government to being all things to all people. Because all members do not care deeply about all issues, it is possible for a few who are strongly concerned about some matters to gain an acquiescent majority. A legislature represents some interests well at times and ignores others; is open to some views and closed to others. It may rise to unexpected heights of responsibility or degenerate to shabby political infighting. It makes laws that settle controversies and enacts others that beget confusion and turmoil. Its debates and deliberations produce wide consensus on some matters and exacerbate conflict on others. In its finest hours, the legislature can be a model of representative democracy at work: in its worst it is rabble at play.

This most representative of the branches of government is never still, never the same from session to session or even day to day. Yet it takes on a character, a culture, a set of corporate values and roles that shape its ways of working and its product. There are common patterns in the way in which it transacts the public's business.

Information and Policy: An Overview

In the many functions that a legislature performs—representing people and interests, resolving policy conflicts, enacting statutes, overseeing the administration of public policies, serving as ombudsman and constituent caseworker—there is a common element: information. The legislature consumes enormous amounts of information, reprocesses it, and spews forth a great mound of new or different information in the form of reports, laws, resolutions, statements by its officers, leaders, and members, and requests for still more information to use in the next round of policymaking.

All public agencies are information machines, but few others have as many working parts as a legislature to gather, sift, sort, filter, reshape, bury, or regurgitate information. No other part of government has as much power to form the information it consumes into measures that govern the future behavior of people and institutions.

Legislation is information about the policy of the state. At the same time it reflects the way the legislature gathered and used information to arrive at a statement of policy. Thus, by focusing on how a legislature gathers and uses information, we can begin to understand something of how well it comes to grips with public problems and how well it performs its function of deliberation and making policy choices.

Dealing with Problems, Framing Issues for the Legislative Agenda

In thinking about how a legislature gathers and uses information, it is useful to distinguish between problems and issues. A problem is a set of independently verifiable conditions that some people may want to change because it adversely affects their interests. A problem may be resolved by actions that remove its cause or ameliorate its effects. In public life, the resolution of one problem can produce others.

Problems can be classified as tame or wicked (Rittel and Weber, 1973). A tame problem can be solved. It is subject to rational analysis and specific action. The resolution has few, if any external consequences. An increase in asphalt prices for road improvements is a tame problem if the state has plenty of money and the legislature quickly passes a supplemental appropriation to keep work on schedule. If money is tight, however, rising prices can become a wicked problem, the resolution of which implicates other programs that could lose their resources to meet road needs. A wicked problem does not have simple, ready answers, tends to defy rational analysis, and becomes politicized; and any resolution of it is likely to produce other problems in the future.

An issue is a structured formulation of a matter on which a public choice is required. While problems may exist but remain unrecognized by legislators, issues have no life independent of their expression. All problems do not present issues; there may be no disagreement about what to do. A snow emergency is always a problem in Minnesota. It would be an issue only if government did nothing about clearing snow after a blizzard. Not all issues are capable of resolution; some are designed for other purposes, such as changing the distribution of power in the electorate or the government. The issue of legislative salaries, for example, is framed not to allow an equitable salary to be set but to attract attention and support for those who make pay increases an issue.

Technical and Political Information

Making this distinction between problems and issues helps us understand another important distinction in the two principal kinds of information that a legislature processes. A great deal of *technical information* is funneled into a legislature. This includes data; analysis of data; and expert opinion on the character, incidence, and extent of problems. Technical information helps define and explain problems in substantive terms. The several volumes of reports from the Minnesota Tax Study Commission, for example, were full of technical information about the economic and tax problems of the state. They also contained a lot of information about tax issues as framed by the commission, such as the proper mix of income, sales, and property taxes; impacts of particular taxes on business, jobs, and farming; and the stability of the tax system. The reports of the legislative auditor, the Departments of Finance and Revenue, the state economist, the state demographer, etc., are additional important sources of technical information for the Minnesota Legislature. More technical information is produced at legislative hearings by witnesses who provide data and descriptions of conditions that they want legislation to address.

Political information consists of public opinion—that opinion officials find it prudent to heed (Key, 1961). Political information includes data about elections or surveys of various public attitudes. It also consists of intelligence and gossip, information on the positions of peers, legislative or other governmental leaders, interest groups, supporters, and opponents. In general, political information is concerned with the public significance of a problem or issue, while technical information is more concerned with the matter itself. Information describing the tax system and its effects is technical. Information about the commission, who supports its recommendations and how strongly, or about the perceived impact of taxes and attitudes toward them, is political.

These two kinds of information enjoy a symbiotic relationship in the legislative process. They feed on, affect, and shape each other. Perception of a problem by legislators may generate an issue, which in turn produces a demand by the protagonists of the issue for both technical and political information about it. As the problems brought to legislative attention become more complicated in their characteristics and effects, legislators need higher quality technical information to understand what can be done to frame issues and deal with them. They also need political means for translating the technical knowledge they develop into forms that produce a feedback of political information that enables them to act in ways that are technically sound as well as popular.

Thus both kinds of information about problems and issues have profound effects on how well the Legislature functions in its roles as maker and legitimator of policy. Inadequate technical information, or poor use of good information, can produce ineffective or even dysfunctional policies. Poor political information can cause misjudgments of priorities and public interests.

Legislatures are increasingly confronted with policy problems that are technically complex and issues that are politically controversial. Virtually all information that the Legislature receives about problems and issues, whether technical or political in nature, must pass through a politically charged field. Values and interests are screens that affect perceptions. Consequently, not all matters that a disinterested jury of state government experts might consider important will be perceived by legislators in positions to do something about them as politically salient. By the same token, not all matters that the legislators regard as politically salient would be thought important by some disinterested group.

Whether a problem makes it through the political screen depends to a considerable extent on how the issues it suggests have been framed, and by whom. There was, for example, a considerable body of information on child sexual abuse and the problems such behavior presents for the individuals involved, for welfare and law enforcement agencies, for courts, and for schools long before it became a legislative issue. The problem is clearly an important one by any measure of the number of people involved, the long-term effect of such practices on the victims, the costs to the state, and the interest of society at large in preventing and correcting antisocial, abnormal, and illegal behavior. The problem became salient for legislative action in 1985 as a result of a series of notorious child sexual abuse cases in Minneapolis and Scott County, after which the news media and the state's law enforcement officials framed the issue as a question of how to balance the rights of defendants with the interest of the state in their effective prosecution and the rights and interests of the victims.

Explaining a problem, such as child sexual abuse, is not the same as framing the issue for legislative purposes. The problem can be explained clinically without too much reference to criminal law and procedure. As the issue was framed for the Legislature, however, it did not deal with the clinical problem of child abuse, but rather with the policy issue of how the state should govern the reporting and prosecution of child abusers.

The objective of framing an issue is to produce a particular response from the legislature in the form of policy (Nelson, 1984), or in some cases, to prevent the legislature from devising any language capable of winning majority support. The way an issue is framed suggests the answer (Polsby, 1984). The 1985 farm legislation debates illustrate this point. The advocates of a mortgage moratorium framed the issue as a need for a temporary extension of credit to farmers who would otherwise face foreclosures—in other words, the political issue was survival of the family-owned and operated farm. A vote for the moratorium was a vote for family farming. A vote against was a vote for its destruction. Opponents of the moratorium framed the issue as one of finding a practical state response to a problem that the state could neither control nor cure. Thus, they argued that a moratorium would do little if anything to help farmers solve their financial problems and might be instead counterproductive by reducing creditor interest in making farm loans.

In many instances, the ability of a group to frame an issue in a way that compels legislative action may depend on the availability and quality of competing technical and political information on the subject and on the skill of those participating in the process in getting that information through the screens and in reformulating the issues. Access to critical decision makers is crucial. Because a legislature is a highly pluralistic institution, the critical actors are not the same on all matters. Legislative leaders, committee chairs, members regarded by their colleagues as experts or advocates of certain types of legislation, the governor, agency heads and representatives, highly regarded executive staff, lobbyists, legislative staff, the media, influential constituents such as business, labor, community, or religious leaders—each is important as both a source of and a screen for information that can be decisive on any matter. All are actively involved in framing issues in ways they hope are compelling enough to get on the legislative agenda. This generally means framing them so as to attract substantial public attention so that legislators receive the political information that the issue is of concern to a large and intensely interested number of people or to strategically important ones.

Legislatures make decisions on several thousand issues every session. Each decision has its own history. No study of legislative decisions can be complete if its aim is to describe how 201 members interact to produce about 300 laws from over 3,000 bills in 120 days. We can grasp essentials of the process, however, if we reflect on selected examples of the process and infer from them some broader patterns of behavior.

Setting the Agenda: The 1985 Session

The 1985 session of the Legislature provided a good test of the decision-making process. It was a session that placed legislative institutions under stress, and one that considered a number of highly politicized and very complex problems.

For the first time since the advent of partisan elections, the Independent-Republicans seized clear control of the House of Representatives in the 1984 midterm elections. As Senate terms were for four years and coterminus with the governor's, the Senate remained in the firm control of the DFL. The shift in control of the House brought an end to more than a decade of relatively smooth cooperation between the two houses of the Legislature.

The Independent-Republicans had campaigned in 1984 on a theme of opposition to high state tax rates that allegedly damaged the state's business climate. They promised a massive billion-dollar tax cut designed to encourage businesses to locate and expand in the state and to compel a reduction in the scale of public spending. While Governor Rudy Perpich (DFL) had made improvement of the business climate and tax reform top priorities for his administration, he had not advocated tax cuts of the magnitude proposed by the new House majority and Speaker David Jennings.

The IR program took its cues from the campaign of the Minnesota Business Partnership, consisting of the chief executives of many major Minnesota-based corporations, which sought legislative action to improve the business climate. Their top priority was tax reductions, but they also sought changes in the state's unemployment compensation laws and its stringent "Superfund" law that provided for the cleanup of toxic waste sites. For his part, Perpich had anticipated these issues. He had appointed a blue-ribbon tax study commission headed by St. Paul Mayor George Latimer to study the state's tax system and its effect on the economy, and to recommend a program of tax reform to make the system more efficient, equitable, and more favorable to industry and employment in the state. The commission obliged with a mammoth set of studies of all aspects of the tax system and an extensive set of recommendations for reform, including a substantial reduction in the income tax, expansion of the sales tax, rationalization of the property tax, and simplification of tax forms. The commission report, however, was issued a month after the elections had produced an Independent-Republican majority in the House with a tax agenda of its own. The IRs had won the initial round. The tax issue was to be framed as one of providing a big tax cut rather than as a tax reform.

The governor had also commissioned a study of the Superfund law, with the aim of finding changes that would reduce business fear of its adverse legal and financial effects. This commission ultimately recommended changes in the law to create a state indemnification fund for victims as a means of reducing business insurance costs, and otherwise to limit the liability of polluters for damage caused by actions taken in the past.

In the Senate, the DFL majority leadership was also concerned with the tax issue, but was attempting to frame it as a fairness question, with an eye to the party's labor and farm constituencies and to the interests of users of state services. To a considerable extent the DFL leadership had accepted much of the adverse business climate argument advanced by business interest groups, but sought a way to deal with the issue that would not damage employment opportunities and state services.

The Business Partnership also commissioned a study of the state's education system. Shortly before the Legislature convened, it issued a report that recommended sweeping changes in secondary education, including opportunity for high school students to exercise free choice in attending any public school in the state, with the state per-pupil subsidy to school districts following the student rather than staying in the home district. The idea was to restructure the incentives to school districts to encourage improvements in educational quality without simply increasing school expenditures across-the-board. The concept of "free choice" within the public school system was warmly endorsed by other business and civic groups, particularly the Twin Cities Citizens League. The governor quickly seized the proposal and became the principal political champion of the public school freedom-of-choice proposal of the Business Partnership. He embraced the idea with enthusiasm, and put his administration and his personal political clout behind it, ensuring it a place on the legislative agenda. For the governor and his allies, the issue was to be framed as one of educational quality. For the opposition, composed of organized education groups, particularly teachers and school boards, the issue was seen as one of adequate resources and local autonomy.

Every session of the Legislature has before it some matters that represent a new agenda and some that are drawn from the "gunny sack" of leftover matters from prior sessions, ideas that were premature when originally introduced, and perennial proposals that occupy time but are destined to go nowhere. While the tax and Superfund issues had legislative histories from prior sessions, they were newly framed for the 1985 session. The broader business climate issue was a continuing one that had played a central role in at least two earlier sessions. The free-choice enrollment issue was entirely new.

The Legislature itself had directed the State Health Department to construct a comprehensive study of health care cost containment. Since the issue was nonpartisan, both houses were expected to consider legislation to require prepaid health plans for state welfare clients.

Pressure was also building from other quarters that would affect the issues on the legislative agenda. The most volatile issue, other than taxes, would arise from the precipitous fall in the value of farmland and a resulting crisis in the availability of farm credit in the state. As the time for the 1985 session approached, militant farmers organized to march on the Capitol and demand state action to help them save their farms from foreclosure.

During the months before the Legislature convened, two child sex abuse cases had erupted in the media. The first involved the director of the Minneapolis Children's Theatre. The second produced a mass of indictments in Scott County that were eventually dismissed and produced an investigation by the attorney general into the handling of the cases.

Then, shortly before the Legislature met, a judge voided as unconstitutionally vague the provisions of the Minnesota child abuse statute that required professionals to report suspected child abuse. These cases built an expectation that the Legislature would have to address the problem in some manner.

Unemployment compensation was a gunny sack issue that the 1984 Legislature had been unable to resolve due to the irreconcilable differences between business and labor interests. The issue remained high on the agenda of business interests, and high on labor's agenda of things to prevent. A considerable range of proposals on employment and training legislation were being floated in the months before the session began. The most urgent problem was the sunset of the state's emergency employment program, which had been enacted during the recession. Labor and interests groups representing low-income and structurally unemployed workers wanted the act to be extended. The state had also pursued controversial policies for the economic revitalization of the Iron Range in the wake of massive job losses in the mining, forestry, and steel industries. Some of these programs were under attack as expensive and ineffective.

The 1983 Legislature had enacted a new formula for state aid to local governments, which had been especially beneficial to the state's larger cities, but had reduced the level of entitlement of many of the suburbs and smaller cities. Resentment among those that had not benefited fueled an effort by the League of Municipalities and an ad hoc coalition of cities and towns to revamp the formula to favor them.

In addition to these matters, most of which could easily qualify as genuine problems that needed some kind of legislative attention, and all of which were fairly skillfully framed as issues, there were the usual myriad of proposals and requests for legislative action and funds.

Decisions on three issues made by the 1985 Legislature can provide some insight into the legislative process: (1) the tax cut, (2) revisions to the 1983 Superfund law, and (3) an amendment to the health and human services appropriations to prohibit exclusive agreements between health maintenance organizations and providers of services or products.

The first two were "big" issues during the session and offer a picture of how the Legislature deals with high-visibility matters. The third was important to a more limited public, and did not receive much legislative or public attention, although its impact on other important health legislation was significant. It provides an example of how "little" bills may have a large impact on policy. All three matters were wicked problems, in that they were complex, controversial, and not subject to straightforward analysis and solution; and that any resolution of them was likely to produce a further problem that would need future legislative attention. While it is too much to claim any of them are typical of legislative decision making, each captures and illustrates important aspects of how the Legislature gathers and uses information in making significant decisions.

Making Superfund Safe for Business

1983 Superfund Act

The issue of how to deal with the cleanup of toxic waste disposal sites not covered by the federal Superfund act (42 USC §9601 et seq., 1980) had been before every session of the Minnesota Legislature since 1981. The issue grew out of increasing public awareness of serious threats to public health and the environment from hazardous materials found in waste disposal sites throughout the country, including several in Minnesota.

To address the gap between what the federal government's program could be expected to accomplish in the state and the danger to the public from the remaining hazardous waste sites, Senator Gene Merriam (DFL) introduced the Minnesota Environmental Response and Liability Act (MERLA) in the 1981 session. Referred to the Committee on Agriculture and Natural Resources, it was amended by opponents to delete everything but the title. Merriam withdrew the bill from further consideration.

The 1982 session was more hospitable to the bill and a revised version was enacted. It created a $4 million fund, of which $1.5 million was to be raised by a special tax on the state's 2,000 hazardous waste generators. The remainder came from the state's general revenues. The bill made it easier for parties injured by exposure to hazardous waste to recover damages from the firms that generated, transported, and disposed of the wastes.

Governor Albert Quie (IR) vetoed the act, arguing that "if it became law it would further damage Minnesota's already troubled economy and encourage businesses to leave our state" (*Minneapolis Star and Tribune*, March 20, 1982). An effort to override the veto failed in a special session. In part, the failure was attributed to the feeling of House DFL leaders that an override would deprive the party of a potent campaign issue in the 1982 elections.

With the election of Rudy Perpich (DFL) as governor in 1982, and DFL control in both houses of the Legislature, enactment of a state Superfund law in 1983 was assured. Passed by large majorities in both chambers, Perpich signed the act (*Minn. Session Laws*, Ch. 121, 310–42, 1983) on May 10, 1983, in spite of intensive lobbying by state business firms and organizations, particularly the 3M Company, the state's largest employer. 3M Chairman Lewis Lehr declared that his company might not build or expand plants in the state if the bill became law.

The 1983 act did several things:

(1) It imposed a statutory standard of strict liability, retroactive to 1973, on generators, transporters, and disposers of hazardous wastes. Under strict liability, a plaintiff does not have to prove that the defendant behaved in a negligent manner to collect damages.

(2) To facilitate trial of claims against those responsible for hazardous wastes, the act reduced the requirement for proof of "causation", i.e., the burden on the plaintiff to show that the injury suffered was caused by specific acts of the defendant. The theory behind this change was that in an improperly protected hazardous waste site many materials from many sources may be deposited. Requiring a victim to link its particular injury to any one user of the site is an unreasonable requirement, the determination of which is beyond both scientific and judicial certainty.

(3) Those responsible for hazardous wastes were made jointly and severally liable for injuries. This meant that in cases in which several codefendants were found to be liable for damages awarded to a plaintiff, a defendant might have to pay more than its proportionate share if others could not pay their share. In addition waste depositors were made jointly and severally liable for damages arising from acts committed between January 1, 1960, and December 31, 1972, if the acts would have been abnormally dangerous at the time.

(4) A limit of $1.2 million was set on the liability of any municipality for a single hazardous waste occurrence.

(5) The state was given authority to regulate the disposal of hazardous wastes and to enforce standards of disposal and transportation.

(6) A $5 million revolving fund was created to pay for the cleanup of sites not covered by the federal Superfund law and to provide for the 10 percent match required by that law. The fund was to be replenished at an estimated rate of $850,000 a year from a tax on waste producers and handlers. In 1984 the act was amended to exempt firms from the tax if they incinerated hazardous wastes.

In the three-year struggle to enact the state Superfund law, its advocates succeeded in framing the issue as one of environmental health and justice for the victims of improperly disposed hazardous wastes. Although a different perspective had been advanced that viewed the issue, at least in part, as one of changing the state's business climate, that view had not prevailed in the Legislature. Governor Quie accepted it, however, in his 1982 veto of the bill. Now that Superfund was law, the focus would change to its enforcement and its effect on businesses operating in the state.

Reframing the Issue for the 1985 Session

For several years, business interest groups had directed an organized and well-financed campaign aimed at changing tax, spending, and environmental policies that allegedly damaged the business climate in Minnesota. By 1983 they had generally succeeded in persuading the leadership of both parties that some decisive actions would be necessary if Minnesota were to be competitive with other states in attracting and retaining industries and jobs. The Independent-Republican party seized the business climate issue as the backbone of its successful campaign to seize control of the House of Representatives in the 1984 elections. A key point of criticism of the state's business climate was the state Superfund law. Throughout 1984, business leaders attacked the law as an onerous burden on the cost of doing business in Minnesota.

In February 1984, the 3M Company appeared to make good its warning to the governor when he signed the Superfund law. Chairman Lehr announced that the company would build a major research and development complex in Austin, Texas. At about the same time, the Sperry Corporation announced that it would expand its St. Paul division in Colorado. Both actions were attributed to the poor business climate in Minnesota. In March a *Minneapolis Star and Tribune* poll reported that a majority of Minnesotans agreed that the state did not have a good business climate (*Minneapolis Star and Tribune*, March 15, 1984). A month later, Alexander Grant and Company released its annual rating of states in terms of their business climates. Minnesota had fallen from 32d to 43d in its system.

Business groups now sharpened their attacks on the liability provisions of the Superfund law. They avoided criticism of the cleanup provisions of the law, and concentrated on their fears that the strict liability and other changes from common-law rules on causation and joint and several liability would generate a flood of costly lawsuits. They argued that these changes in law were making it impossible for Minnesota firms to obtain environmental impairment liability insurance that they needed to protect themselves against lawsuits. And they insisted that the retroactivity provisions of the law were inherently unfair to corporations that may not have done a good job in disposing of wastes in the sixties and seventies, but had complied in good faith with the law as it then existed. Responsibility for these old waste disposal sites, and the injuries that they produced, should be a problem for the state at large, they argued, not just the corporations involved.

Despite the dire predictions of a flood of litigation, few cases were filed under the Superfund law, and none had been decided by mid-1985 (Minnesota Department of Commerce, 1984). Later, business lobbyists would shift their ground, arguing that such lawsuits take time to work through the legal system, but that in any event, the provisions of Superfund would work to produce more settlements favorable to plaintiffs than at common law, and that the cases that eventually got to juries would set precedents for large judgments for the plaintiffs.

The insurance problem seemed to have some substance. In February 1984, Lloyd's of London announced that it would exclude Minnesota companies from its environmental impairment liability coverage (*Wall Street Journal*, October 23, 1984). Lloyd's later pulled out of this market altogether, but maintained if it were to reenter, it would still exclude Minnesota. In December of 1984, the state Department of Commerce issued a study that pointed out that the number of companies writing such insurance in Minnesota had dropped from eight to four (Department of Commerce, 1984).

While business interests mounted their campaign against Superfund in preparation for the 1985 session, environmental and labor groups prepared to defend the act. Basically they defended the liability provisions of the law as necessary changes to overcome the inadequacies of the common law in compensating victims for injury they suffered as a consequence of exposure to hazardous wastes. They attacked claims of runaway litigation and business costs as unfounded in experience with the act, pointing to the absence of cases. Refutation of the insurance problem argument was more difficult. Opponents of change argued that the Commerce Department study proved that insurance was in fact available, and that the difficulty in obtaining it was not remarkably different in Minnesota than elsewhere in the United States, due to an embryonic market and lack of demand.

It was clear from the arguments of both the advocates and defenders of change that the terms of the debate would be on the business climate issue. To this extent, the business groups had, by the time the Legislature convened in January, reframed the issue to their advantage. Perhaps the strongest evidence of this was the decision of the governor in December of 1984 to appoint a 17-member task force headed by Tom Triplett, the state planning director and a key aide of the governor, to review the liability sections of the law and recommend changes that could be proposed to the Legislature. Previously, the governor had staunchly defended the law. Just prior to the opening of the session, the Minnesota Poll showed a majority of legislators favoring revision of the liability provisions (*Minneapolis Star and Tribune*, January 2, 1985).

Merriam Proposes a Compromise

The stage was finally set for change when Senator Merriam announced that he would offer revisions to the law. Merriam decided to co-opt the revision effort rather than fight it because he had become convinced that the business interests had the votes to change the law. He reasoned that, as the chief sponsor of Superfund legislation, he could strike a deal with business interests that would save what he regarded as the essential provisions in return for his support of changes that addressed the most serious problems raised by businesses. His compromise proposal, therefore, eliminated the causation, joint and several liability, and retroactivity sections, but left the strict liability provisions and the cap on municipal liability (SF 300).

Representative Steve Sviggum (IR), an assistant majority leader in the House, introduced a companion bill (HF 268). This compromise won the support of big business, but environmental groups withheld endorsement. The governor offered general support to the Merriam-Sviggum bill, but called for the creation of a victims compensation fund to protect those injured before the bill's retroactive liability date of July 1, 1983. The original House cosponsor of the 1983 act, Representative Dee Long (DFL), and other DFL representatives denounced the bill, saying that they saw no real problems with the existing law.

Meanwhile, the governor's task force was having trouble agreeing on revisions. It agreed to the repeal of the causation and joint and several liability sections. It could not agree, however, on changing the date for retroactive liability or on the need for a victims compensation fund.

House and Senate Action

The Senate Agriculture and Natural Resources Committee, now chaired by Senator Merriam, approved the compromise bill on February 14. Environmental groups opposed the bill at the public hearing. Senator Collin Peterson (DFL) also opposed the bill and announced his intention to introduce a bill to provide a victims compensation fund.

On the same day, the House Environment and Natural Resources Committee cleared the Sviggum bill by a vote of 12 to 10. Seven attempts by DFL representatives on the committee to retain features of the 1983 act were defeated. One IR representative, John Hatinger of Coon Rapids, whose district included a hazardous waste site, joined the DFL members in voting against the bill. The principal opposition testimony in the House committee was from the state AFL-CIO.

The committee hearings produced no new technical information on the subject. They essentially underscored the political information that a formidable array of political and opinion leadership was joining business leadership in advocating changes in the law. Editorial opinion from around the state also appeared to favor the changes.

The only major interest groups in opposition were the AFL-CIO and the environmentalists. The revisions had, however, spawned a new, subsidiary issue: how to deal with the claims of victims who were injured before the effective date of the proposed new law but who had been covered in the 1983 law. Thus, the introduction by Senator Peterson of a victims compensation fund bill became a significant turn in the fortunes of the legislation, which had seemed, to this point, to be on a smooth path toward adoption.

Peterson's bill (SF 571) provided for a $2 million dollar fund, initially to be provided by a state appropriation, but also imposing a tax on waste generators at a level that would require them to bear half of all damages awarded. The bill was referred to the Senate Committee on Rules and Administration, chaired by the majority leader, Senator Roger Moe. This committee promptly reported the bill without amendments. The governor, in endorsing the Merriam-Sviggum bill, had also urged the Legislature to consider establishing a victims compensation fund.

Opponents Try to Revive the Health Issue

At this point, the first heavyweight editorial against the changes in the law appeared in the *Minneapolis Star and Tribune*, entitled: "Don't Gut Minnesota's Superfund Law" (February 22, 1985). The *Star and Tribune* also increased its news coverage of the issue, and its headlines tended to frame the legislation as action to favor business. The February 22 story, for example, was headed: "Altering Superfund for Business Is Formally Supported by Perpich."

Action on the Merriam-Sviggum bill now moved to the Judiciary committees, which shared jurisdiction with the environmental committees because of the legal issues involved. In the Senate judiciary hearing, some new evidence on the effects of the bill was produced by a witness who stated that his waste-handling firm had acquired a Mississippi company rather than expand operations in Minnesota, because of the requirements imposed on it by the Superfund law.

In early March, the Minnesota Department of Health issued a report finding an unusually large number of lung abnormalities among residents of the Iron Range. A *Star and Tribune* story, "Lung Study May Help Fund Get Support," reported speculation among legislators that the findings might increase resistance to the Merriam-Sviggum bill and build support for a victims compensation fund (March 3, 1985). Two days later the Minneapolis paper printed another editorial inveighing against the revisions in the law and seeking to revive the environmental frame for the issue. Nonetheless, the House Judiciary Committee reported the bill on the same day with only one IR member defecting.

The Fight over the Victims Compensation Fund

Now it was the turn of the House Committee on Environment and Natural Resources to hear testimony on the House companion to Senator Peterson's victims compensation bill (HF 156). The principal business witness, Shirley Brantingham, representing the Minnesota Association of Commerce and Industry (MACI), argued that revenues for the fund should come from general taxation rather than business, since hazardous chemical wastes should be viewed as a societal problem.

On March 7, the Sviggum bill reached the House floor. It was basically unchanged by the committee process, which had adduced no substantial new technical or political information on the subject since its introduction (other than some show of support, mainly in the DFL, for a victims compensation fund). The DFL leadership in the House sought unsuccessfully to amend the bill to provide for the elimination of the causation section, or alternatively, to drop the causation provisions and add a compensation fund. The retroactivity section of the bill was amended on the floor to allow Superfund lawsuits for the period before July 1, 1983, if the plaintiff could show that polluters knew or should have known that the dumping of hazardous wastes would cause serious harm.

On March 14, the House passed the bill as amended and sent it to the Senate by a vote of 81 to 44. Fifteen DFL members voted for the bill, and only 3 IR members voted against it.

Although the House defeated amendments that would have attached a victims compensation fund to the Sviggum bill, the House Environment and Natural Resources Committee approved the fund (HF 156) and referred it to the Judiciary Committee, which also had before it a "clean" bill on the subject introduced by

Representative Sally Olsen (HF 876), which it substituted for the original bill. The committee then amended the compensation fund bill to force individuals to choose whether to pursue compensation from the fund or to seek relief in court, and passed the bill on to the Committee on Government Operations, which in turn cleared it and referred it to Appropriations for its last review by a House committee.

During this round robin of House committees, the only new political information to come to the attention of the Legislature was another editorial in the *Minneapolis Star and Tribune* (March 22, 1985) and the action of the Judiciary Committee requiring victims to choose between applying to the fund for compensation or going to court to seek damages. This amendment was urged by business interests who sought to prevent victims who were compensated by the fund from taking a "second bite at the apple" by suing polluters for additional damages above those recovered through the fund.

Meanwhile in the Senate, Senator Peterson's compensation bill was overwhelmingly approved by the Senate Judiciary Committee on the same day (March 22) that the *Star and Tribune* editorial urged its passage. It then received, in turn, endorsements from the Senate Government Operations and Taxes and Tax Laws committees.

The Olsen bill came to the House floor in early April, where it was amended to allow a victim to bring court action even though an award had been received from the compensation fund. Finally passed by a vote of 130 to 1, the bill, which now provided for a fund of $1 million, drawn from general revenues of the state, was sent to the Senate.

The Senate substituted the House bill for Senator Peterson's bill, and referred it directly to the Taxes and Tax Laws Committee. There the bill was amended to increase the fund to $2 million, part of which was to be raised by a tax on hazardous waste producers. It was then sent to the Finance Committee, where a limitation was added providing that compensation from the fund would be limited to $250,000 for any one award.

As the compensation bill moved smoothly through the committees of the Senate, the Merriam bill amending the 1983 Superfund Act was being debated in the Judiciary Committee. It was approved on an 8 to 5 vote, after an amendment was defeated that would have made polluters retroactively liable before July 1, 1983, if they knew or reasonably should have known that the hazardous waste they disposed of could be reasonably expected to cause serious harm to others. Thus, the bill sent to the Senate floor did not contain this provision, which had been added to the House bill.

Both the Merriam bill and the compensation bill were now before the full Senate. The latter was taken up first and amended to restore the requirement that a victim make a binding choice between seeking relief from the fund or from litigation. Senator Peterson announced that he would withdraw the bill if this amendment were not removed. His position was reinforced by an editorial in the *St. Paul Pioneer Press and Dispatch* (May 4, 1985). In the face of Senator Peterson's threat, the Senate backtracked and watered down its binding choice amendment to preclude a victim from seeking additional relief from the courts only if an award from the compensation fund had been received and accepted. In addition, the Senate restricted the use, in a subsequent lawsuit, of evidence gathered to determine the amount of an award from the fund. With these final changes, the Senate now passed the compensation fund bill by a vote of 59 to 7.

Both Senate and House had now passed compensation bills, but in different forms. On May 13, a coalition of business interest groups, including the Minnesota Association of Commerce and Industry, the Business Partnership, and the Chambers of Commerce of Minneapolis and St. Paul, called a news conference to denounce the Senate version of the bill. They were particularly critical of the failure of the Senate to retain the binding choice amendment, the maximum limitation of $250,000 for awards from the fund, and inclusion of the tax on waste generators to supply half of the financing for the fund. They asserted that businesses in the state would prefer the Superfund law as it stood to the victims compensation bill as passed by the Senate.

The next day, a new piece of significant political information was delivered to the Legislature. The AFL-CIO and the Clean Water Action Project (an environmental interest group) held a joint news conference to chide the business spokesmen, calling their opposition to the victims compensation fund "blackmail."

The House and Senate leaders now entered the controversy. First Speaker Jennings refused to appoint conferees to settle differences on the compensation bill before the Senate passed the Superfund revisions. Senate Majority Leader Moe, in response, refused to bring up the Merriam bill for final Senate action until the two houses settled their differences on the compensation bill. The St. Paul paper editorialized on the stalemate, urging the leaders to break the deadlock over Superfund amendments before the session ended.

The Senate responded by passing the Merriam bill, but only after amending it to include the entire Senate compensation bill. At this point, however, only three days remained in the regular session of the Legislature. Although both houses now appointed Conferees—Sviggum and Olsen from the House and Merriam and Peterson from the Senate—they could not reach agreement before adjournment on May 20.

The Compromise Bill

During the month between the regular and special sessions, a number of meetings occurred among the conferees and members of the governor's staff, led by Tom Triplett, the commissioner of planning, and business lobbyists. Environmental and labor representatives did not participate in the negotiations. A final compro-

mise was hammered out, which was introduced when the special session convened. Both houses passed it without amendments and it became law.

Merriam made a spirited defense of the revisions, arguing that the critical
cleanup provisions of the original MERLA had not been touched; that victims
would have a better chance of compensation under the new law, which incorporated the victims compensation fund; and that "the business community will feel
better." Merriam admitted that:

> [i]f I had my druthers I wouldn't be doing this. . . . But this is the real
> world and it became clear changes were going to be made. . . . I had
> the option of taking the high ground and fighting every change or of
> negotiating and trying to minimize the changes to MERLA.

As enacted, the amendments repealed the causation section of the original law,
thus requiring plaintiffs to prove causation under common-law standards. Liability was made retroactive to 1983, the date when the original MERLA went into
effect. Finally, the joint and several liability section was repealed. The victims
compensation fund was established, funded at $2 million to be provided from
general revenues. The state, however, could subrogate polluters who caused injuries that were compensated from the fund. The standards for determining eli-
gibility for compensation by the fund were far less strict than would be required
at common law. A cap of $250,000 was placed on the amount of compensation
for which victims would be eligible, and individuals who received a judgment
from a lawsuit or compensation from the victims compensation fund could not
subsequently seek damages through the other process.

The Role of Political and Technical Information in the Decision

The problem Superfund was created to address and the problems it generated
were quite suitable to the development of technical information to illuminate the
extent of the problems and possible resolution of them. Technical information as
such, however, played almost no role in the process. Instead, political information held the center of the legislative stage and was far more influential in determining the outcome.

At the outset, the business interest groups framed the issues before the Legislature as a matter of improving the state's perceived poor business climate. So
effective was this framing that the environmental and labor groups were unable to
revive, even with the help of the state's largest newspaper, the health and safety
frame that had led to the initial passage of the law in 1983. The factual evidence
adduced to support the allegations of injury to business was at best weak, at
worst nonexistent. Yet the business climate frame was so powerful that the DFL
governor and the chief sponsor of the 1983 act became prime movers in the effort
to revise the bill.

The governor and others who were concerned with balancing probusiness revisions with some means of protecting victims were able to offer a powerful framing of this issue—providing fair compensation for the innocent victim who would be left uncompensated for injuries—to develop wide support for a victims compensation fund. They ultimately had to settle for financing the fund from the state treasury, conceding a counterargument that it was "unfair" to tax the "good" waste handlers along with the "bad" ones to support the fund.

There was no significant technical information presented to either house on the question of the size that the fund should be in order to provide adequate relief for prospective claimants. Like the other revisions, the fund itself and amendments to it were mainly propelled by political information about the sponsors and opponents of particular provisions.

In many respects, the Superfund revision is a case in public values. The 1983 law addressed a problem that became a national and state environmental health issue. The business complaint was not that the problem should not have been addressed, or even that polluters should not pay—at least once the law was enacted. Rather they argued that the law went too far; that it was "unfair" to "good" business, and that the consequences would endanger the public value of employment opportunities. While evidence for this position was scant, the fact that it was believed and might be acted on by businesspeople in the location and expansion of firms was enough to gain for the bill a place at the top of the legislative agenda. Since enactment of the revisions, there has been little complaint about the law from business, victims, or environmentalists. In this respect, Merriam seemed to have correctly assessed the consequences of revision—no significant impact or effect, but business was happier. The Legislature may not have solved a problem, but it had satisfied the issue.

The Legislature Cuts Taxes

The Tax Problem

Minnesota has historically been a "high-tax" state, with a high level of public services and a strong inclination toward using the tax system for redistribution among income groups and local jurisdictions. The Minnesota Miracle of the early 1970s, for example, was made possible by use of the state tax system and a school aid formula that provided a substantial level of state support for all school districts.

When Albert Quie was elected governor in 1978, he was determined to correct what he, other Republicans, and some DFLers saw as an imbalance in the tax system that was stifling economic growth in Minnesota. Although the Legislature was controlled by the DFL, several reforms were enacted in the tax system that borrowed from theories of supply side economics that taught that reductions in the marginal rate of taxation would result in stimulation of investment by businesses and high-income taxpayers, thus producing both an expansion of economic activity and an increase in revenue collections, albeit at lower rates.

As the recession of 1981–82 gripped the state, however, it was soon apparent that the theory did not hold for such a sharp economic downturn, particularly in state government, which had no control over international and nationwide economic forces that were producing a simultaneous shift in the economic structure of the state and a severe recession. Unanticipated revenue shortages and indecision on how to fill the $1.813 billion gap between revenues and appropriations for state programs led to six special sessions of the Legislature during the last two years of the Quie administration. A patchwork of tax increases, appropriation cuts, payment shifts, and revenue collection speedups was enacted. Among these stopgap measures was a 10 percent surcharge on income taxes, which was to expire by June 30, 1985, a 2 percent increase in the general sales tax, and an increase in the motor vehicle excise tax from 4 to 6 percent.

Framing the Tax Issue

When DFL Governor Rudy Perpich took office in 1983, the economy was beginning to rebound, and he made his first priority the reestablishment of fiscal stability in the state. The major industries of Minnesota had also organized to fight high taxes through the Minnesota Business Partnership. Its priority was purely and simply a cut in taxes affecting corporations and higher-income residents of the state as a means of improving the state's business climate. The partnership pointed out that the state had climbed from 14th to 6th highest in public expenditures per capita, and that it had the highest nominal income tax rate in the country. Perpich was quite concerned about the business climate issue, as he was deeply committed to the creation of more jobs in the state—especially in depressed communities—but as governor, he also wanted to get the state off its fiscal roller coaster by making the tax system less susceptible to cyclical impacts. By the 1984 session of the Legislature, Perpich felt confident enough of the revenue forecasts of the state Department of Finance to recommend repeal of the surtax on incomes.

Seizing the business climate issue, the Independent-Republicans in the Legislature demanded that the repeal be made retroactive to January 1; after some considerable skirmishing on the issue, Perpich agreed, and the Legislature made the repeal retroactive.

Several months before the 1984 session Perpich appointed a blue-ribbon tax study commission, chaired by Mayor George Latimer of St. Paul. The Republicans, who were not consulted or represented on the commission, were skeptical that it would produce anything of value to the business community. Since it was not due to report to the governor until December of 1984, after the elections, it did not figure in the 1984 debates over tax policy.

The mandate of the commission was sweeping. It was to evaluate the entire state tax system and consider possible alternatives for the major tax sources, using standard criteria. The commission took its mandate seriously, hired an experienced study director after a nationwide search, and proceeded to conduct a thorough analysis of the state's tax system.

As the commission moved methodically ahead with its tax study, the 1984 election campaign was in high gear. The Independent-Republicans seized the tax/business climate issue and promised a billion-dollar tax cut if they gained control of the House. For the first time since legislators were elected by party in 1974, the Independent-Republicans won a clear majority in the House of Representatives. Taking the election as a mandate for a tax cut, the new speaker, David Jennings, began selecting a team and developing a strategy to achieve that result.

A month after the election, the Latimer commission issued its report, recommending a comprehensive reform of the state tax system in line with a set of criteria for efficiency and equity. The major recommendations of the commission included a 20 percent reduction in income taxes; elimination of federal deductibility on state tax returns; expansion of the general sales tax of 6 percent to include clothing and services; reduction in the number of property tax classes from over 60 to 3; and elimination of various property tax credits and refunds allowed by the existing tax code. The commission also proposed a one-page, simplified tax form that could be used by most taxpayers. The most important aspect of the commission proposal, however, was that it was a package—the individual elements made sense primarily because of their relationship to each other. The recommendations were not intended by the commission to be examined one at a time in isolation.

That, of course, was their immediate fate. The governor, who had appointed the commission, began to form his tax strategy even before it reported. Determined not to allow the IR party to have sole possession of the tax-cut issue, he did not wait for the commission's report to state his support for a tax cut of $500 million as the "single most important thing in the 1985 legislative session." He also endorsed the idea of a simple, one-page tax form. The other major position staked out by the governor in his own fiscal strategy was his insistence on a budget reserve of half a billion dollars as a "rainy day" fund to avoid the kind of unanticipated budget crises that had afflicted his predecessor. He also expressed considerable disinterest in expanding the reach of the sales tax to clothing and services.

Organized interest groups were quick to pounce on specific recommendations of the tax study commission. Labor, long an important constituent of the DFL, opposed any expanded coverage of the sales tax. Others, especially farm groups, opposed some of the property tax recommendations and urged instead even more exemptions or reductions in rates. Given particular objections by interest groups and the broad attack on the income tax by the new House majority, the governor put distance between himself and the tax commission. In his State of the State address to the Legislature on January 10, Perpich did not mention the commission or its work. He proposed three major tax initiatives: a large cut in income taxes, a simplified one-page form, and the establishment of the $500 million budget reserve.

To a considerable extent both the governor and the IR party were framing the 1985 tax issue in the same way: as a major tax cut. The principal difference was in the size of the cut proposed and the resulting size of the budget reserve. An important subissue in the debate that was to ensue centered on reducing the nominal income tax rate. Perpich accepted the tax commission recommendation for ending federal deductibility, but did not mention it in his address to the Legislature. This allowed the top nominal rate to fall from 16 percent to 9.9 percent, and incidentally would squelch the argument that the state had the highest tax rate in the country.

By the end of January, the IR caucus in the House had decided to oppose the elimination of federal deductibility, sensing that it had a strong political position by opposing a "tax on a tax." The IR also took the position that the size of the projected revenue surplus did not warrant a $500 million reserve and that $250 million would be sufficient. The lower reserve also made it possible to maintain advocacy of a billion-dollar cut, consistent with campaign promises.

Information for Tax Policy

As the Legislature convened to begin its work, there were two principal sources of technical information on the tax problems of the state and the issues they raised. The first was the Latimer commission, which had produced an impressive stack of reports by its consultants and staff. The second was the Department of Finance, which made quarterly revenue forecasts and conducted other analyses of the tax system. Both were regarded by many legislators as prejudiced sources, either as responsible to the governor and designed to support his viewpoint, or as extensions of the fiscal philosophy of the DFL.

The election was the principal source of political information on the tax issue. The defeat of a number of DFL legislators by Independent-Republicans espousing a big tax cut was a compelling bit of information. It was also clear that the governor favored a substantial cut, and that while DFL leaders in the Senate were less than enthusiastic about major cuts in state services to make a big cut in taxes possible, they also recognized that it was politically desirable, whatever their misgivings about it as a matter of state policy. Finally, the governor and the DFL leadership carried with them an important political memory — the six special sessions that had undermined the credibility of the Quie administration. They were determined, therefore, to ensure a budget reserve sufficient to guard against the vagaries of revenue forecasts that would otherwise produce a need for a special session of the Legislature to maintain a balanced budget for the biennium.

Given the narrow margin of four votes by which the IR party controlled the House and the inexperience of the new majority in leading the House, the Senate DFL leadership decided to follow a strategy of giving the House enough rope to hang itself on the tax issue, but to be ready with its own plan and depend on the greater experience of senators in the conference process to achieve the major DFL tax objectives and at the same time let the House leaders appear inept. The governor had already laid out the basic position of the party: a big cut, a half-billion-dollar reserve, and a simplified form, with some modification in property taxes.

The House Produces a Tax Cut

The House leadership was, in any event, eager to seize the initiative on taxes. The first step, which the new speaker had begun to put in place immediately after the election, was to change the rules of the House to create a Budget Committee dominated by the IR (7-3) and charged to recommend a budget resolution setting a limit on the total level of general fund spending for the state. This resolution would bind the House and allow the speaker to rule out of order any appropriation bill or amendment that would bust the budget by producing an expenditure that would exceed the limitation set by the resolution. The spending cap set early in the session would also make it possible for the IR to determine the level of taxation that would be required to fund the budget. Thus, by setting the budget resolution at the appropriate level, the IR promise of a billion-dollar tax cut could be set and maintained. The resolution would also put the House in a strong bargaining position with the Senate on both tax and appropriation bills.

Although the DFL minority objected strenuously to both the merits of the budget resolution and to the tactics of the majority in imposing it on the House, the leadership prevailed, taking along a few DFL members in the process with a solid IR party-line vote.

With a budget and tax target set, the development of the House tax package became the task of the Committee on Taxes, chaired by Representative William Schreiber. Schreiber was a veteran member of the committee and considered a strong, if low-key leader and a shrewd strategist. In many respects, the Tax Committee is the most partisan of the substantive committees of the House. Although there may be some consultation with the minority leader in making minority appointments to the committee, the speaker is free to ignore the recommendations of the minority leader. Those appointed from both parties, however, tend to be highly regarded by their colleagues in the House as among the brightest and most capable members.

On the average, Tax Committee members in 1985 had a year more experience in the House than the membership as a whole. While all served on two other House committees, many of them claimed to spend upwards of 60 percent of their time on Tax Committee issues. Even with this edge in experience and extra time, several of the committee members would readily admit that they did not understand some of the issues discussed by the committee because of their technical nature.

Because of the technical character of many of the matters before the committee and the need to understand quickly the implications of changes in the tax code for different classes of taxpayers and for the amount of revenue generated, the Tax Committee tends to depend more heavily on staff support than other committees of the House. This dependence created a special problem in the 1985 session. When it took control of the House, the new IR leadership dismissed a large number of staff members, including the fiscal analysts who had been assigned to the Tax Committee. Thus, the new committee staff had no previous experience in a legislative session. The House Research Department staff had not been regarded as partisan by the new leadership, and it was retained, so there was some continuity in staffing through research staff assigned to the committee. In addition, members relied on the party caucus staffs to advise them on the political aspects of tax policy and on some substantive matters as well. In general, members of both parties appeared to accept the information supplied by the Research Department staff as of high quality and as nonpartisan. As a consequence, this staff was most heavily relied upon for technical information. For the most part, however, the staff for the House Tax Committee played a relatively passive role in the formulation of tax policy. They supplied information on request, but did not assume an active role in shaping the major aspects of policy for either the majority or the minority on the committee.

The passivity of the legislative staff made the committee depend heavily on nonlegislative sources for technical information and for ideas about tax policy. The most important of these sources was the state Department of Finance. Strongly staffed with fiscal analysts, and the governor's chosen instrument for the development of fiscal policy, the department was not only the maker of the official forecasts of revenue and spending requirements, but the advocate of a point of view about tax policy for the state. This open advocacy of the governor's fiscal program made the information suspect among the IR majority on the committee and in the House. There was always the suspicion that revenue estimates were being doctored to support the governor's view. Consequently, the opinions and other information of the Finance Department and other state departments were often discounted by the majority. Even with this suspicion, however, the fact that the department had a virtual monopoly on technical information produced by its computer models and expert staff made all members somewhat reliant on it for an understanding of the complexities of the tax system and its impacts on taxpayers.

The other major source of information to the committee was lobbyists representing interest groups concerned with particular aspects of tax policy. Constituents made up another important outside source of information about taxes. Members of the committee interviewed for this study, however, reported that they spent relatively little time talking about taxes with lobbyists and constituents.

Of all the sources of information available to the committee, perhaps the most important was discussion with colleagues regarded as experts on tax matters because of their track record of interest, reliability, or political judgment on this most sensitive of policies. A number of members appear to have discussed the issues only slightly with others, however, thinking of themselves as playing an almost judicial role. They felt that their job was to listen to the information brought before them and to exercise their best judgment based on experience and conscience.

The Latimer tax commission, which had compiled an unequaled lode of information about the tax system, its effects, comparisons with other states and with ideal criteria, and a mass of expert opinion on alternative proposals, played almost no role in the deliberations of the committee. Few, if any, members of the committee had read the voluminous technical reports of the commission. Some had not read its final report. All were of course aware of the important political fact that the governor, who had appointed the commission, had distanced himself from it. The commission had gone out of existence with its report, and neither its chair nor the members were inclined to spend much time lobbying legislators on behalf of the measures they had recommended. They tended to let the report speak for itself and to assume that in time, its wisdom would be more widely accepted.

In January, soon after the Legislature convened, the Tax Committee held hearings on the Latimer commission report. While there was some admiration expressed for the work of the commission, most committee members of both parties thought that the recommendations were politically naive and impractical to adopt in the 1985 session. The name of the game was cutting taxes, not reforming the system. Beyond the perfunctory hearing, little more was heard of the commission and its recommendations.

The governor's tax recommendations got little more respect from the committee majority. In February, Representative John Tomlinson, who had chaired the committee when the DFL controlled the House, brought the governor's proposals before the committee. While testimony was taken from the Departments of Revenue and Finance, it was clear that the majority intended to develop its own tax package independent of the governor's recommendations.

The specifics of the IR plan were slow to develop. While continuing to assert that taxes could be cut by a billion dollars, only two specifics emerged by the end of February. The first was to reduce property taxes by $173 million, including a reduction in the mill levy for schools. The second was the proposal to reduce the budget reserve to $250 million (as opposed to the governor's proposal to raise it to $500 million) from the 1983–84 level of $375 million. In early March, Chairman Schreiber said that the IR proposal would give more across-the-board relief to single parents than the governor's proposal and that the IR property tax package would simplify property taxes, although not to the extent proposed by the Latimer commission. He suggested that the number of classifications be reduced to nine, and the allowable credits would be consolidated to two, for homesteads and agriculture.

In part, the slow pace in formulating the IR tax proposal was a result of the need of the committee to deal with an unanticipated political crisis. The financial problems of Minnesota's farmers came to a political head early in the session as hundreds of farmers descended on the Capitol demanding that the Legislature take action to prevent foreclosures and ease financial burdens brought on by collapsing international markets and farmland values. In addition to a moratorium on mortgage foreclosures, the farmers demanded some kind of tax relief to reduce their operating expenses. As the demonstrations at the Capitol continued, the DFL and the IR vied for identification as the farmer's friend. The DFL leadership favored tax legislation to reduce farm property taxes and to reduce or eliminate sales taxes on farm equipment and replacement parts. The IR supported another bill, which, as reported by the Tax Committee, lowered sales taxes from 4 to 3 percent on new and used farm equipment and lowered the sales tax rate on machinery replacement parts from 6 to 3 percent. When the bill reached the floor, the DFL was able to persuade six IR representatives to vote for an amendment to completely eliminate the sales tax on used machinery and parts.

On March 29, Schreiber announced the IR income tax plan to the committee. Taxes were to be reduced by 18 percent, producing a cut of $919 for the biennium, and dropping the maximum rate from 16 to 14 percent. Federal tax deductibility would be retained. The bill's sponsor argued that if federal deductibility were eliminated it would be too easy for the Legislature to raise taxes in the future by gradually easing the rate back up to the old levels. The bill also provided a $198 million retroactive tax break for contributions to Individual Retirement Accounts (IRAs) and other retirement plans made between 1982 and 1984.

DFL members of the committee, while not advancing an alternative plan of their own, denounced the IR plan, claiming that federal deductibility disproportionately benefited higher-income taxpayers, and that the IRA deductions would give the break only to the few who could afford to make such investments.

Speaker Jennings urged the Tax Committee to report a bill to the House as early in April as possible so that the Appropriations Committee would know how much money was going to be available and would have enough time for its subcommittees to do their work. Although the tax subcommittees worked diligently, it was not until after a full committee meeting that lasted into the early morning hours of April 24 that a tax bill was reported to the full House.

The Tax Committee bill included major changes in state income, sales, and property tax laws. Personal income taxes were to be cut 16.7 percent, reducing the top rate to 14 percent. The general sales tax and motor vehicle excise taxes were lowered from 6 to 5.5 percent. All new and used farm equipment was exempted from sales tax — a move opposite to the direction recommended by the tax commission. Together with various miscellaneous revisions, the total cut in sales taxes would be $350 million. The homestead credit on property taxes was raised from $650 to $700, again contrary to the recommendations of the tax commission. The committee also recommended, however, that the homestead credit itself be reduced from 54 to 50 percent of the property tax bill. The agricultural tax credit was increased from 33 to 50 percent of the gross tax on the first 320 acres. Overall, property taxes were cut by $173 million. The total tax cut in the committee bill was $1.364 billion — if adopted, the largest tax cut in the history of the state.

A week later, after surviving a barrage of DFL attempts to amend it, the committee bill passed the House with only one significant change. The one change was an amendment proposed by Schreiber to create a dual system of determining the amount of homestead exemption credit. Under the Schreiber amendment, homeowners in the Twin Cities metropolitan area would be able to take a 1 percent credit on the market value of their homes, up to a maximum of $700. Homeowners in other parts of the state, however, would receive a homestead credit of 49 percent of their gross property tax bill, up to the $700 maximum.

DFL representatives cried foul at the Schreiber amendment, which had not been discussed by the Tax Committee. They were concerned that the dual system would create significant inequities in the way the homestead credit was allotted. The matter was of no small political significance, as the metropolitan area was the DFL stronghold. The day after the amendment was adopted by a vote of 70-61, a House Research Department analysis predicted that under the amendment, homeowners could expect property tax increases of up to 46 percent and property taxes on farms could rise as much as 60 percent. Schreiber had to admit that such a result was unacceptable. The bill had passed the House, however, and would go to conference with this acknowledged flaw in it.

The Senate Alternative

In the Senate, the lead senator was Douglas Johnson, the chairman of the Tax Committee. Johnson was a veteran senator and a close ally of Governor Perpich, having been elected to Perpich's seat when the latter became lieutenant governor. In cooperation with the majority leader, Roger Moe, Johnson's strategy was to wait for the House to act before developing an alternative Senate plan.

The committee had plenty of work on other measures. From February to May, it dealt with about 50 other measures referred to the committee. Of these, the most important, from a political viewpoint, was a proposal to extend the property tax deadline for farmers and to eliminate sales taxes on farm machinery. The committee also considered a project strongly favored by Johnson, to permit the operation of a gambling casino in Ely. The committee approved the measure after considerable debate and a good bit of arm twisting by Johnson. In another demonstration of his power as chair of the committee, Johnson succeeded in defeating a proposal, favored by the governor, to authorize construction of a state convention center in Minneapolis. Johnson opposed the measure (which later was restored to the Senate tax bill) because of his displeasure at the tax-cutting campaign of metropolitan area business leaders, who also were prime advocates of the convention center.

Although the committee was not working on an omnibus tax bill during the first four months of the session, Johnson, Moe, and the Senate staff assigned to the Tax Committee had been hard at work on the development of tax policy since the summer of 1984. Initially, staff work concentrated on the progressivity of Minnesota's income tax and on the effects of exclusion of pension income from taxation. Committee staff also met with executive agency staff to keep themselves, Moe, and Johnson informed about the administration's tax reform plans.

Before the session began in January 1985, the staff and the committee leadership had identified income tax cuts and reforms and the elimination of federal deductibility as major priorities. The prospect of a tax cut was reinforced by the position of the House leadership, the desires of the governor, and the forecast of a revenue surplus for the coming biennium. In December, a caucus of DFL members of the Tax Committee added two more priorities: a tax plan that would maintain the current tax incidence pattern for both property and income taxpayers, and tax relief that would be as widespread as possible.

During the four months that the committee devoted to other matters, the staff and Johnson continued to work on a prospective Senate tax package, following the objectives agreed on by the caucus and earlier discussions. By early March a staff proposal had been developed that incorporated some of the incentives for local spending reforms sought by both the governor's staff and some legislators. Computer analyses of probable effects showed that the goals of maintaining the existing tax incidence could be attained. Johnson took the proposal to key members of his committee, and after receiving their endorsement, circulated the proposal to the remaining DFL members of the committee. All members of the DFL accepted the proposal, but it was not publicly announced until it could be fine tuned once the April revenue forecast was issued by the Departments of Finance and Revenue.

Because the Senate lacked the computer capability to handle the analysis on its own, the actual running of the analytical model had to be done in the Department of Revenue. Given the turnaround time for manipulating the data under different assumptions, it was late April before a package could be firmly in place and the Senate leaders could have confidence in "the numbers." The delay, however, gave them time to assess public reaction to the governor's proposals and to the tax plan beginning to emerge from the House of Representatives. Johnson was determined to go ahead with federal deductibility, regardless of public sentiment, because he believed it to be a needed reform, which incidentally had the desirable political effect of further reducing the nominal state income tax rate. But the waiting and watching also allowed the Senate to drop measures such as taxation of military pay, which had been included in the House package, and produced opposition from military families who were directly lobbying House members.

The Senate DFL proposal was announced by Moe and Johnson at a press conference on Sunday, April 28, although it had never been presented to the Tax Committee. Johnson submitted it to the committee the following day in a scripted presentation in which all DFL committee members had a role, and it was approved by the full committee on Tuesday.

The plan had five objectives: (1) target the income tax cut to middle-income taxpayers; (2) simplify the income tax form to a single page; (3) eliminate the discrimination against one-income married couples; (4) reduce nominal tax rates from 16 percent to 9 percent, eliminating the high tax rate "barrier to growth" opposed by business groups; and (5) provide property tax relief for farmers and homeowners. Like Perpich, Johnson did not mention that much of the decrease in the income tax rate was due to the elimination of the deductibility of federal income taxes from state returns. He did, however, point out that the House plan would keep the state income tax rate the highest in the country. He further condemned the House measure as one that would increase property taxes for one of every seven taxpayers. Johnson argued that any revisions passed by the 1985 Legislature should be permanent, and not so large that future Legislatures would have to repeal some of the cuts or reforms. Finally, he underscored the importance of maintaining a $500 million reserve, as recommended by the governor.

The Senate proposal was more complicated than the House plan. It drew more heavily on technical information from the Senate committee staff, the Departments of Revenue and Finance, and, to a very limited extent, the Latimer commission. Support of federal deductibility, for example, was at least in part a response to nonpartisan analysis. It was also strongly informed by political information. The fact that making federal income taxes nondeductible from state taxes would lower the nominal tax rate considerably was not lost on the DFL leadership. The determination to retain the $500 million reserve was clearly in support of the governor's position. The plan was calibrated by responses to the interests of the DFL caucus, so that while it was reformist in approach, the basic distributional benefits of the existing tax system were not seriously disturbed. In fact, some of the elements of the plan, if measured against the criteria proposed by the Latimer commission, were counterreforms. These included increases in homestead and agricultural tax credits, lowering of the sales tax, tax incentives for enterprise zones, deductions for natural ore, exemptions of some forms of charitable gambling, authorization for casino gambling in Ely, and the Minneapolis Convention Center. Most of these items are clear examples of "distributional politics," in which coalitions are built by cobbling together diverse interests into a common bill so that everyone gets something they want.

The nature of the Senate DFL bill made framing the tax issue more difficult for its sponsors than for sponsors of the House bill. In the House, the issue was clearly presented as a tax cut. The Senate bill also offered a tax cut, but because of the other things included in it, was also represented as a tax reform package. But the packaging of the reforms with tax-related projects of interest to particular DFL senators muddied the issue. The bill was particularly vulnerable on this count due to the heavy price that Johnson exacted in the provisions for Ely casino gambling and deductions for natural ore. Both measures were matters of personal concern to the Tax Committee chair. The Ely gambling provision was hotly contested on the floor, and defeated when several DFL senators either voted against it or abstained so that the motion to strike the section passed by a vote of 33 to 32.

Three days after the committee approved the bill, Moe brought it to the Senate floor. He urged that the Senate remember recent state fiscal history and not vote for too great a tax cut, and that it provide an adequate reserve against fluctuations in the economy that might reduce revenues below the levels forecast. He also warned against heavy cuts in state programs. Johnson then presented the bill, using the same speech he had given in the Tax Committee.

The IR Minority, led by Senator Glen Taylor, offered an alternative plan, which, like the House plan, proposed a $1.387 billion tax cut, including a 19 percent across-the-board income tax cut, a 20 percent reduction in property taxes, and a 24 percent reduction for property taxpayers. Although Taylor was at pains to distinguish the senate minority's plan from the House proposal, the debate was, except for the deletion of the casino section, clearly an exercise in party politics. After the deletion of that provision, the bill passed the Senate on a straight party-line vote, 42 to 25.

The Tax Conference

The smooth progress with which the respective tax bills passed each house under strict party discipline evaporated when the two quite dissimilar measures came to conference. The different approaches taken by the House and Senate not only reflected different institutional positions of the chambers on tax policy, but also symbolized fundamental cleavages between the Independent-Republican leadership of the House and the DFL leadership of the Senate. Thus, the prestige and power of each House was at stake as well as the future electoral fortunes of the two political parties.

The partisan cleavage was emphasized by the appointment of conferees. No minority conferees were appointed from either house. The House conferees were led by Schreiber and the senators by Johnson. While all members from each house were strong loyalists to their respective causes, the House conferees included John Himle, a skilled polemicist, whose job was to bait the senators and focus public and media attention on the tax-cut issue. At this point, the basic House strategy had been successful: to focus on the tax cut, and force the governor and the Senate into a bidding war on the size of the cut. The second aspect of the House strategy was to stall on any agreements with the Senate in the appropriations conferences until the size of the tax-cut was determined. The House did not want to be in the position of having to recede from its tax cut mark in order to fund programs to which it had agreed. Rather, it wanted to cut state programs to match the level of projected revenues that would be available.

The Senators expected, as they had assumed from the start of the session, that the crucial decision would be made in the tax conference, where their greater experience, the competence of their staff, and their skills at negotiation would give them an advantage over their less experienced House counterparts.

Three substantive issues separated the two houses: the size of the tax cut (the House version proposed $1.3 billion, the Senate $814 million); the elimination of federal deductibility; and the size of the budget reserve. While there were other issues, such as the incidence of the resulting tax system and the extent of property tax reform, or the one-page form, these were not issues of enormous controversy or complexity. In any event, they were dependent on resolution of the central issues.

The Senate conferees first attempted to focus public attention and discussion on the disparities between House tax proposals and House proposals for spending. This attempt failed, basically because the only tactic used by the senators was to try to bring pressure on the House by walking out of the conference and refusing to negotiate. House conferees refused to accept Department of Revenue and Department of Finance statistics and forecasts as a basis for discussion, and they would not accept the Senate's premise that spending levels should either precede or be determined simultaneously with decisions on revenues. They framed the issue by analogy to a household: the state should find out what its income was going to be, then cut the budget to live within it.

Essentially, the conferees did not negotiate, but carried out performances, remonstrating with each other, walking out of sessions, holding press conferences, and denouncing the other side as being unwilling to find a solution. Private meetings with the speaker and majority leader, and occasionally the governor, did not produce a compromise by the end of the session; so, the Legislature adjourned its regular session without acting on either taxes or appropriations for the next biennium.

It was clear that the governor would have to call a special session. He refused to do so until he could be assured that the major outstanding issues on which the Legislature should have acted in regular session had been resolved, so that the session could be a short one of two or three days. Since the adjournment technically terminated the conferences still in progress, the governor's insistence on agreement before reconvening the Legislature put considerable pressure on the leadership to reach agreement.

Since the tax and spending issues were paramount, the leadership intervened extensively in the development of agreements. The conferences continued to meet informally, but the real negotiations were carried out by Moe, Jennings, the governor, and the cochairs, Schreiber and Johnson.

Although these negotiations took almost a month, during which the governor personally appeared before the conference to propose a compromise, the final result was probably more satisfying to the House than the Senate. The House won the bidding war. Taxes were cut by roughly a billion dollars, the initial IR target. This was achieved when the Senate and the governor conceded to a reduction of the budget reserve to $450 million. The Senate, by failing to explain the importance and utility of nondeductibility of federal taxes early in the session, could not frame the issue successfully for the conference against the House claims that it was "a tax on a tax." Consequently, the Senate and the governor had to be content with a compromise that allowed taxpayers the option of deducting federal taxes from their state income tax returns and paying a higher rate, or not deducting them and paying a lower rate.

Thus, Minnesotans received the biggest tax cut in the state's history, but very little tax reform. By the time the Legislature convened for its 1986 session, new revenue forecasts showed the state facing a probable deficit that would require use of the budget reserve and require either tax increases or spending cuts. Both houses attempted to fashion budget cuts and some tax adjustments to cover the projected deficit, but again, they could not agree on a common solution before the Legislature had to adjourn. A special session was required to complete other business, but the budget issues were left to the governor to resolve through the state's "unallotment" process, whereby the governor reduced the amount of money that had been allotted to agencies by a proportionate amount.

Is This Any Way to Make Tax Policy?

As tax policy, the 1985 tax bill left a great deal to be desired. While it achieved a substantial cut in tax rates and assuaged the interests of those complaining of the effect of state taxes on the business climate, there is little subsequent evidence that the cut had a discernible effect on business locations or expansions.

Politically, the cuts did not benefit the IR party, although it had succeeded in achieving most of its legislative agenda. In 1986, Perpich won reelection by a landslide, the DFL regained control of the House by a margin of almost 30 seats, and DFL control of the Senate was increased. The state was still confronted with the same basic problems in its tax system that had existed in 1984.

The experience of the Legislature in tax policy suggests that the role that technical information can play in the decision process is closely related to the credibility of those who provide it. Credibility is far more important than the inherent worth of the material that is provided. Timing is also critical.

The Latimer commission, for example, provided a wealth of well-researched information and expert advice on the Minnesota tax system. This information, while available about a month before the Legislature convened and five to six months before decisions were made, was essentially ignored by both houses and the governor. Although headed by a prominent politician and populated with substantial DFL personalities, the commission lacked credibility in the Legislature. It simply did not address the problems and issues as the legislators perceived them. The commission attacked some of the canons of DFL faith, principally the belief in regressivity of the sales tax and homestead exemptions. The commission proposals spoke primarily to reform, when the major concern of legislators was cuts. These matters, and a growing distance politically between the governor and Latimer, caused the governor to disavow implicitly his commission, further undermining its credibility. The IR leadership had almost no interest in reform, except as a means to the end of cutting taxes.

The commission's timing also contributed to its legislative irrelevance. Operating on the assumption that the DFL would continue to control both houses after the 1984 elections, its report was published after the IR had won control of the House, largely on the issue of a tax cut. There was no audience for reform. The governor sensed that he was in a bidding war with the House leadership for tax cuts and, by the time of his State of the State address, had made a tax cut the centerpiece of his policy.

A major difference appears in the use of technical information by the House and the Senate. There is little evidence that the House committee involved its staff substantially in the development of its tax proposals. In contrast, the Senate staff was heavily relied upon by the DFL in the development of its proposal. The senators also depended to a considerable extent on the Departments of Finance and Revenue for information about the tax system and the probable effects of changes. The Senate staff had a long working relationship with Johnson and Moe, and were trusted by them. On the other hand, they provided no support to the Senate minority in the development of its tax plan. Similarly, the executive departments had credibility with the DFL, but virtually none with the Republicans.

In the clutch, political information was more important than technical knowledge in shaping both the House and Senate versions of the tax bill, and in the final resolution reached at the special session. The positions of the governor, the leaders, and committee chairs were dispositive in almost all instances. The positions of key interest groups were also critical, but related to the way in which the issues were successfully framed. The business lobby saw the culmination of several years of work on public opinion and legislation. They had carefully framed the tax cut benefiting them as a business climate issue. An extensive advertising campaign, orchestrated threats by business leaders to move their companies from the state, and strong financial support of the IR campaign for the House of Representatives paid off in 1985. The business interest succeeded in forcing the political leaders of the state to compete with each other as champions of improving the business climate and, incidentally, of tax cuts.

The case also illustrates the general observation made earlier that in important matters, the informal, private negotiations among very few leaders and the governor are usually necessary to reach resolution. The need for this level of intervention is partly due to the adjournment deadlines that provide little time for serious discussions among conferees. It is also a function of the increasing centralization of power in the leadership of both houses. But in this system, much of the most important work is left for the conference process, guided by the leadership.

A Stalemate on Health Policy

Most of the 3,259 bills introduced during the 1985 session of the Minnesota Legislature were neither as pervasive in impact nor of as much widespread public interest as the Superfund amendments or the tax cut. Most of them were little bills, of importance primarily to their sponsors and beneficiaries. Other bills, while important in their effect, gained little public attention and excited little interest in the Legislature because they were relatively noncontroversial. Finally, there were bills that were complex in terms of the subject matter they dealt with and they may have been hotly contested, but only by a small number of legislators and lobbyists who had a deep interest in their enactment or defeat. Very often, bills of this sort arose in the context of broader areas of legislation.

In terms of its effect on the people of the state, few areas of public policy could be more important than health policy. Since the mid-seventies, the Minnesota Legislature has devoted a considerable amount of its energies to many aspects of health care. Generally, the Legislature has moved state policy from a basically regulatory approach to the health care industry to one that features competition among providers. Minnesota has, in large part due to policies enacted by the Legislature, led the nation in the reorganization of its health industry, so that by the early 1980s a larger proportion of medical care than in any other state was handled through health maintenance organizations (HMOs).

The state has also been a leader in health cost-containment legislation. This included, in 1984, a law placing a moratorium on new hospital construction, relocation of existing hospitals, or certification of new hospital beds. The bill, though opposed by the industry, was part of the garbage slipped into a conference report in the final days of the 1984 session. The state has also enacted rate review legislation, but the most significant cost-containment measures in recent years have dealt with the costs of health care provided by the state itself through employee benefit plans.

The result of this legislation has been to increase the options available to employees, and to provide financial incentives to employees to select the most cost-effective plans. In addition, state law allows the commissioner of health to distribute data on the prices of treatment and on the financial status of hospitals, and practitioners are required to post their prices for treatment of common ailments. Finally, in anticipation of a need for a comprehensive approach to cost containment, the Legislature directed the Health Department to report to the 1985 session its recommendations for an integrated, comprehensive cost-containment program for acute care health services.

Thus, as the 1985 session approached, it was anticipated that health care cost containment would be a major priority for the session. The issue is one of considerable technical complexity, both financially and institutionally. Politically, it involved the conflicting interests of different parts of the health care industry, as well as the interests of those receiving the care and those who pay for it through employee benefit programs in the public and private sectors.

The Legislature was not especially well equipped to deal with the merits of the issue. Legislation dealing with the problem was within the jurisdiction of the House Subcommittee on Health Care of the Committee on Health and Human Services. As the IR now assumed control of the House, the subcommittee chair, David Gruenes, beginning his third term in the House, was new to his job. He had an interest in the subject of cost containment, but had no professional background. The only members of the committee who brought personal knowledge of some aspects of the problem from their past experience were Brad Stanius (IR), Ralph Kiffmeyer (IR), and Karen Clark (DFL). Stanius was a pharmacist, serving his first term. He was also a member of the Human Services Division of the Appropriations Committee. Kiffmeyer was a nurse anesthetist. Clark, in her third term, was a professional nurse.

In the Senate, the Health and Human Services Committee was chaired by Senator Linda Berglin (DFL), who was regarded by her colleagues as the Senate's expert on health policy. She had served four terms in the House and was in her third term in the Senate. Berglin served on the Subcommittee on Income Maintenance, chaired by Senator Ronald Dicklich, who depended heavily on Berglin to deal with the technical issues in health care policy. The subcommittee included a physician, Senator A. W. "Bill" Diesner, and several other senators with strong interests in the subject and considerable legislative experience.

In January, the Department of Health presented its comprehensive report on cost containment for acute care services to the full House Committee on Health and Human Services. Going beyond its mandate, the report contained recommendations for state government, consumers, employers, insurers, and providers. Comments at the hearing from health care organizations were generally favorable, although there was not full agreement with the recommendations. The full committee also heard in January from the commissioners of health and human services on issues they would like the Legislature to consider during the session. The Health Department, however, did not prepare a bill embodying the recommendations of its cost-containment report.

The Death and Life of the Exclusive Agreements Issue

With no one on the committee or the administration pressing the issue, and with the majority caucus occupied with business climate issues, the House Subcommittee on Health Care turned its attention to other bills. The most significant of these was HF 294, introduced by Representative Kathleen Blatz (IR), who chaired the Committee on Crime and Family Law. Blatz had introduced the bill at the urging of two groups who had drafted it, Physicians Health Plan (PHP), a health maintenance organization, and the Minnesota Medical Association. Basically, the bill prohibited certain exclusive agreements between HMOs and providers of health care, such as physicians, hospitals, or pharmacists, to reimburse them for services or products they dispensed if they agreed to work only with that HMO.

The subcommittee considered the bill in two meetings, on February 28 and March 12. At the first meeting Blatz presented her bill as an effort to foster competition through prohibiting the exclusive agreements. She argued that if the agreements were allowed to continue and become pervasive, monopolies could develop in particular areas, particularly rural communities, if one HMO contracted for exclusive rights to the services of all local physicians.

A representative of the medical association framed the issue as protecting physician-patient relationships. Exclusive dealing contracts, he argued, prevented physicians from competing with an HMO because patients were forced to choose between their HMO or their physician when the latter refused to enter into an exclusive contract with the HMO. Representatives of PHP, the Pharmaceutical Association, and the Dental Association also supported the Blatz bill. They framed the issue as one of choice between monopoly and competition, and questioned whether current practice violated antitrust law. Representative Stanius strongly endorsed the bill, citing his experience as a pharmacist and stating that the patient was the main concern addressed by the bill.

Opposing witnesses accepted the idea that competition versus monopoly was the issue. They argued, however, that such agreements were not widely used, but that the right to use them was important to preserve because they allowed HMOs to compete with each other and with private physicians through product differentiation. The principal witness against the bill was a representative of MedCenters Health Plan, one of the state's largest and most successful HMOs.

Stanius took vigorous exception to the competition argument of the opponents, contending that an HMO should not be allowed to refuse to participate with a provider or pharmacist, and that this was the problem the bill would resolve. Opponents responded that if all providers could participate in any plan, there would be no competition at all. Other members of the committee expressed considerable confusion since both sides seemed to be arguing that their position would best advance competition.

At the second meeting, Blatz tried to shift the subcommittee's attention back to the problem she feared would develop in rural communities. Some of the testimony of both proponents and opponents suggested, in light of questions from members of the committee, that the problem might be more theoretical than real. Another witness emphasized that the bill would favor one kind of HMO over others—the independent practice associations, like PHP, that include a large number of physicians who draw a minority of their patients from HMOs, as opposed to HMOs that employ physicians directly or group plans where physicians are members of a partnership or corporation that contracts with the HMO to provide physician services.

The Health Department testified, but took no position on the bill, although its representative stated some reservations about the language of the bill and its enforcement. Various members of the committee continued to express skepticism about the need for the bill and again complained of their inability to understand the conflicting claims about it. A motion was offered to postpone the bill for interim study, but with opposition from Stanius, who again invoked his expertise in health care, the motion failed. Although the committee deferred to him in not killing the bill outright, it was not prepared to take positive action on it, either.

To this point, the House subcommittee had received information that appeared to be technical in nature, in that it dealt with the substantive matters, but the information was provided with a political slant. The bill was the product of interested groups, PHP and the organized medical profession and pharmacists. It was opposed by other obviously interested groups—other HMOs and some consumer groups. The committee received no technical information from disinterested sources. The Health Department expressed reservations, but took no position. It provided neither useful technical nor political information, except to the extent that this meant there would be no pressure from the department on either side of the issue. On the other hand, the bill was sponsored by an influential and re-spected member of the majority party, but there was no caucus position on it. This meant that it would have to be dealt with on its merits independent of the House leadership. Within the subcommittee, only Stanius was a fervent advocate of the bill. With key members, especially Clark, expressing confusion and doubt, the bill was set aside.

But it did not die. At the end of March, the IR caucus, realizing that there was little time left for the committees to discuss and produce a health bill, put to-gether a Comprehensive Health and Welfare Policy Act, which included numer-ous health-related proposals, job and training measures, and a controversial pro-posal to cut welfare assistance to employables. This bill was sponsored by Representative Tony Onnen, chair of the Health and Human Services Committee. The House research staff prepared a summary of the bill for the committee, which approved the bill after a marathon meeting on April 4. The bill, however, provoked protests and rallies at the Capitol from welfare recipients and other cli-ent groups of the health and welfare systems. The demonstrations and protests were supported by the mayors of Minneapolis and Saint Paul, and received ex-tensive media coverage. The House leadership decided to back off. The Health and Human Services Division of Appropriations Committee canceled hearings that had been scheduled for the bill. The chairman concluded that with 112 amendments offered to it, the bill "may be beyond rescue. It is seriously flawed as it is." Onnen declared the 224-page bill "dead."

On April 19, however, the Health and Human Services Division of the Ap-propriations Committee approved a bill, strongly supported by the administra-tion, but not considered a partisan issue, concerned with prepaid health plans. This bill was shortly incorporated into an omnibus bill being prepared by the di-vision, which ultimately looked very much like the Onnen bill that had been so recently declared dead. One of the provisions of the new bill, inserted by Stanius, who was also a member of the division, contained the prohibition of exclusive agreements between HMOs and health care providers. The omnibus bill passed the House with the support of the IR majority.

The revival of the Blatz bill through the Appropriations Division on Health and Human Services was a result of persistent lobbying by PHP and the continu-ing interest of Representative Stanius. A private meeting among the chairs of the health subcommittee, Onnen, and a representative of the Department of Health had produced an amendment dealing with the concerns of the department. Onnen had initially agreed to attach the provision to the caucus bill, but when that bill was set aside, Stanius succeeded in attaching it to the omnibus bill.

The Senate Counterattacks

The early weeks of the session in the Senate were also devoted to educational meetings and hearings of the Health and Human Services Committee. The Income Maintenance Subcommittee was busy with bills concerning nursing homes and home health care licensure, a measure sponsored by Senator Berglin. A number of related, noncontroversial measures were combined in a bill by Senator Berglin. Several measures to contain health costs were also heard, including proposals by the Departments of Health and Human Services.

The most important measure before the subcommittee was the administrations's proposal for prepaid health plans, sponsored by Senator Eric Petty (DFL) and strongly supported by Berglin. The bill was supported, as it had been in the House, by technical studies by the Departments of Human Services and Health. The administration estimated that one of its provisions, a requirement that general welfare assistance clients be required to enroll in prepaid health plans, would save the state government about $5 million annually.

As this bill was being considered by the subcommittee, Senator Diesner, the physician who was a member, offered an amendment to add the exclusive agreement prohibition. Although it was approved by the subcommittee, Senator Berglin proposed an amendment at the next meeting to delete the Diesner amendment. The subcommittee took testimony, which substantially duplicated that given in the House. The Health Department again professed neutrality, but subtly suggested that the bill was not necessary.

Berglin strongly opposed the prohibition of exclusive agreements, and over Diesner's objections, his amendment was deleted. On a broader front, Berglin organized hearings before her committee on the House IR caucus bill, even though it had not yet passed the House in any form. IR senators protested the hearings, claiming the bill was dead, and walked out of the hearing.

As the House did not pass a comprehensive health bill, as such, but incorporated its package of substantive measures in the appropriations bill, the Senate had to prepare to preserve its health legislation by attaching various Senate bills to House bills in order to compel conferences on the issues. The Senate also began to prepare for the major confrontation with the House on health and welfare policy through the conference on appropriations. Berglin, anticipating the Stanius amendment, added a provision to the Senate appropriations bill that would essentially put PHP out of business. Two major HMOs, MedCenters and Group Health, had in the meantime announced that they would not participate in prepaid health plans if the exclusive agreements prohibition passed.

The Conference and the Sacrifice of Prepaid Health Plans

The House conferees on human services appropriations included only one legislator with much legislative experience, the cochair, Bob Anderson, who had served five terms in the House. Only one of the remaining four members, who included Stanius, had served more than a single term. In contrast, the Senate conferees were led by Senator Don Samuelson, who had served six terms in the House and was in his second Senate term. He was an experienced union negotiator. In addition, Berglin and the other senators were all seasoned legislators, with many conference committees behind them. All but Berglin were also members of the Senate Finance Committee.

As the committee worked through the conference report, it was clear that there would be strong differences over the exclusive agreements provision. Berglin and Stanius were assigned as a subcommittee to see if they could reconcile their respective amendments, and thereby salvage the prepaid health plan, which both houses and the administration favored. Neither would yield, however, which resulted in a final bill that excluded the prepaid health plan legislation. The House conferees would not agree to it without the Stanius amendment, which was unacceptable to Berglin and the Senate conferees. In fact, the conference was unable to complete the remainder of its work before the session adjourned, and like other conferences, continued to work informally to prepare bills for the special session.

The Price of Intransigence

It seems likely that the Legislature could have enacted legislation on prepaid health plans had this proposal not been held hostage to the exclusive agreements amendment. The prepaid plans bill had been framed basically as a cost-cutting measure, and there was very little opposition to it. The exclusive agreements measure, by contrast, was hard to understand. Both proponents and opponents held that their position was best for competition. Politically, there were no sure touchstones, and the technical information was conflicting. Some health maintenance organizations opposed it; one was strongly for it. Lacking unambiguous technical information and political consensus, most members shied away from it. It got as far as it did because few members cared very much and the one who did was persistent and determined. In a caucus with little experience or independent knowledge of the issue, Stanius was able to parlay his own professional experience and zeal to telling effect, attaching the measure first to the caucus bill, and when it failed, to the appropriations bill for health and human services.

The interest groups, especially PHP, were also effective, arranging individual meetings with committee members, with Onnen, and with Senator Diesner. They refused to take no for an answer, and kept moving the bill to a new forum when it ran into trouble.

On the Senate side, the most salient piece of political information was Senator Berglin's outspoken opposition. She did not allow the bill to be heard in her committee and when she discovered it on a subcommittee bill, she took immediate steps to delete it. Moreover she sponsored a bargaining chip amendment to endanger PHP's business. Berglin's reputation with her colleagues was enough. If she was against it, so were they.

In the conference, the prepaid health plan had to be sacrificed for the 1985 session to Stanius's intransigence on the exclusive agreements provision. Although the differences between the House and Senate on prepaid plans as such were small, Stanius would not yield, knowing that the measure was important to Berglin. The other House conferees were not willing to forsake Stanius, and thus, sacrificed the prepaid health plan, which would have saved the state $5 million a year. The political costs of not agreeing were not perceived as high. While the governor and the Department of Human Services were supporters of the prepaid plan, they had not framed the issue in politically compelling terms, even for a legislative session that was determined to cut taxes and the costs of government.

Decisions and Information; Institutions and Policy

In thinking about how the Legislature gathers and uses information, we must understand the institutions that structure legislative deliberation. While the sum of a legislator's activity suggests that every member is compelled to become a generalist on state affairs, the Legislature in fact operates through specialization. Only a few members, primarily the party leaders, are truly generalists who try to grasp the fundamentals of all major legislative matters as well as to master the rules of procedure. Even they must filter out some things and leave them to others.

A second tier of members serves as committee chairs and specialists on particular kinds of legislation. These members develop reputations for expertise and reliability among their colleagues and are likely to be deferred to as authoritative sources of technical and political information in their areas of perceived knowledge. It is not uncommon to hear, in discussions with legislators, the comment that, "there are only two people in the whole House who understand the local government aid formula," or only a handful who know what's in the school aid bill, or that but a few can decipher the tax system. Committee and floor debate and conference committee negotiations are frequently transactions among this little club of in-house experts. The larger membership tends to serve as a jury (to the extent that there are no party instructions on how to vote on a matter), listening to the expert advocates and choosing the more plausible side or the side their political information suggests best suits their interests.

A third tier of members may possess expertise in a particular area growing from their nonlegislative experience or from interest in a cause they wish to advance. A trial lawyer, for example, may find courtroom experience both useful and influential in dealing with amendments to the criminal code. An insurance broker, pharmacist, nurse, physician, banker, or teacher may be able to use knowledge gained in a prior or concurrent occupation of great value in dealing with related legislation. Such members often become important sources of information for their colleagues, and points of access to the process for groups that share their perspectives. Although not in the leadership or experts in an area of legislation such as taxes, natural resources, or health policy, these members are often effective sponsors of particular bills because they can assert a practical expertise to which many other members will defer. The "I'm from Milwaukee and I ought to know" approach to information is not without effect in the Legislature, where common sense and reasoning from example, experience, and analogy is far more common than mathematical modeling.

Finally, every legislative body contains some back-benchers, members whose level of activity and interest in most legislation is low, and who tend to take their cues on how to vote from the governor, their leaders, or from interest groups in their constituencies or elsewhere. They have little need of technical information, since they are likely to spend little time contemplating it or trying to frame issues for decision. Rather, they are primarily consumers of political information—who is for or against the proposal, how strong is the support or opposition, what do the interests that matter to them think of it?

In Minnesota, as in most legislatures, the information-gathering process focuses on the committee system. The principal formal method of gathering information on proposed or potential legislation is the public hearing or informational meeting. Hearings are open to the public, but no written record is kept of them. Tape recordings are made and retained in the Legislative Reference Library. For the most part, however, the only record of the information disseminated at legislative hearings is in the memory or notes of members, staff, and others present when testimony is given. Therefore, the premium is on testimony that is memorable. While witnesses may present written materials to members, most testimony is oral. Hearings tend to be loosely structured, with opportunities provided for any person who wishes to testify. The time allowed for presentations may be limited to a few minutes, however. It is possible for interest groups to stack hearings by registering large numbers of witnesses who repeat essentially the same technical information and, though sheer numbers, convey an important form of political information—who is concerned and the intensity of concern. Outside the committee rooms, demonstrations provide dramatic statements that reinforce political information about who is for or against a measure.

The committee system also provides the primary focus for lobbying by interest groups and state agencies. Both in formal testimony and in private conversations with the chair and experts on the committee, group representatives seek to influence legislators' perceptions of the problems and issues and the legislative language that is chosen by the committee to deal with the issues. It is at the committee stage in particular that framing of issues is the most important. What the sponsor of legislation or a lobbyist seeks is to have the committee accept as its own the frame presented. If that is accomplished, then the advocate's view becomes the committee's cause, and goes to the floor with the prestige of the chair and the leading committee experts behind it. This is, in itself, an important piece of political information for the less involved members.

The committees are also the place where much of the staff work for the Legislature is concentrated. Research staff may prepare materials for members that provide technical information on legislation. Caucus staff may also prepare both technical and political information for the use of members in questioning witnesses and in devising strategy for work sessions and the markup of bills. Unlike congressional hearings, where staff normally organize the hearing and may even take an active role in the proceedings, Minnesota legislative staff tend to operate in a more responsive mode. Questions of fact, impact, or law may be raised by members, and it is the task of staff to provide responses to many of these questions. Research and legal staff may also be available to assist in drafting and revising language to meet the objectives of committee members. Committee members may be provided with reports compiled by research staff, by the legislative auditor, and by other public agencies and private organizations that bear on legislation at hand or on the general jurisdiction of the committee.

In the Minnesota Legislature, the party caucuses are a forum of great importance in legislative processing of information. While their prime focus is on gathering and disseminating political information, they are also significant consumers of technical information. It is in the caucus that the party leaders frame the major issues they will press during the session and devise the strategies for advancing them. Members bring with them to the caucus political information about their constituencies and their own agendas for legislative action. Legislators and caucus staff draw on their knowledge of problems, on staff studies, on contacts with interest groups that have been or could be persuaded to become associated with the party in legislative and electoral endeavors, to make choices on positions and strategies, and to establish legislative priorities.

Some of these priorities may be quite clear. In 1985, the first priority for the Independent-Republican caucus was a billion-dollar tax cut. Such a decision automatically limited the need for technical information to that which supported the decision. There is, in fact, an interest in limiting the development of information that might suggest a contrary view and in exploiting any information that appears to corroborate the decision. The caucus is also a disseminator of information to both the Legislature and the public in the hope of generating a feedback of political information that suggests that the position taken is a popular one.

The single most important source of information for the Legislature is the executive branch of state government. In the case of state financial information, the Legislature is virtually dependent on the Departments of Finance and Revenue for technical information about revenue collections and revenue forecasts. Other departments, such as the Departments of Transportation, Health, and Natural Resources, exercise a virtual monopoly over certain kinds of technical information. While there are always anecdotal sources available to legislators, systematic information about most state government activities is in the possession of the executive agencies. Legislative staff or other study groups may analyze some of the data, but the agencies themselves provide most of the analyses available to the Legislature. Agencies also tend to enjoy a close working relationship with the committees of both houses that have jurisdiction over legislation and appropriations of concern to them. They almost always have access to the committee chairs and key members, who provide an open channel for information to the committees. In addition, individual legislators often act as patrons to agencies in whose activities they have taken an interest. Such members can usually be counted on to introduce departmental bills and be attentive to agency concerns in the committee process.

The governor and members of the cabinet and administration play key roles as providers of both technical and political information. The position of the governor or a major cabinet officer on a matter before the Legislature is of central importance to all legislators, and particularly to members of the governor's party. The governor also plays a central role in setting the legislative agenda through the State of the State address to the Legislature, the budget message, and other special messages or speeches delivered before and during the course of the session. Because of the wide audience they can command and the base of support that was built in order to gain election, governors can often set the terms of debate by framing issues that are compelling simply because they have identified them as matter the Legislature should address. In the 1985 session, the governor was the most important force behind consideration of legislation to permit high school students freedom of choice in attending any public school in the state. Although the legislation was not enacted during that session, knowledge of the political information that the governor supported it kept it alive almost to the end of the session. In the 1987 session, the governor's support for a state arts high school was the most salient piece of political information available to legislators, many of whom felt the project was of dubious merit. It was ultimately included in the conference report on the bonding bill, largely because of the knowledge that the governor wanted it.

The Legislature meets each year for a constitutionally limited period. This limitation on time produces a fairly predictable rhythm to the flow of information. The first several weeks of a session may be looked upon as a time for the gathering of information. The filters are relatively open to ideas in the form of bills and testimony. The pace is leisurely, and there is time for some study, contemplation, and trial framing of issues. By the midpoint of the session, committees are at work in earnest in revising bills and reporting them to the floor. It becomes more difficult for new technical information to reach key members and have an impact on their thinking. The amount and velocity of political information, however, tends to increase as members and outside interests must choose sides on specific language. By the final weeks of the session, political information dominates consideration of major proposals. The major concern is on finding enough votes to pass high-priority bills and on the political effects and appearances of proposals on constituencies, clientele, and the members themselves. Considerations based on technical information may intrude, but only if they are of such a nature that they raise significant political issues.

8

The Legislature at Work: Budgeting

Of all the work the Legislature does, none is more complex or more time consuming than enactment of the biennial budget for the state. Since the late seventies, the budget has been the primary focus of public attention on the Legislature, and taxing and spending have become the major subjects of dispute between the party caucuses in the Legislature.

The Changing Fiscal Environment

During the generation covered by this study, the fiscal environment of the state underwent a substantial change. Since the Floyd Olson administration during the Great Depression, Minnesota has been a "high-service" state. Both political parties were generally responsive to demands for high-quality education, roads, health services, and social welfare programs. Both were relatively progressive in tax policy, gradually placing more emphasis on income taxes than property taxes as the principal basis for state revenues. The DFL has traditionally been the champion of progressivity in income taxation and the implacable foe of expansion of the sales tax to food and clothing purchases. Both parties have competed to reduce property taxes, especially for farmers and the elderly, and both have supported the use of state transfer payments to school districts and local government to reduce their reliance on property taxes.

For most of the postreapportionment era, there was an underlying consensus in the Legislature, at least among the leadership of both parties, that the state should perform an active and innovative role in the provision of public services of a high quality. Although there was frequent disagreement over specific programs or specific taxes to pay for them, the focus of fiscal politics was on the merits of programs more than on the overall level of expenditure. This consensus was based on the assumption that the state's economy would grow enough to provide fairly regular and modest expansions of services without wrenching adjustments in tax rates. Thus, incremental growth of expenditures was tolerable, so long as it was accompanied by an incremental and modest increase in taxation. By and large, legislators of both parties believed that their job was to decide on the services the state should provide, and assuming they believed they were well managed, to then bite the bullet and raise the taxes necessary to finance them.

During most of this period, state expenditures were devoted primarily to the operation of state agencies and the support of public education. The public schools themselves, as well as local governments, were supported principally by local taxation of property, supplemented by revenues from the state sales tax.

The Minnesota Miracle and the New Fiscal Regime

A new fiscal era for Minnesota began in 1971, with enactment of the Minnesota Miracle, the package of educational and local government aid, tax levy limitations, and agricultural tax credits, sponsored by Governor Wendell Anderson and ultimately supported by the conservative leaders, Stanley Holmquist in the Senate and Aubrey Dirlam, the speaker of the House. The resulting compromise retained the underlying consensus, but changed forever the nature of fiscal politics.

The basic feature of the Minnesota Miracle was to use the statewide income tax, collected from a growing economy, to redistribute revenues to local governments and school districts and to allow them to reduce local property taxes. In addition, the Legislature provided further property tax relief to classes of taxpayers, particularly farmers, homesteaders, and the elderly. Thus the new system shifted the aggregate costs of state and local government from property and sales to income.

Second, the miracle changed the nature of the state budget. The budget had been a device that was primarily devoted to financing direct state services, where the Legislature could biennially control both the character of service offered and the level of support each received. It became a device for transferring revenues raised by the state, via a formula determined by prior Legislatures, to other units of government for uses not directly under legislative control. Whereas in 1957, intergovernmental transfer payments were only 38 percent of the state budget, by 1975, they had risen to 50 percent of outlays. When combined with other formula-driven assistance to local units and property tax relief, 60 percent of the state budget was essentially beyond control by the current Legislature. By 1982, 80 percent of the budget was consumed by seven programs that were either formula-or demand-driven. By 1987, transfer payments consumed 85 percent of state spending from general revenues, leaving only 15 percent available to finance direct state government operations.

Recession, Restructuring, and Devolution

The consensus that had supported the Minnesota Miracle began to unravel in the late 1970s. Minnesota was not subjected to the more extreme versions of the tax-and expenditure-limitation movement, which produced Proposition 13 in California and similar constitutional budget or tax caps in other states. Business interests, however, began to chafe at the high nominal and actual corporate and personal income tax rates needed to support state programs and the wide range of transfer payments.

In 1978, Albert Quie, the IR candidate for governor, defeated the DFL incumbent, Rudy Perpich. The Senate remained solidly in the control of the DFL, but the House was evenly divided between the two political parties. Quie was determined to rein in state spending, and to make substantial changes in the tax system. His main objective was to limit revenues as a brake on expenditures. The primary means of doing this was to index tax brackets to inflation to prevent "bracket creep" and the automatic increase in revenues that followed inflation. This inflationary "ratcheting" of revenues had made it possible for the DFL administration and Legislature to expand programs during the 1970s without raising the tax rate. Independent-Republicans and business leaders in the state saw this as a painless inducement to overspending. Quie did not attack the level of services then being offered. Without a majority in either house, however, Quie needed DFL support for his indexation package. The price exacted by the DFL Senate leader, Nicholas Coleman, was homestead relief. Thus, Quie's main objective was to slow down the rate of growth in state spending. Assuming continued growth in the economy of the state, he believed that lower tax rates would continue to produce revenues sufficient to fund all of the major programs of the state, but that they would necessitate a slower rate of growth in the total level of state expenditures.

He was wrong. Indexation reduced the rate at which revenues flowed into the state treasury, but double-digit inflation, accelerated by the 1979 oil shock, pushed up the costs of state government and increased the demands on formula-based programs. The state, which had seemed recession-proof during the seventies, now slumped into a serious recession, exacerbated by structural changes that decimated employment in mining, construction, and durable goods manufacturing. Between 1979 and 1982, employment in mining declined 62 percent. Construction jobs declined by 26 percent, and 17 percent of durable goods manufacturing jobs were lost. Even wholesale and retail jobs declined, and while employment in services continued to grow, the rate was flat. The rise in the value of the U.S. dollar, on top of the Soviet grain embargo declared by President Carter, precipitated a recession in the agricultural sector of the Minnesota economy, which had become heavily dependent on its export market (Roden, 1986).

The recession in the state produced greater demands on state programs designed to aid the unemployed. As these tend to be formula-driven programs, the budget for them was virtually out of the governor's or the Legislature's control. The agricultural recession produced demands that the state do something. Since the causes were beyond the power of state government to manage, the only direct amelioration the state could offer farmers was more tax relief, thereby further widening the gap between revenues and expenditures.

If the recession was not enough to upset the budgetary apple cart of Governor Quie, he was faced with the further irony of the triumph of Ronald Reagan in the 1981 federal budget, which cut back a wide range of federal domestic programs and began the process of devolution to the states of primary financial responsibility for them. Thus, the state found itself stuck with a larger bill for recession-related welfare costs than would otherwise have been the case.

Quie was now locked into a policy spiral that would not stop until he left office. He was forced to call six special sessions of the Legislature to plug the revenue gaps that arose as revenues did not meet predicted levels, producing imbalance in the state budget. Because of the linkage that existed between state taxes and transfer payments to other units of government, cuts in state taxes tended to produce pressure on localities and school districts to raise their taxes. Rather than face this prospect, income tax rates were raised in 1982, although indexation was not repealed. A short-term surtax, which was to expire in 1984, was placed on income taxes. The Legislature also slightly broadened the coverage of the sales tax to include the sales of candy and soft drinks, and raised the rate from 4 to 6 percent.

Revenue Instability; Rigid Entitlements

The lesson of the Quie administration was that Minnesota's tax system was highly sensitive to cyclical fluctuations in the national economy. Over 40 percent of general fund revenues came from the individual and corporate income tax. As the recession deepened, revenues dropped. At the same time, a large proportion of state expenditures was beyond the control of the governor and Legislature. Instead, the level of spending required for a number of social programs was driven by levels of unemployment or other factors, which were determined by the number of citizens who became entitled to some form of assistance, in direct benefits, transfer payments through local governments, or tax relief. Another part of the expenditure system was rigid, driven by formulas for redistribution of state revenues written at a time when revenues were expected only to rise with inflation and growth.

When the combination of indexation and recession stopped the growth of the revenue stream, the budget could not easily be contracted because the amount of discretionary expenditure was very small. Even the 15 to 30 percent of the budget that might be theoretically considered discretionary was not in fact so. At best, only a small increment of this part of the budget could be cut without serious damage to important state functions. Like the federal budget, the Minnesota state budget was getting "out of control" (Wildavsky, 1988).

Changing Expectations and the Rise of Budgetary Conflict: From Minnesota Miracle to Minnesota Mess

From Legislative Control to Formulas

The establishment of formulas for the redistribution of state revenues to localities represents a strong consensus that the people and functions being supported are both legitimate and deserving. Although any Legislature had the power to amend a formula, and amendments were occasionally made, the dynamics of budgeting were fundamentally changed.

First of all, the formulas represented entitlements to their beneficiaries. The recipient agencies and governments became dependent on the state transfer payments, which were built into their annual budgets on the assumption of full formula funding. Property tax levels for municipalities, counties, and school districts were based on the assumption of a continuing flow of state aid. The major cities, the associations of government officials, and the school boards all developed lobbying staffs and programs designed to perpetuate, and if possible to increase, the flow of state funds to their budgets. They were joined by agents of interest groups representing the ultimate clients of the formula-funded programs: teachers and parents, welfare recipients, contract service providers, and public employees. Statutory limits on the millage localities could levy built in additional pressure on them to seek full formula funding from the Legislature, especially as they reached or came near the cap on their taxing authority.

Due to formula-driven entitlements, the Legislature, instead of dealing with a state department head who had a strong interest in pleasing the governor or the Legislature, and who may have had at least some discretion in rearranging priorities and programs to meet either a policy change or a revenue shortfall, faced elected and appointed officials of political subdivisions who had counted on the transfer payments as part of their "given" revenues, and other beneficiary groups who counted the payments as income. What's more, they all lived in the districts of the legislators. Thus, instead of working on the budget of an agency that works for it, the Legislature increasingly found itself working on the budgets of those for whom it works.

Any major change in policy threatened the consensus on which entitlements were originally based. As the political support for the established entitlements became stronger, the formulas became more sacrosanct, creating a bias in budgetary politics toward making cuts first, if any were necessary, in the "discretionary" 15 percent of the budget that financed the state bureaucracy. Cuts in the traditional state agencies do not involve other units of government and their powerful interest groups. Nor do they require hundreds of autonomous governments to adjust their budgets. The problem with a "surgical strike" against the state agencies is that there is rarely enough "fat" to meet the appetite of a substantial revenue shortfall (Jernberg, 1988). It then becomes necessary to consider tax increases if the entitlement programs are to be left unmolested.

Dissensus about the Role of State Government

By 1982, the budgetary consensus that had started with the Minnesota Miracle had been dissipated. The experience of the IR minority in the House of Representatives with the compromises and conflicts that had consumed the divided House and had soured the promise of the Quie administration to reduce the role of government and lower expenditures, had produced a minority leadership with a markedly different approach to budgeting, based on a different view of the role of government.

The Business Climate vs. the Service State

The new IR leadership of the House (and to a lesser degree that of the Senate) began to challenge frontally the notion of the service state to which both parties had previously subscribed. David Jennings, the new minority leader, made it clear that he and his caucus intended to try to reduce the *size* of state government, not just its rate of growth. They planned to do this by restricting the revenue the state could spend, following the same strategy of large tax cuts that had been successful for the Reagan administration at the national level. The progressive tradition, which had been at the core of Minnesota politics for almost 50 years, could no longer be taken for granted.

As discussed in Chapter 7, the issue chosen by the IR leadership was the state's business climate. The argument was that Minnesota was losing businesses and jobs because its income tax rates were forcing businesses to go to other states. The only cure was a big tax cut—a billion dollars. And that could occur only if the state disciplined itself and cut spending, particularly spending on social programs. Countering the DFL argument that such a policy was kicking the jobless and poor when they were down, the IR contended that tax cuts would stimulate the economy and bring jobs back to Minnesota through private investments, in contrast to the misguided efforts in public subsidy that were busting the state budget.

Instead of a bipartisan consensus that the function of the budget was to provide adequate funding for state services and transfer payments to other units of government to equalize tax burdens, there was now dissensus. Only part of the Legislature retained its allegiance to this benign view and to the idea that disagreement should be confined to the relative merits of specific programs, and that once these were decided, funding should follow policy.

The new minority (which became the House majority in 1985) turned the idea of the budget upside down. They insisted that the main task of the Legislature was to reduce taxes to stimulate the state's economy and promote business. Once that was accomplished, the budgetary task for the Legislature was to cut state expenditures to a level that could fit within the available revenues. Instead of placing primary legislative emphasis on specific programs, they wanted to put the policy focus on the overall total levels of taxation and expenditure. The House majority realized, however, that there was strong popular support for the transfer payments to localities and school districts. This meant that the budget cuts would have to come from the 15 percent of the budget that was "discretionary," and from less than universally popular entitlement programs, such as welfare or the formulas that provided higher levels of local government aid to St. Paul, Minneapolis, and Duluth (all DFL strongholds) than to suburban and rural cities.

The Minnesota Budgetary Process: An Overview

The Minnesota budgetary process is not well designed to facilitate a legislative focus on the total package, or a comparative evaluation of the merits of different programs. It is a good example, at the state level, of what Wildavsky (1988) calls "classical" budgeting.

In Minnesota, the constitution commands that the governor submit and the Legislature enact a balanced budget for each biennium. If the revenues anticipated when the budget is enacted fail to materialize, the Legislature must return to raise taxes or cut expenditures to restore the balance by the end of the biennium. If the Legislature does not act to bring the budget into balance, the governor must use the "unallotment" process, making across-the-board cuts in agency budgets to reduce expenditures to levels that will restore balance with anticipated revenues. The biennium may not end with a deficit, although it is possible to allocate excess revenues (if the Legislature approves it) to a reserve or "rainy day" fund for use to defer future deficits.

The process relies heavily on consensus about state priorities, so that governors are unlikely to demand wrenching changes in the allocation of resources unless there is substantial support for a shift in direction in the Legislature as well. The system is historical, in that its norms tend to be imbedded in the collective memories of the executive bureaucracy and the senior members of the tax and spending committees of the Legislature.

The process is fragmented. No single budget bill is submitted to the Legislature, and consideration of the budget is divided first between the taxing and spending committees of each house, and within each committee the process of review and deliberation is further dispersed among the subcommittees or divisions of the major committees.

Changes in levels of expenditure for specific agencies or programs tend to be incremental. Past levels of activity tend to be accepted as the base from which the review proceeds, in both the executive and legislative branches, with attention focused on changes in programs or levels of expenditure. The process relies on simplification of the budget issues, with a few serving as symbols or examples for decision makers, and providing voting cues for the vast majority of members from both parties who are too occupied with other legislative duties to devote their full attention to the complexities of the budget. Thus, the process is also social, with most members accepting the judgment of more experienced colleagues, who themselves make up a social elite within the Legislature. Within this elite, even partisan disagreements on budget policy are vitiated by members' common immersion into the arcane mysteries of financing formulas and long association with each other and the agency heads and lobbyists who make up the extended budget ''family.''

The product of compromise, the Minnesota budget is a satisficing document when completed, not one that optimizes policy desires. Few agencies or legislators get all they want; most get something. The budget itself and the review process in the Legislature is basically nonprogrammatic. While committees may use hearings and work sessions to examine programs and policy implementation, the more common practice is to focus on specific problems and on the overall size of the work force, executive salaries, or total expenditure increases over past experience. Budgeting is repetitive and sequential. The same steps are retraced each biennium, and they are taken in an established order: The governor prepares and submits the budget, it is divided and distributed to committees, thence to subcommittees, which act and send their parts back to the full committees, then the entire body, the other house, conference, and back to the respective houses for final action before going to the governor.

As an instrument of state policy, the budget involves a higher degree of continuing interaction between the governor and the Legislature than any other measure. But the perspectives of the two branches are quite different. The governor does attempt to view the budget whole. The Legislature, by contrast, has historically approached the budget through the medium of specialized subcommittees, and has never debated the entire budget.

Preparation of the Governor's Budget

Minnesota uses an executive budget system. The governor is responsible for submitting a balanced budget to the Legislature, which must also enact a balanced budget for the biennium. The budget contains the governor's recommendations for each program or agency. It also contains, in the same document or a separate one, the requests for spending that each department submitted to the governor. This practice was carried over from the era when departments submitted their budget requests directly to the Legislature, without mediation by the governor. When the modern system was adopted, part of the price paid by the executive branch for its ability to prepare and submit a budget was the requirement of transmitting the departmental requests. Most observers of the Minnesota process appear to agree that this is a desirable practice. It provides useful information to legislators without forcing state administrators to engage in the charades resorted to by federal department heads to avoid breaking the president's budget discipline by admitting that they had requested more for specific programs than the amount contained in the executive budget.

The budget process begins in the spring of even-numbered years. The Finance Department issues the governor's preliminary spending guidelines to all state agencies. These guidelines generally contain instructions for determining the base that may be used for calculating any increases or other changes. The guidelines also state the limits placed by the governor on incremental increases in overall departmental totals. The base for the next biennium normally is the level of authorized spending for the current two years. The governor's guidelines may, however, adjust the base from which departments can estimate their expenditures for the next biennium. For example, in 1986, the guidelines did not allow agencies to build inflation into the calculation of their base budgets, as had been done in past years. The guidelines also permit the governor to control the overall level of requests that will be generated. In 1984, Governor Perpich instructed agency heads not to exceed an increase over current year budgets of more than 14 percent for the biennium.

The Finance Department serves as the governor's principal adviser and agent in the preparation of the budget. It performs the budget examination function, reviewing department requests and making recommendations to the governor. This intimate executive staff function complicates the department's parallel role as the monopoly provider of financial information to the Legislature during the budget process. Because of its institutional relationship to the governor, many legislators are suspicious of the department's reliability in providing accurate and "uncooked" information. This suspicion tends to be heightened when the governor and the majority in either house are of different political parties. In spite of this tension, however, the department retains generally high ratings by legislators for the accuracy and usefulness of the information it provides (Backstrom, 1986).

Quarterly Forecasts

The revenue forecasts prepared by the Department of Finance are a principal source of executive-legislative and partisan tension in the budgetary process. The forecasts are important because they provide the basis for determining whether the budget submitted by the governor is in balance. But the revenue forecasts are a moving target. They are made quarterly, to take into account changes in the national and state economies that can have an impact on revenues. Because they must forecast conditions up to 30 months in the future, they are subject to all the vicissitudes and errors of the art of economic forecasting. These normal problems are exacerbated when the most recent forecasts seem to support the position of the governor and his party and undermine the position of the opposition party on the budget.

Responsibility for the revenue forecast lies with the state economist and the staff of the Economic Analysis Division in the Department of Finance. Their official forecast contains revenue estimates, a review of national economic events of significance to the state economy and revenue base, an analysis of economic conditions in Minnesota, and revised expenditure estimates for entitlement programs and borrowing costs. The Legislature has no independent economic analysis capacity, although at least one staff member of the Senate Office of Legal Counsel and Research and the House Research Department monitor the use of the state's economic model to try to verify the accuracy of the numbers.

Because of the volatility of the Minnesota revenue system, any forecast errors are magnified by changes in the economy from conditions assumed in the econometric model used by the state. That differences in the economic forecast from quarter to quarter can be explained on technical grounds does not, however, do much to reduce the political tension. An April forecast that shows an increase in revenues over the January forecast will still be suspect by those who have staked their political fortunes on cutting the budget to meet the earlier mark. Similarly, a new forecast that shows a decline in revenues below that which was originally forecast, will be suspected as a trick by the governor's staff to subdue any effort at tax reduction. In 1986, the department offered three alternative forecasts in an effort to provide a range of assumptions about the state's economy and to stimulate a risk-analysis approach to determining the overall level of spending. Speaker Jennings promptly attacked the innovation, demanding that the department produce a single forecast on which the Legislature could depend. This exchange illustrates the political significance of the forecasts. Legislative leaders as well as the governor base their budget strategies on certain fiscal and economic assumptions. When they are wrong, as in Governor Quie's case, there is almost always some political embarrassment and loss of credibility; there can be loss of power.

Piecemeal Review: The Six-Pack Budget

There is currently no public review of the budget as a whole. Until 1984, the Department of Finance held open hearings on the departmental requests. Some legislators, and certainly legislative staff, attended. Since 1984, Governor Perpich has elected to close the executive process to protect his options from public and legislative view as long as possible. The Legislature still receives the departmental requests in the late fall, when they are transmitted to the Department of Finance. This allows the committee staffs to prepare some analyses for their members.

In assembling the budget, the governor is the only elected official who must systematically engage in weighing programs against each other and against his own policy priorities. But even the governor's discretion is limited, not only by the statutory mandates to fund entitlement programs, but by the fact that most state agency functions are also mandated and continuing in nature. For all practical purposes, the current budget is the base for almost all programs. The governor must focus attention on the increments. Because of the balanced budget requirement, governors must also give attention to the total level of expenditures and the balance among the various parts of the tax system.

The governor's budget is submitted to the Legislature, however, as a collection of documents (including a single volume containing the governor's budget message, a summary narrative, and charts, tables, and graphs) designed to provide a broad overview of the governor's fiscal expectations and priorities for the next biennium. The detailed budget recommendations and supporting information, including agency requests, are submitted in six volumes, which correspond to the jurisdictions of the four divisions of the House Appropriations Committee and the subcommittees of the Senate Finance Committee, and the Education committees of each house. The tax recommendations are referred to the Tax committees of the respective houses. These documents provide a very high level of detail, and provide analyses of expenditures organized by program, activity, and objects of expenditure (personnel, operating expenses, travel, etc.). The budget never again appears before the Legislature as a unified statement of fiscal policy.

There is no governor's budget bill. It is up to the members of each legislative unit to draft the appropriate appropriations or tax bill for its part of the budget. With the exception of the agency requests, which are available in November of the prior year, and the possibility that the governor may have discussed some of his recommendations with the leadership or the chairs of the committees, members of the subcommittees and divisions have not seen the material they now must review. They must hold hearings and work sessions and produce bills that can clear the full committees by late April or early May, roughly 3 months later. This compression of time for legislative review is regarded by many legislators, including the leadership of both houses, as one of the most serious problems the Legislature confronts in exercising adequately its financial power. Basically, the Legislature has 3 months to review and act on a budget that it has taken the executive branch 10 months to prepare. And it must act 27 months in advance of the end of the biennium for which the budget is made, using fiscal forecasts with a half-life of 90 days.

Although executive budgeting appears to be a relatively calm and rational process, this is largely a product of it being conducted out of public view, and the fact that it is a highly centralized process controlled by the governor. The legislative budgeting process, by contrast, is open and often raucous, even chaotic. The hearings proceed simultaneously in both houses, forcing administrators and lobbyists to scurry from one side of the Capitol to the other, offering repetitive testimony. Staff members try to monitor activity in the other house, as time and schedules permit.

The quality of review given its part of the budget can vary widely among the respective subcommittees. Depending on the experience, forcefulness, and respect given the chair, the subcommittee review may be searching and thorough, or it can be superficial and tangential to major policy concerns for the allocation of state resources. One committee can focus on the total level of expenditure, the growth in spending, and the priorities of the departments and programs it reviews, while another spends its time on the pet peeves of its members. In some cases, it appears that Parkinson's Second Law (1957) is fully in force. Parkinson argued that the amount of time a government committee spends on a budget item is inverse to its importance. The House State Departments Division of the Appropriations Committee in 1987, for example, spent 20 minutes deciding whether a new position in the office of the secretary of state should be a clerk stenographer II or III, but only 10 minutes to approve a request from the Department of Revenue for new compliance initiatives that totaled $16 million. The governor and the legislative leadership had decided, without debate or discussion, that the money was needed, based on a departmental estimate that it could produce $48 million in additional revenue, thereby helping to balance the budget. No one from the Department of Revenue who appeared before the division could explain how these figures were determined.

On the other hand, committee review can sometimes check leadership decisions that are ill considered or too generous. In 1988, the leadership agreed, without any public airing of the issue, to allocate $3.5 million to the National Guard to pay every member a $100 bonus and reimbursement of tuition, as an aid to recruitment and to compensate guard members for loss of their tax exclusion in an act of the 1987 Legislature. After hearings, the State Departments Division reduced the appropriation to $2.2 million, and placed reporting requirements on the guard to see if the new benefits actually improved recruitment.

Ultimately, five separate spending bills are produced in each house, which, after approval by the House Appropriations and Senate Finance committees, come before the respective houses for floor debate and action. In addition, the Tax committees produce one or more revenue bills, and there may be a separate capital budget bill to finance state public works.

Reporting of appropriations bills to the floor is usually held up until the April revenue forecasts are made available. If the forecasts are favorable, the governor may recommend new spending initiatives or restoration of cuts he originally made in agency requests. Agencies and interest groups may seek additional funding for pet programs. If the forecasts suggest less revenue than originally suspected, protagonists square off to cut or defend programs, to push some spending into future years (juggle the books), accelerate tax receipts, or (if all else fails) raise taxes or "enhance revenues." After these revisions are made, the committees begin reporting bills to the floor.

In each house, the leadership coordinates the committee process and the floor debate, orchestrating the schedule, guiding the committee chairs, and taking the pulse of the caucus or giving it clues on how to vote in committee and on the floor. There is little attempt to coordinate action between the two bodies until later in the session, when time is running short and action in one house depends on the ability of the other to finish its work, or when the leaders are jockeying for policy position. Ultimately, the leadership of each house, working with the tax and spending committee chairs, put the pieces of the budget together, first for each house, then for the whole Legislature. One senator described the process: "The decisions are made right there in that office. . . . The office of the majority leader. He parcels out figures to committee chairs, and he decides how to cut a deal with the speaker."

The House Budget Resolution

Until 1985, the committees began their deliberations in both houses without any instructions or guidance from their chamber as a whole. When the IR caucus gained control of the House in 1985, the new leadership, under Speaker David Jennings, pushed through an amendment of the House Rules to create a Budget Committee, whose function was to prepare a House resolution setting spending and taxation levels. Once adopted, the new rules gave the speaker power to rule out of order any bill or amendment that busted the budget by exceeding the limits set in the resolution. This gave the divisions of the Appropriations committee guidance on the overall levels of expenditure the House could be expected to approve. The Budget Committee had the further power to adjust downward any committee bills that exceeded the ceilings set in the budget resolution.

The Budget Committee was dominated by the majority caucus. It was chaired by the speaker, and contained the majority leader and the chairs of the Appropriations and Tax committees. The budget resolution it produced was entirely the product of the leadership, designed to carry out its pledge to produce the billion-dollar tax cut.

Although the DFL objected to the new budget process, it maintained the system with minor variations when it returned to control of the House in 1987. The Budget Committee was replaced by a Ways and Means Committee, dominated by the majority party and chaired by the speaker.

The Senate refused to follow suit, however, and continued to rely on the informal mediation of the majority leader to coordinate the overall process and the bottom line of the budget. As a consequence of the asymmetry in the processes of the two houses brought about by the House budget resolution, it has not fulfilled the expectations of its advocates. In practice, the budget resolution governs House budget decisions only in the earlier stages of the legislative process. As the session progresses, negotiations between the speaker and Senate majority leader vitiate the resolution's effect, even in the House. Since there is no formal agreement, by way of a joint budget resolution that binds both houses to an overall total, that issue, as well as differences in the specific appropriations and tax measures, must still be resolved in conference. In 1985, for example, the House had to ignore some elements of its resolution to achieve agreement with the Senate. The resolution played an important role in those negotiations, however, by strengthening the position of the speaker and the House conferees in negotiations with the Senate and the governor.

A second problem with the use of the resolution was that it was initially designed to apply only to programs financed from the general fund. Thus, programs supported by earmarked taxes could escape the constraints of the resolution. This led to some "creative bookkeeping" by legislative supporters of particular programs, transferring them from the general fund to special funds.

The use of special funds and other devices, such as accelerating tax collections or deferring expenditures, have become fairly regular gambits in budgeting, making the balanced budget something of a chimera.

Appropriations and Tax Conferences

After establishing the new Budget Committee and budget resolution process in 1985, Speaker Jennings told reporters "Final tax and spending bills will still be decided in conference. . . . " The speaker was merely recognizing the central fact of Minnesota legislative life described in Chapter 6: the basic and most important decisions of the Legislature are made in conference. This is nowhere more true than in budgeting. Consequently, the work on the budget by each house is seen by all those involved as preliminary to the conference, strategic preparation for the negotiations that will take place largely in private among the leaders of the two houses—the chairs of the six spending and tax conferences, and the governor and his agents.

As Chapter 6 points out, the money conferences are the most important, not only because they deal with the budget, but because the complexity of their subject matter makes them the ideal place to place garbage. The fact that the negotiations are often intense and under the deadline for sine die adjournment of the legislative session means that few members see, much less understand, the conference reports before they must be voted on under rules that forbid amendments and conditions that sharply constrain the time or inclination for debate. Although the governor in Minnesota has the power of item veto, its use to excise the various bits of garbage inserted in conference is unlikely because of his deep involvement in the agreements that produce the final bills.

The leadership, using estimates prepared by the Department of Finance, keeps a running total of all expenditures and all revenues being generated by the six conferences, and directs them to report a set of bills that will in the aggregate produce a budget that meets the constitutional mandate for balance and secure the signature of the governor. But the total budget does not come before the Legislature for final action. Each house acts only on the six pieces. The Minnesota Tax Study Commission labeled the low level of attention devoted to the overall level of spending and taxation the most critical shortcoming of the budget process (Minnesota Tax Study Commission, 1986:46).

The Short Session

The budget process in Minnesota is, at least in theory, a biennial process. As pointed out in Chapter 3, the Legislature has operated since 1973 under the flexible-session amendment, allowing it to sit for any 120 legislative days each biennium. This period is usually divided into a long session of 90 days in odd-numbered years, and a short session of 30 days in the even-numbered years. The governor presents his budget for the biennium to the long session. Theoretically, the short session should be used to fine tune any budget problems, such as lagging revenues; handle a few urgent issues that cannot wait for the next long session; and perhaps consider the state's capital budget, as a special piece of fiscal and public works policy.

In reality, the short session has become an opportunity for new legislative initiatives and political posturing, especially in the House, where all members face election in the fall. In the 10 weeks of meetings ending in April, the budget tends to get reopened if there is any latitude in the revenue forecasts, or if a separate source of off-budget funding can be found for a new program. Thus, in 1988, the Legislature created a homeless housing fund, using interest from certain escrow accounts held by mortgage bankers.

In 1986, the IR House majority sought to avoid the short session altogether. The Legislature had included the capital budget in its 1985 packages, so it was not necessary to meet for that purpose. The governor lent support to the idea, but the combined interests of the Senate, the administration, and the House majority itself eroded support for forgoing the session. When it convened, its main business was revisions to the budget. New revenue forecasts suggested that the state was facing a deficit, and programs would have to be cut to keep the billion-dollar tax cut enacted in 1985.

From a fiscal perspective, and from the perspective of maintenance of the legislative power of the purse, the session was unsuccessful. Agreement could not be reached in the limited time available on budget cuts or tax increases to rebalance the budget. As a result, when the House adjourned without acting on the budget bills, the governor had to implement the unallotment process and cut agency budgets across-the-board. The alternative would have been another special session, but in the absence of agreement on approach to the deficit, the governor did not call one.

The short session has become an uncertain echo of the long session. The legislative machinery and rules are not geared to its effective use, particularly in fiscal policy. The result is a free-form forum that lacks the time for deliberation that is available during the long session.

Special Sessions

A discussion of the budgetary process in Minnesota is incomplete without some attention to special sessions, as they have become, in recent years, a common if not regular part of the process. Special sessions on the budget have been called for two basic reasons. First, they have been necessary when the budget has come out of balance because of unanticipated declines in revenue, due to economic conditions. Given the instability of the Minnesota revenue system, combined with the use of biennial budgets, special sessions can be seen as normal, rather than aberrations. The fact is that the state of the art of economic forecasting has not developed to the point that 30-month prognostication is of great value as a guide to keeping revenues in balance with expenditures.

The best way to ameliorate the need for special sessions is to provide a substantial reserve fund, which the governor can use to supplement current revenues as a source of support for authorized expenditures. The obvious problem with a reserve fund is that it requires a level of taxation higher than that forecast as strictly necessary to finance the government for the next biennium. It is, therefore, a sitting duck for those hunting a way to cut taxes. A growing reserve fund can be an even greater political problem. It invites criticism as an unnecessary cause of higher taxes and offers a "painless" way to increase expenditures by simply reappropriating the money it contains to provide for new or expanded programs.

The second and increasingly dominant reason for calling special sessions to deal with budget issues is that the regular session simply does not provide enough time for the complex negotiations and adjustments necessary for decision to take place. The experience of recent years suggests that, especially when there are strong partisan differences over the budget between the two houses, that conference committees need more time than is usually available to finish their work. As budgets become larger and more complex, and as some of the entitlement programs come under sharper challenge, or as the Legislature demands more attention to overall spending levels and the balance among revenue sources, deliberations on the budget can be expected to consume even more time. In many respects, the special session is the necessary consequence of arbitrary deadlines set for adjournment.

While special sessions are often regarded as evidence of legislative failure, the policies they produce are often quite highly regarded. The Minnesota Miracle, for example, was the product of the longest special session in the history of the Legislature — 151 days. The work that precedes such sessions is usually clearly focused and organized, so as to keep the session to a minimum number of days. This means that the leadership and the committees must do their homework carefully to keep agreements from falling apart once the session convenes. The narrow focus of the special session also helps concentrate legislative attention on the matter at hand, in contrast with the hundreds of other matters that come before a regular session.

The point is not that special sessions are desirable. Rather, it is that special sessions are not necessarily undesirable. They are increasingly necessary devices for providing some flexibility in an otherwise rather rigid legislative system.

The Capital Budget

With the exception of 1982, when bonding authority of only $4.7 million was authorized, and 1980, 1986, and 1988, when no bill passed, there has been a major capital budget bill every year since 1975. The capital budget contains bonding authority for state public works projects, major repairs and rehabilitation of facilities, and acquisition of property by state agencies. It also contains an appropriation of money from the general fund to pay debt service on the bonds that are issued for the authorized projects. The bill is an important instrument of state government, as it provides for the development of public infrastructure. It is of considerable economic importance, totaling $265 million for the 1985–86 biennium, and $470 million in 1987. While its impact on the current budget may be slight — governors and Legislatures have historically agreed to limit debt service to no more than 3 percent of the operating budget of the state — its political significance is enormous. The capital budget provides for the expenditure of money in legislative districts for public works projects. The projects included in the bill, therefore, are of great interest to members of the Legislature, to the agencies that provide the facilities, and to the army of contractors, workers, employees, and clients who build, operate, and use them.

Prior to 1973, the capital budget bill was prepared by the Legislative Building Commission, consisting of five senators and five representatives. With the advice and assistance of the commissioner of administration, the commission reviewed the long-range needs and expansion plans of agencies, conducted site visits of facilities for the Legislature, and prepared the capital budget bill. Typically, it conducted its business in the interim between sessions of the Legislature. Its bills were considered, after adoption of the flexible-sessions amendment, in the short session during even-numbered years.

While this system, by all reports, worked well, it was abandoned in 1975. There were concerns that it was working outside the bicameral system, and that legislators were producing a bill that should be produced by the governor. There was also concern that the role of the commissioner of administration might violate the separation of powers doctrine.

Since 1977, the Department of Finance has prepared the capital budget, which the governor submits to the Legislature by April 15 of odd-numbered years. There is, however, no regular process for presenting it to the Legislature, or for legislative consideration. For some time, there was a tacit agreement that the capital budget would be considered in the short session, enabling the Legislature to continue to use the interim for review of projects and site visits to facilities. This agreement has not always held. In 1985 and 1987 the governor pushed for action on the capital budget during the long session. In 1988 the Legislature refused to pass the bill because leaders were concerned that there was danger that the proposed bond authorizations would exceed the 3 percent guideline and that too many projects were being pushed into "out years" for financing, thereby committing future Legislatures to financing them.

When it reaches the Legislature, the capital budget is dismembered like the rest of the budget, and sent to the various Senate Finance subcommittees and House Appropriations Committee divisions for review. This loss of coherence makes everyone and no one responsible for its passage. The leadership must usually exert its authority to get the bill put back together in time for passage. The chairs of the Appropriations and Finance committees may take on the assignment, or pass it to another senior member. Site visits, which are an important part of legislative oversight of the capital program of the state, are not coordinated. Each subcommittee chair schedules such visits during the interim, or may decide that there is more pressing business before the subcommittee. No single group of legislators or staff is responsible for examining all the various types of capital needs and comparing the relative merits of proposed projects against any long-term program or plan. Typically, members, including the leadership, complain that there is insufficient time in the long session to give adequate consideration to the capital budget.

The upshot of the lack of regular processes for review of the capital budget is that it is put together through the conference process in the final days or hours of the session. Once again, its content is determined by the private negotiations of the leadership and the governor, and the need to obtain a three-fifths vote in both houses for enactment. There is rarely any debate in the Legislature over the priorities reflected, their economic significance, or the total and trends in capital spending.

The Budget Game:
Rules, Strategies, Actors, Roles

The budget is the major partisan battleground in the Minnesota Legislature. Fiscal issues have provided the principal and continuing differences between the DFL and the IR during the last decade. These differences have escalated from disagreement over particular taxes and the balance among different sources of revenue and debate over the relative merits of specific state programs to sharp cleavages over the overall size of government and the role of government in the state's political economy.

The Legislature has not yet adjusted its own institutional processes to enable itself to manage this sharper and broader conflict while still exercising its historic power of the purse. Continuing to use the traditional processes of fiscal review and decision geared to an age of incremental expansion of the service state, the Legislature has been largely unable to come to terms with the politics of decrementalism and the bottom line. The formal processes of a generation ago are basically unchanged. But the game has changed, and it is played by different rules. Increasingly, the Legislature must depend on the informal power of its leaders to engineer enough agreement to allow a session to end. Most of the power to allocate the state's resources has been surrendered to the deux ex machina of formula funding, such that over 80 percent of all spending is preauthorized. And the Legislature has surrendered its power to make midcourse corrections when it cannot agree on them to the governor, using the across-the-board formula of the unallotment process.

We turn now to an analysis of the new budget game, its strategies and unwritten rules.

The Forecasting Game

When the issue to be decided was simply how to finance what the Legislature agreed the state needed to provide in the way of services, the revenue forecast gave legislators necessary information about whether they could pay the bills within existing tax rates, or whether new taxes might be needed or increases scaled back or spread out to avoid a tax increase. Economic growth and bracket creep generally kept tax growth in rough synchronization with expansion of services, so long as there was consensus that the tax burden was about right, and reasonably equitable.

But, due to the collapse of this consensus with recession and an ideological shift in the IR party and among more conservative members of the DFL, the revenue forecast has taken on a different significance. The forecast has become a symbol of tax burden: a surrogate alarm warning about the total size of the public sector by drawing attention to the growth in revenues available to the state. Specific programs and needs take on a secondary importance. The critical issue is not the parts (although there may be considerable debate about some of them), but the whole.

This places a lot of political freight on the revenue forecast, changing it from a technical aid in balancing the books to an index of the state's economic and governmental health. Thus, a forecast of a revenue shortfall sends a political signal that spending cuts are in order. A revenue surplus, on the other hand, provides political justification for arguing that taxes have become excessive.

Because the parties are so sharply divided on the issue of the service state, the forecasts take on an almost talismanic significance, and they are seen increasingly in partisan terms. Forecasts that appear to support the view of the governor and his party are immediately suspect by the opposition as "cooking the books," to support the budgetary position of the administration. When forecasts are consistently rosier than the case turns out to be, as during the Quie years, they become an object of legislative distrust. But absent any participation in the forecasting process or any alternative source of information, the Legislature remains dependent on the administration's forecasts.

The new rules virtually compel the opposition party to question the integrity as well as the accuracy of the revenue forecasts, but ultimately to rely on them. The challenge, however, tends to undermine the process of legislative calculations, which requires agreement among members on the basic numbers on both the revenue and spending sides of the budget.

The Formula Game

Since the Legislature has systematically limited its discretion by creating programs that are funded on a formula basis, the power of the appropriations committees has declined and that of the authorizing committees has grown. While new authorizations must be reviewed by the Appropriations and Finance committees, they are normally accepted and reported out in their initial year with "no appropriation." They may then be inserted, with funds attached, in the conference report. Even if not funded in the year they are passed, they provide mandates for funding in future years. If they involve transfer payments to other governments or to individuals, then the formulas go into effect in the next biennium, and the governor will normally allocate the mandated amount of funding to them.

Formula funding and tax expenditures as the principal approach to budgeting has increased the power of the Tax committees. Tax credits or other forms of tax relief have become a major activity of the committees. Since these measures merely reduce the flow of revenue into the state treasury without increasing the amount that has to be appropriated from the general fund, the spending committees are "out of the loop." Thus, the Tax committees are the focus of a great deal of interest-group activity, seeking benefits in the form of credits and exemptions, as well as special taxing authority for local programs and interests, such as convention centers, casinos, or economic development programs. Once enacted, tax abatements or privileges are hard to control. Their incidence is determined by the number of taxpayers or other entities that meet the qualifications. The back door to the treasury in the form of tax expenditures has become a major way of increasing public support of programs favored by members of the Tax committees without raising the issue of the total size of government. It thus is a convenient strategem for both the proponents and opponents of the service state. For the liberals, it is a way around increases in the level of expenditures. For conservatives, it offers a way of giving with one hand while taking away with the other.

The Omnibus Game

From the perspective of the leadership, the most important gambit in the budget game is the use of omnibus bills to enact the budget. These large bills force a centralization of authority in the leadership. They facilitate discipline and cohesion in the crucial last days of a legislative session, because each bill contains something dear to the heart of almost every member. They also produce legislation that is virtually veto proof, because the governor becomes party to the compromises that produce the bills.

The use of separate bills rather than a single budget act prevents the Legislature as a whole from debating the entire budget, and consequently, from debating the relative priorities represented by each bill. It may be possible for the Appropriations and Finance committees or for the House or Senate to debate the relative priority of health, human services, or corrections programs in the state departments bill, but there is no occasion for debating the relative merits of expenditures on these activities as opposed to education or transportation.

This leaves the setting of overall budget priorities in control of the leadership and the governor. By forcing the resolution of serious disagreements into conference, the leadership also has the opportunity to load the bills with any other measures that they feel are important or desirable, but were unable to make it through the regular legislative process. Few other conferences provide so many opportunities for construction of garbage bills, because few others are as large to begin with, and so comprehensive in coverage that some "germane" connection could be found with a slight suspension of disbelief.

End-of-Session Chicken

The end game of a legislative session tends to be dominated by the budget. To a considerable extent it is a game of chicken. First, House and Senate conferees spend considerable time in the early stages of the conference, after agreeing on the easy parts, bluffing each other to try to gain concessions in favor of the position of their respective houses.

This game may be escalated to involve the tax and spending conferences, as a decision ultimately has to be made whether to decide on the level of expenditures first, forcing the Tax Committee to provide enough money to finance the budget, or to first set the tax policy, and cut the budget to fit the available revenues. In 1985, for example, this was a source of dispute between the houses, with the House insisting on setting tax policy first, and the Senate preferring to follow the traditional practice deciding first on expenditures. The governor may also enter the process, using the threat of veto to force the inclusion of some item he favors or the exclusion of something he opposes from the final packages that are being prepared.

The basic political situation at the end of the session is that each of the three parties — the House conferees, the Senate conferees, and the governor — has the independent power to prevent an agreement and force a special session to complete the work on the budget. Each, however, is under a great deal of social pressure from colleagues, the media, and each other to find a basis for agreement. This pressure and the pressure of time facilitate compromise. No one wants to bear the blame for the collapse of the process at the brink of adjournment.

Follow the Leader

As in so much of the Minnesota legislative process, the most important rule in the politics of budgeting is "follow your leader." Although almost 70 percent of the members of the Senate and 60 percent of the members of the House are on a committee that deals with some aspect of the budget, this most important of legislative functions is closely held by the leadership. It is they who determine the basic posture of their caucuses on the budget, and with the committee chairs work out the basic outlines of the taxing and spending bills that will be reported from committee. Ultimately, it is the leaders, working with each other and often with the governor, who balance the budget, for only they hold all of the information necessary to that task.

Budgetary Dilemmas:
Information, Institutions, and Leadership

The Minnesota Legislature has moved, in recent years, from a preoccupation with budgeting to a near obsession with it. In ten years, it has dealt with the budget not only in every regular session, but in seven special sessions. Budget issues have become the most pervasive and divisive issues to confront the members. Most members support some changes in the budget process (Backstrom, 1986), suggesting that they may sense that the present process is not quite up to the task. The Tax Study Commission saw as the critical issue the lack of overall review of the total budget, but also recognized problems in the movement of the critical choices about the budget from the main stage of the Legislature itself into the shadow of semiprivate deliberations by the leadership.

This analysis suggests other problems and dilemmas that confront the Minnesota budgetary process. The biennial process appears to produce serious problems in achieving balance and in regularizing the process so that members and the public can follow it and increase fiscal accountability. The loss of control by the Legislature over the bulk of state spending to formula-based programs has surely changed the character of the process and the ultimate power of the Legislature over the public purse. In a strong two-party state like Minnesota, bicameralism complicates the budgetary process. And the capital budget has, in recent years, become something of a policy orphan—no one seems to know quite what to do with it.

The Costs and Benefits of Biennial Budgeting

The instability of the Minnesota revenue system places a serious burden on biennial budgeting. It is hard enough with stable revenues. When the procedures used by the Legislature are not flexible enough to make adjustments for unforeseen shifts in the state's economic fortunes, and consequently its revenues, the problems are compounded.

Twenty-nine states now budget on an annual basis. One clear advantage of annual budgeting is that it is not necessary to make such long-range forecasts of revenues, and it is easier for the budget enacted by the Legislature to stay put. While state agencies have to go through the entire budget cycle more frequently, they do not have to work so far in advance of actual operations. On the other hand, there would conceivably be less tendency to pad budgets to allow for unforeseeable contingencies. Annual budgeting would also cure the serious problems of inefficiency and morale that occasion the go-and-stop process that now too often characterizes agency operations that start a biennium with a clear legislative mandate to operate at a particular level, only to be halted in the second year by an across-the-board cut through unallotment or a switch in legislative signals due to a looming deficit.

In some respects, Minnesota has a de facto annual budgeting process. But it is far from a fully developed one. Basically, the second year of the biennium is one in which the Legislature tinkers with the budget, making adjustments in spending or taxes to account for changes in tax or spending rates, or adding a few things as supplemental items, or working on the capital budget.

An annual budget would mean more budgeting by the Legislature as well as the executive. Full hearings would be held each year. Committee members would probably develop more expertise with agency budgets. If anything, the time the Legislature spends on the budget would increase. The short session would probably prove impractical for a full budget review, leading either to a different distribution of legislative days between the two years of the biennium or the expansion of the short session to a full 90 or more days.

Any discussion of extending the number of days the Legislature meets raises the question of the continued viability of the citizen-legislator. We have already seen that the duties of the leadership have made those positions virtually full time. The spending and tax committee chairs are close behind in time devoted to the Legislature. For those most affected by such a change, the transition to full legislative employment has already occurred. The question is whether an additional 30 or 60 days a biennium would materially change the character of the Legislature. There is considerable evidence from other states that even where sessions are considerably longer than in Minnesota (New York, for instance) the idea of a citizen-legislature is not wholly impossible.

One of the uncertainties in state budgeting these days is the amount of federal funds that will be available to finance state programs and local activities receiving transfer funds. Since the federal government budgets annually, there is some advantage to a state in following a budget cycle that increases its knowledge of available federal funds, or lack thereof. Localities also have annual budget cycles and, with their heavy reliance on state transfers, need to know what levels of support will be provided. In this sense, biennial budgeting has some advantages for localities, at least so long as revenue instabilities do not force unallotments or legislative retrenchments of previously authorized transfers.

Those who are concerned with the rising costs of state government see annual budgets as doubling the opportunities for agencies and lobbyists to advocate more spending. An examination of the budgets of states that use annual budgeting, however, reveals no faster rate of growth in government expenditures than occurs in states that budget biennially.

One of the apparent advantages of biennial budgeting is that it encourages longer-term planning by agencies and more time between budget cycles to evaluate agency performance. Increasingly, the lack of long-term planning is seen as a major problem of annual budget cycles, which do tend to focus the attention of administrators on short-range objectives and changes since their last appearance before a legislative committee. It may be, however, that the difference between a

year and two years is relatively insignificant when it comes to long-range thinking by agencies.

Bicameralism and Legislative Budget Policy

The bicameral system complicates the budget process, adding to its overall disorderly appearance, and contributing to the chaos and air of crisis that pervade
the closing of the legislative session. The virtues of bicameralism—dual access
to the legislative process, the second look at proposals, the necessity of compromise, the slowing down of action—apply to the budget process as well as to other
legislation. The problems of bicameralism are also highly visible in the budgetary process, particularly the use and abuse of the conference.

The polar partisanship of the Minnesota House of Representatives is amelio-
rated to some degree by the more consensual politics of the Senate (which is not
free of partisan animus, particularly on the budget). It is fair to say, however, that
so far as the budget is concerned, bicameralism does not provide a second look so
much as a different look. This is because of a legislative schedule that is too tight
for one house to complete its action before the other takes up the budget. As a
matter of necessity, both houses consider budget issues simultaneously. Committees on one side may wait to find out what their counterparts are doing, especially
if there is partisan advantage to be taken in acting last, but there rarely is time for
the houses to act sequentially.

More than on any other matter, the Legislature resorts to the conference to
make the crucial decisions on the budget. The expectation that this will be so
tends to diminish the quality of committee work in both houses and promotes
action by each house that is geared to staking out bargaining positions on taxes
and spending, in preparation for negotiations in the conference.

While informal discussions usually occur between the leaders of the two
houses, there is no formal and regular mechanism for the development of joint
policy on or approaches to the budget prior to the conference stage. Minnesota
has no common budget staff serving both bodies, or as in the case of Wisconsin,
a Joint Committee on the budget. There is no mechanism for regular legislative
participation in the development of the budget, such as the Maryland General
Assembly's Affordability Committee, which makes recommendations to the governor on total spending levels. In general, Minnesota has not used these or other
devices in use in other states that ameliorate the effects of bicameralism on the
coherence of the legislative budget process.

The Whole vs. the Parts

A joint budget resolution is another device to overcome both the effects of bicameralism and the further fragmentation of the budget through the committee
system. Although it has not been fully successful, the establishment of the House

Ways and Means Committee (previously, the Budget Committee) has forced the House money committees to take up their work in the context of overall spending and taxing totals. The absence of a parallel process in the Senate continues to frustrate any attempt to produce a meaningful debate—both early in the process and near its end—in the overall budget, its priorities, and the relative merits of different programs or activities.

The absence of a comprehensive budget bill, whether prepared and submitted by the governor, or prepared by the Legislature, further impedes the ability of the Legislature to focus on the overall fiscal picture. The lack of a legislative budget staff with a mandate to provide both comprehensive analysis of the state's fiscal condition and trends as well as specialized analyses responsive to questions from the committees is also an impediment to effective review of the governor's recommended budget.

The use of separate budget packages, prepared by different conferences, orchestrated only by the leadership of the two houses, institutionalizes not only fragmentation of the budget, but the practice of using the budget bills as the vehicles for the great collections of garbage that influential members can insert, notwithstanding its relevance or legislative status. A process that produced a "clean" and comprehensive legislative budget in time for meaningful debate about levels and priorities of expenditure would be a less attractive cover for unrelated amendments.

There is, of course, much to be said for a process that directs legislative attention to the parts of the budget. It is through the budget process that legislative oversight of administrative operations most regularly occurs. While the scrutiny given programs and agencies is uneven and often idiosyncratic, it does keep agencies alert to any problems or issues that might attract unflattering attention from the Legislature.

The Capital Budget

Finally, the Legislature and the governor clearly need to do something about the capital budget to end its orphan status. The submission of the capital budget in March of odd-numbered years generally means that it arrives too late for action in that year. Yet there are almost always projects that the governor or members of the Legislature feel are too urgent to wait for another full year to authorize. At a minimum, there is no apparent reason why the capital budget could not be submitted at the same time as the operating budget. It could probably even be published during the interim, to allow site visits and committee study before the session begins. And there would seem good reason to create either a joint committee on the capital budget or at least distinct committees in each house to review it and propose an annual or biennial capital budget bill for enactment by the Legislature. If the capital budget were prepared by the governor as an annual annex to the budget, and as the implementation of a long-range capital program for the state, as is done in many city governments, it could be reviewed as the regular incremental implementation of the capital program of the state.

The Need for Budgetary Reform

Budgeting is at the heart of the legislative process. The power of the purse is a central legislative function. Its exercise establishes priorities among state policies that require resources for implementation. It also gives the Legislature its best regular insight into the operations of executive and other agencies of state government, making budgeting central to the oversight function. As state government has become larger and more complex, the need for an effective budgetary process has increased, but the Minnesota Legislature has, for the most part, retained the processes and practices that were more appropriate for a simpler time.

9

Legislators at Work: How They View Their Jobs and Their Legislature

The work of the Legislature, as earlier chapters indicate, is complex, time consuming, and often controversial. Serving the Legislature places demands on members that are sometimes hard for citizens, who are concerned primarily with the legislative results, to appreciate. Turnover in recent years is in part a reflection of the extraordinary pressures of legislative service. Members frequently talk of ''burnout.''

Legislative service also has rewards: a sense of community service and accomplishment, enhancement of personal reputation and recognition, an opportunity to participate in important affairs of state. It sometimes is a stepping stone in a longer political career or to an influential position in private business or practice.

The pluses and minuses of legislative service are important because they influence the kinds of people who are willing to serve in the Legislature, and, thus, the quality of the Legislature itself. The Legislature makes laws for everyone, but for its members it is also the place where they spend much of every working year, and almost all of their time when the Legislature is in session.

If the Minnesota Legislature is to succeed as a competent policymaking body for the state, it must be a place where good people like to work. They must have whatever assistance they need to make sound decisions, and must operate in an organization with procedures that are efficient and acceptable. This means that the organization and procedures of the Minnesota Legislature facilitate the work of its members sufficiently that able people are willing to continue to serve in it.

To assess how its members view the Minnesota Legislature as a workplace and to identify things members would like to change to improve their effectiveness and that of the Legislature as a whole, a mail survey was conducted among persons who had served as members of the Minnesota Legislature from 1980 to 1985. Responses were received from 173 of 287 legislators, an overall return rate of more than 60 percent. Those responding were a well-balanced sample of all members. The full report of the survey, including the questionnaire, has been separately published (Backstrom, 1986), and many of the specific findings have been incorporated into other chapters of this book.

How Members Spend Their Time

Most members work very hard at their legislative jobs, averaging 65 hours per week near the close of the session, and 53 hours even during the midsession committee hearings stage. Members' "regular" occupations added another 12 hours on average to the workweek, except between sessions, when legislative activities constituted only one-fourth of a nearly standard workweek (11 of 45 hours). Some members claim to work on state business 70 hours per week regularly, and this rises to 90 hours at the end of the session. Just over a quarter (28 percent) of the members said they now work full time as legislators.

Back in their districts when the Legislature is not in session, the most typical member reported working about 5 hours a week on legislative business. Half of the members worked 8 hours, one-quarter 12 hours or more, and a few up to 40 hours. The average was almost 11 hours per week. Two members said they did no legislative work in the district. Leaders as a group (this includes committee chairs and vice-chairs) reported working only 2 more hours per week than nonleaders between sessions on legislative matters.

During the session, most time is spent on committee work, which consumed one-third of members' time. Floor sessions took another one-fifth, while one-seventh of their time was spent on constituent matters, and one-eighth in studying bills.

Nine of every 10 members want more time to prepare and study bills. More than half also want more time for committee work, their major specialized responsibility.

In addition, 4 of 5 legislators desired to spend more time on another part of the legislative job—representation, such as can be accomplished by constituency contacts and services. Nearly two-thirds said they do not have enough time for a third major responsibility, oversight of the executive branch through contacts with the governor and state agencies.

Where could more time come from? Giving up the outside occupation that two-thirds of them now pursue might seem obvious, but only 1 in 10 legislators thought the Legislature should officially be made a full-time job. Even the leaders of the Legislature, whom everyone recognizes to have vast time commitments, are no more willing to recommend moving to full-time status.

Reorganization of their scheduled responsibilities is not likely to yield more time for study of bills. Two-thirds of the members would like floor sessions shortened, but this is the place of highest public visibility in the lawmaking process, and where the principal public record of legislative intent is registered. About the same proportion of legislators would like to spend less time with lobbyists and media, but both are entitled to generous access to lawmakers.

Rather than trying to do more study of the language of particular bills individually, the Legislature could set aside time before the specific work of the session gets underway for general orientation sessions on major subject-matter areas. Such study sessions could be led by staff with participation by executive agencies and outside experts. Programs like this—once called "Minnesota Horizons"—have occasionally been mounted. Similarly, wide-ranging studies of certain problems by study commissions could be arranged in the interim.

The other obvious source of assistance to members in understanding bills is capable staff.

Adequacy of Information

Effective legislation requires accurate, deep, and timely information delivered in understandable form to the policymakers, who then must weigh the costs and consequences of action or inaction. Legislators were asked how much help they received in deciding how to vote on matters before them from various possible sources. Table 6 shows the results.

Looking to the Governor and the Leadership

At present legislators rely most heavily on the governor for information on which to make up their minds as to how to vote. More than three-quarters of the members rely on information from the governor, even though that person may not be a member of their own party. This could be a cause for concern in a separated powers system where different branches of government are supposed to take independent looks at policy before it is enacted. But it may only reflect the expectation that the governor should provide clear leadership on significant policy issues and the fact that the position of the chief executive is an important political cue for legislators, regardless of party affiliation.

Nearly one-fourth of the members said they relied a great deal on their caucus leader for information in deciding how to vote, an indication of the strength of legislative parties in Minnesota.

Only 1 in 6 members reported that they relied much on committee staff, nearly the same proportion as counted that heavily on lobbyists and on executive agencies, and on discussions in their party caucuses. One in 12 sought much help from caucus staff. Only about 1 in 8 relied much on their own reading of bills,

Table 6. Percentage of Legislators Relying on Various Sources of Information
in Deciding How to Vote

Source of Information	Little Help	Some Help	Much Help
Governor of the other party	1	22	77
Governor of their own party	8	51	41
Own party's caucus leader	9	69	22
Committee staff	41	42	17
Executive agencies	14	70	16
Lobbyists	12	73	15
Discussion in caucus	18	67	15
Own reading of bills	27	61	12
Own caucus staff	48	44	8
Key individuals in own district	46	47	7
Another legislator	48	48	4
House or Senate Research	60	38	2
Public testimony at hearings	49	50	1

with senior members twice as likely to depend most on their own reading of bills than were junior members. Only 1 in 14 said they have key individuals in their district on whom they relied heavily as sources of information.

One in 25 said they got much help from other legislators to fill them in on bills before them, although nearly half did some of this. Committee hearings were at the bottom of their sources for substantial information—only 1 in 100 relied much on them.

The Legislature's own principal staff agencies—House and Senate Research offices—were much relied on by only a very few members (1 in 50), while 3 of 5 depended on them only a little.

Dissatisfaction With Staff Support

Since logically the greatest possible assistance in getting members on top of their work should come from their own staff, a close look is required at this disturbing finding. Table 7 reports the data.

Members expressed widespread dissatisfaction with the quality of their legislative staff agencies. A substantial majority—nearly 3 in 5—found the House Research Department (a general professional resource) less than adequate, and a bare majority believed the Revisor of Statutes office (bill drafting) was inadequate. The balance was on the side of adequacy of the other staff departments, but more than 2 in 5 of the members found inadequate the Legislative Reference Library and the Office of Senate Research and Counsel. More than one-third were dissatisfied with their own caucus staff (partisan publicity and campaign assistance), their secretarial or legislative assistants, and the Office of the Legislative Auditor (spending and program postaudit). Committee staffs were regarded as the most satisfactory, this being the only kind of staff to be rated as more than adequate by as many as 1 in 10 legislators, but a quarter of the members thought even they were inadequate.

Table 7. How Legislators Rate Their Staff Support

Type of Staff	Percentage of Legislators Rating		
	More than Adequate	Adequate	Less than Adequate
Own committees' staff	11	65	24
Legislative Auditor	5	62	33
Secretary, Legislative Assistant	8	57	35
Own caucus staff	7	54	39
Senate Counsel, Research	1	54	45
Legislative Library	5	48	47
Revisor of Statutes	7	42	51
House Research Department	5	36	59

The inadequacy of staff does not primarily stem from having too few assistants. Three in 5 legislators thought the size of the legislative staff was adequate, but about one-fifth said there should be more, while 1 in 6 thought there were too many staff already. Only a handful of legislative leaders thought the staff was too small; in fact, 1 in 10 Senate leaders and twice that many House leaders thought the staff was too big.

Yet there are a few types of assistants members want more of. A majority of members wanted the legislative staff augmented in two areas. Nearly two-thirds — including even a majority of those who believed in general that the present staff was too large — said they should have greater data processing and other computer capability. More of this capacity might also lessen the dissatisfaction with the secretarial staff, since even those who thought the Legislature has in total enough staff were on balance dissatisfied with this elemental service. Also mentioned by one-third of all members was the need for more technical and scientific assistance.

Only 1 in 6 of the members were ready to authorize a professional staff person for each member in the Capitol and only 1 in 8 wanted a staff member in their home district.

More than half of the members wanted the Legislature to have its own budget analysis staff. Legislative leaders in both houses and both parties also favored this development. This is no doubt reflective of the restiveness at the virtually complete reliance on the governor for fiscal forecasts, which have unreliably forecast Minnesota's recent volatile response to the national economy.

It is clear that the reason legislators did not use staff more was that they thought the staff was not adequate. This survey did not ask why members found their staff agencies unsatisfactory. Much of the dissatisfaction with committee staffs no doubt has to do with the necessary responsiveness of any staff to whichever party is in the majority. That fact also results in failure to develop expertise through experience, since a new majority desires a staff it feels it can trust, resulting in heavy turnover when the majority changes.

Two alternative committee staff arrangements are possible: make them nonpartisan, or make them frankly partisan, but add minority staffers.

Although two-thirds of the members thought the present arrangement was satisfactory, the other third of the members want to make the committee staff nonpartisan. This group includes 2 of 5 of new House leaders, who had just brought in new people loyal to themselves to staff the committees.

It is doubtful that a nonpartisan arrangement would ever be fully realized, since, in the year the survey was done, as mentioned, the former House majority's staff, who had thought of themselves as professionals, had been summarily dismissed when control turned over. Of necessity they had to work for the committee chairs and majority who had the responsibility to govern, but they gained the reputation among the then-minority of being in favor of that majority rather than objective fact finders.

A different solution, therefore, would be to add some minority assistants to the committee staffs, as is done in Congress. These people could share factual information with the majority staffers, but could assist the minority to prepare an opposition response to proposals. In addition, they would constitute a small experienced core of the same committee's staff when their party became the majority. Also, since there would be some staff positions retained for the new minority, committee staff people could plan on making a career in that field rather than considering their jobs as mere stepping stones to a more secure position. The experience level of the staff would thus be elevated.

This alternative does not attract widespread support. Only one-third of the rank-and-file members would prefer some minority staff for committees, but fewer leaders would endorse that request — no Senate leaders agree, and only 1 in 5 House leaders. Obviously, current legislative leaders hesitate to arm their opponents with the capacity to provide more effective opposition.

It is more difficult to speculate on the nature of members' dissatisfaction with the central professional staff. Not a single House member said that he or she relied much on the House Research Department, and only 1 in 14 senators relied on their central professional staff. Since by nature most central staff are highly specialized and therefore come in contact with very few legislators, taking a summary measurement from all legislators is likely an unreliable assessment of their objective quality. Yet, if members are dissatisfied with their staff, the concerns must be addressed.

More telling even than rank-and-file discontent is the similar rating by legis-lative leaders, who are certainly well acquainted with the staff resources avail-able, since they hire and supervise them directly or indirectly.

In summary, no majority of legislators can be identified who would support any alternative staff arrangements to the present unsatisfactory situation. But without a reliable staff of their own, legislators must rely on other institutions—meaning either lobbyists or the current administration—to provide information. Members said they did not rely heavily on lobbyists for information, although they admitted to getting some information that way. Instead, Minnesota legisla-tors turned to the governor, whether he or she be from their own party or the opposition party. One might argue that this is the most economical way to get information, by sharing between the executive and legislative branch; but it jeop-ardizes legislative independence, as evidenced by the Legislature relying solely on revenue projections by the Department of Finance. Members show they chafe under this restriction, since just over half urged that the Legislature have its own budget staff.

It is obvious that present staff inadequacies contribute substantially to mem-bers' negative feelings about the Legislature as a place to work.

Relations with the Executive Branch

In a government of separated powers, the Legislature must work out a relation-ship with the governor in order to get anything done. Most legislators surveyed did not think the governor and the Legislature should be adversaries; two-thirds of the legislators of both parties thought the two should act as a team.

Legislators in Minnesota, on balance, supported the governor's role as the principal policy leader of the state, including his budget-making power and his policy direction of state agencies. On the other hand, they believed that the Leg-islature should be more involved in the budget process and in overseeing state agencies.

A majority of both partisan caucuses believed that a governor should be the principal source of policy leadership in the state, and over two-thirds—almost balanced between partisans—did not think making the budget gives a governor too much power. The same proportion would retain a governor's control over the executive department's policy recommendations to the Legislature, but in this in-stance twice as many Independent-Republicans as Democratic-Farmer-Laborites would like the agencies to have a more direct channel to the Legislature than through the governor. (This survey, taken during the tenure of a Democratic gov-ernor, could not assess whether Independent-Republican legislators would have a different view were a governor of their own persuasion in power.)

At the same time, as mentioned, most members would like to see the Legis-lature's powers in these budget areas increased. Three-quarters preferred to have legislators involved in the budget process before it is presented to the Legislature, and two-thirds wanted the Legislature to come up with its own detailed budget.

A bare majority of legislators said they reject leaving administration of the laws to the governor, but even so, seven of eight said they wanted the Legislature to spend more time in oversight of executive agencies. About the same proportion did not think that the present Minnesota arrangement for legislative supervision of administrative lawmaking through regulation (Legislative Commission for Review of Administrative Rules:) was effective in keeping those rules within legislative intent.

A small majority of members would reduce the exclusive power the governor now has over judicial appointments in Minnesota by subjecting them to Senate confirmation. (In Minnesota judges are formally elected, but virtually all initially accede to the bench through appointment by the governor and are thereafter re-elected without challenge.)

In summary, Minnesota legislators cannot be called Whigs, the classical term for those who would exert legislative dominance over the executive branch. Instead, they were fully comfortable with the governor's policy leadership role, his budget-making role, his control of executive agencies. Lack of relative power, then, is not a major source of dissatisfaction for legislators, who nevertheless seek to augment their power to serve as a check against the executive in budgetary and administrative matters.

Views of the Legislative Leadership

Earlier chapters have dealt at length with leadership in the Minnesota Legislature. The survey indicates the extent to which the system of leadership is supported by members, and how legislators responded to their caucus leaders. There is a high degree of acceptance of an important role for the legislative party in organizing the bodies and structuring the agenda.

Attitudes among Minnesota legislators were generally highly positive toward the caucus system. Nine of 10 thought the caucus leaders were not dictatorial but rather were open to the views of the rank and file. Five of 6 believed caucuses should take positions on issues.

Slightly smaller majorities approved of actions of the leadership that control legislators' careers (primarily through committee assignments). Only one-third thought caucus leaders have too much power in this matter. House members were almost twice as likely to object as senators, not surprising given the more concentrated committee appointment powers of the speaker of the House compared to the majority leader of the Senate.

Three in 5 members agreed that caucus leaders should have power over the agenda.

On the negative side, more than half believed that caucuses make many issues needlessly partisan. Again, the largest portion of objectors were found in the minority — nearly two-thirds of the House Democratic-Farmer-Laborites and nearly 9 of 10 Senate Independent-Republicans held such views.

Somewhat over half of all members thought that the existence of strong caucuses weakens the power of special-interest groups, a condition that observers of legislatures usually rate as a strong plus.

In terms of the usefulness of caucus-provided services to individual members (preparation of newsletters, radio and television tapes for use in their districts), almost 9 of 10 members found the materials they got helped them keep constituents apprised of what's going on in the Legislature.

As to caucus fund-raising, only one-third of the Independent-Republican senators and one-fourth of that party's House members thought it essential to their reelection, and even fewer — only about one-sixth — Democratic-Farmer-Labor members acknowledged this dependence.

In summary, the caucus system is well entrenched in the Minnesota Legislature. There was widespread acknowledgment that leadership is necessary to take charge of the organization of the body by assigning members to committee and controlling the agenda. There was also very substantial acceptance of the desirability of the caucus taking positions on issues. The net result is a generally favorable attitude toward the caucus system as it operates.

The Satisfactions and Dissatisfactions of Legislative Life

To have an effective legislature, members must devote enough years to that career to learn the ropes, become expert in the subject matter, and follow through on adjusting policy to new conditions. In order to make continued service in the Legislature desirable, members must on balance find it satisfying. A substantial part of the survey was devoted to assessing the satisfactions and dissatisfactions that come with legislative service.

Six out of 7 legislators saw their role as a legislator primarily as a trustee of their constituents — that is, one who votes as he or she thinks best for them, rather than automatically registering constituent opinion. Just over 1 in 10 saw their representative role as that of a delegate — one who votes in accord with constituency opinion regardless of his or her own views. One in 20 said they mixed the roles. Virtually all legislators said they originally ran for the Legislature because of a general interest in public affairs. Two-thirds wanted to change some specific public policy. One-third were dissatisfied with the sitting member in their district, and the same number were recruited by a political party (multiple answers were permitted). One-fourth thought running for the Legislature was a logical step to advance their political careers, and one-sixth were recruited by an interest group. The only major differences between partisans are that Independent-Republicans were far more likely to have been recruited by their party, and Democratic-Farmer-Laborites were more likely to be seeking a political career.

All members were asked to name their primary career goals. Results are shown in Table 8.

Table 8. Career Goals of Minnesota Legislators

Goal	Percentage Indicating
Serve in the Legislature as long as possible	25
Perfer to be in private life	23
Aspire to legislative leadership	22
Serve in U.S. Congress	16
Serve in statewide office	9
Other	4
Become a lobbyist	1
Total	100

Fewer than half of the members responding wanted to stay in the Legislature as long as possible. A quarter merely wanted to serve a long time, while another one-fifth aspired to a leadership position. Among the others, nearly half had ambitions for higher office. One in 7 hoped to serve in Congress, and 1 in 10 were looking to statewide offices. Only a handful would like to be lobbyists. One-fifth just wished to return to private life.

These results are indicative of the problem of developing a long-term commitment to the Legislature and professionalism in performance, although obviously the existence of higher office will inevitably result in some urge to leave. Obviously, many members do not find serving in the Legislature satisfying enough to make it a life's career.

Probing specific dissatisfactions revealed the data in Table 9. Two-thirds of the legislators felt the most dissatisfaction stemmed from a perceived lack of respect by the public. Well over one-third resented what they saw to be inaccurate or unfair media coverage of the Legislature.

A number of frustrations centered around inadequacies in the legislative process. Three in 5 were plagued by inadequacy of information needed to make decisions, confirming that problem mentioned earlier. More than half were irritated by time conflicts from too many committee assignments.

Half of the members thought the pay was too low pay. Almost two-thirds of the Independent-Republicans felt this way, but only 2 in 5 of the Democratic-Farmer-Laborites complained about it.

Nearly half of the members rebel at the physical demands of long working

Table 9. Dissatisfactions of Legislative Service

Dissatisfaction	Percentage Reporting		
	Little	Some	Much
Lack of respect by the public	6	29	65
Inadequacy of information to make decisions	5	33	62
Time conflicts from too many committee assignments	7	40	5
Too many compromises of principle	7	40	53
Too low pay	8	39	53
Physical demands late in session	16	37	46
Too short a term	26	29	45
Boredom from endless, repetitive debate	22	36	42
Inaccurate or unfair media coverage	18	44	38
Impossible to resolve conflicting demands	14	50	36
Inefficient procedure	23	43	34
Having to campaign	28	38	34
Can't influence policy	24	48	28
Having to raise money for campaigns	46	33	21
Time commitments too great for family	37	45	18

hours late in the session. Despite conventional wisdom, only 1 in 6 respondents mentioned as a negative aspect the time commitment being too great for their families. One-third or more were frustrated by inefficient procedures or bored by endless, repetitive debate.

Another one-third were greatly dissatisfied by what is necessary to get to the Legislature—campaigning—and one-fifth by having to raise money to campaign. At least they wished campaigning did not have to be done so often; nearly half think the terms are too short. Yet elsewhere more than two-thirds said they were not in any danger of defeat; they classified their districts as safe. Only 1 in 10 (11 percent) considered their reelection chances marginal.

A number of members were dissatisfied with inherent aspects of the Legislature. Half did not like the compromises required in bargaining over principles, and one-third were troubled because it is impossible to please people with conflicting demands.

More than a quarter would be satisfied if they had more opportunity to influence policymaking, a feeling understandably more prevalent among minority members.

As to how to eliminate these perceived disadvantages to making legislative service a career, obviously nothing can be done about the inherent nature of the legislative process—the conflict, bargaining, and the compromises. Members who were frustrated by these aspects simply cannot be accommodated, and perhaps should seek other ways of serving their community; likewise with the need to campaign, which is fundamental to gaining democratic consent for submitting to government. Of course, changes in campaign funding could be enacted.

Given the tradition of complete majority-caucus control of the organization, agenda, procedure, and much of the policy output in Minnesota, perhaps nothing can assuage the feelings of impotence of those out of power. Recent rotation of control in the House of Representatives may, however, give hope that any deprivation need not be permanent.

Other causes of dissatisfaction among members, on the other hand, are well within the powers of the Legislature to rectify, namely the complaints about working conditions—the lack of information discussed at length earlier in this chapter, the time conflicts from too many committee assignments, the physical cost of the end-of-session crunch, and the low pay. Leaders could tighten discipline and insist that bill managers and opponents be prepared and better manage the time available for debate. But the terms of House members could be lengthened only by constitutional amendment.

Able members would be more likely to want to continue to serve in the Legislature if the media would strive to improve the balance of its coverage of that body.

And, most important, as constantly repeated here, far better staff support could help members feel on top of their critical information needs.

Attitudes Toward Legislative Reform

Legislators were asked to react to a long list of proposed reforms in the Legislature. Table 10 shows these, with the changes receiving highest support listed first.

Eight of the possible reforms received at least a majority support from those responding. Seven of 10 members would restrict new material in conference reports. Two-thirds thought individual fund-raisers should be prohibited during sessions. The same proposition would like to transfer reapportionment decisions to a nonlegislative commission.

Three in 5 members would like the Legislature to be smaller, although other probes in the survey indicated that many worry about undesirable consequences of a smaller body, such as greater difficulty servicing constituents in huge rural districts, and having a smaller talent pool for doing the work. Three in 5 also would support mixed legislator-and-citizen study commissions to conduct interim studies. Just over a majority believed holding joint hearings of House and Senate committees is worth trying.

Substantial support was evidenced for limiting per diems to actual expenditures, although this did not constitute a majority of all legislators. Likewise, a near majority favored greater public funding for campaigns, but this support was

almost exclusively from the Democratic-Farmer-Laborites, because only 1 in 20
Independent-Republicans wanted more public campaign financing.

Table 10. Approval of Proposed Reforms of the Legislature

Reform	Percentage of Legislators Approving
Prohibiting new material in conference reports	70
Adoption of a legislative budget	70
Prohibition of individual fund-raisers during session	66
Four-year term for House members	65
A nonlegislative reapportionment commission	64
Cut the size of the Legislature	63
Mixed legislator/citizen commission interim studies	60
Joint committee hearings of the two houses	55
Per diems paid only for actual expenses incurred	48
Greater public funding of legislative campaigns	45
Statutory initiative and referendum	43
Return to 90-day sessions every other year	33
Annual budgets	32
Prohibition of caucus fund-raisers during session	30
Pay per diems for legislative work in district	28
Combined legislative staff under professional direction	27
Complete and exclusive public funding for campaigns	24
Cutting legislative staff	21
Enable Legislature to call itself into special session	20
Unicameral legislature	20
Full-time legislature	11
Year-long sessions	4

Backing for statutory initiative and referendum—fewer than a majority—is
also largely a matter of partisan identification; 4 of 5 Independent-Republicans
approve of it, but only 1 in 20 Democratic-Farmer-Laborites. Senior members are
only half as likely to back initiative and referendum as junior members.

Other reforms were supported by one-third or less of the members: return to
90-day biennial sessions, moving to annual budgets, and prohibition of caucus
fund-raisers during the session.

One-quarter of the members favored getting per diems for legislative work in
the district. The same proportion of support was shown for complete public financing of campaigns.

More than one-quarter wanted to combine Senate and House staff. Only one-
fifth would cut legislative staff. One in 4 would also allow the Legislature to call
itself into special session.

The least popular suggestion for change was to go to year-long sessions; only
1 in 20 would tolerate this.

Many of the reforms urged by more than half of the members could be brought about by changing the rules of the Legislature, or simply by dictates of the leadership. This includes the two items desired by most members—regulation of conference committees and of campaign fund-raisers. The leaders could also restrict per diem pay and arrange joint hearings and interim commissions.

The other most-sought reforms would have to be accomplished by constitutional amendment, which must be proposed by the Legislature and approved by a majority of the voters acting on the question: a four-year term for House members and a nonlegislative reapportionment commission.

Other fundamental reforms often suggested that would also require amending the constitution did not have enough support in the Legislature to have any chance. Only 2 of 5 members approved of initiative and referendum, and an even smaller 1 in 5 favored unicameralism. Neither shortening nor lengthening the legislative session had majority support—one-third would like to go back to 90-day biennial sessions, and 1 in 10 were ready to go to a full-time legislature. Whatever changes that will be wrought will likely have to be within the present schedule.

The Lake Wobegon Standard: Somewhat Better than Average

Finally, an effort was made to gain a picture of legislators' overall impressions of the Minnesota Legislature as an institution. This is really another way of assessing institutional pride and loyalty, and therefore a strong indicator of the morale of legislators. That, in turn, may be the key ingredient in determining whether members will wish to continue to serve in the body.

Students of the legislative process have stated a number of characteristics of a "good" legislature—such as being open, fair, free of conflicts of interest, hard working, expert, and broadly representative (Citizens Conference, 1976).

Respondents were asked to position themselves on a scale between pairs of phrases that marked the extreme positions on various ways of characterizing the Legislature. Table 11 shows how many members graded their institution high on each characteristic.

On only two characteristics did members grade their legislature high—being hard working, and being a generally enjoyable place to work.

Members scored the Legislature in a high-middle range on being broadly representative of the state's interests in meeting the needs of the state, and on being open, fair, and free from conflicts of interest. They think the Legislature does somewhat less well in keeping oriented toward state rather than local interests, being free from control by interest groups, and in being generally well regarded by the public. The area in which the Legislature ranks lowest in the eyes of its members is in the level of public understanding.

Table 11. Characterization of the Legislature

	Number Reporting		
Characteristic of Legislature	Little	Some	Much
Hard working	3	35	62
An enjoyable place to work	1	38	61
Open	11	46	43
Representative of all interests in the state	6	57	37
Adequate in meeting the needs of the state	12	52	36
The procedures are fair	14	55	31
Free of conflict of interest by members	18	62	20
Oriented to statewide problems	20	69	11
Independent of control by interest group	26	63	11
Well regarded	17	73	10
Expert	10	84	6
Well understood	40	59	1

In summary, legislators ranked their workplace, like all the children in Minnesota's mythical Lake Wobegon, as somewhat better than average, but far short of excellent. This pervasive attitude reveals a lack of morale that comes from working in a place that they cannot be enthusiastic about. Although the characteristics mentioned here are not specific items of legislative structure and procedure, they are the outcomes of the recruitment, organization, staffing, procedures, and leadership items that have been revealed throughout this book.

Conclusion

This comprehensive account of how Minnesota legislators view the Legislature as a workplace shows a place of intense workers in a very complex environment. They operate quite smoothly with their leaders and relate well to the governor.

But they think that they do not have satisfactory tools to do the job. They are overwhelmed by the need to make decisions without adequate information, and find the present staff unsatisfactory in meeting that need. The decision-making process operates in ways that often frustrates members and makes them embarrassed and angry. They see the Minnesota Legislature as a reasonably independent, responsive, and responsible body, but do not experience the satisfaction of media and public support for their work.

Most members believe that changes could be made to correct the deficiencies they note in the Legislature. Half of them find the job satisfying enough that they would like to keep at it.

And change in these matters is essential, not only to heighten members' job satisfaction and thus possibly encourage more experienced members to extend their legislative careers. A vast improvement in their information supply and their capacity to analyze proposals before them is required before members will feel competent to do their jobs. In particular, major changes in staffing, or at least in assisting members to use effectively the staffing they have, will be required.

Numerous ambivalences within members, as well as differences of opinion among members, conspire to prevent reform. Legislators want more time for important issues but want to keep the part-time Legislature. They desperately need information, but don't want to rely on their staffs to provide it. Most want a somewhat smaller Legislature, but agree that it would cause some difficulties in representation and operation. They think their leaders are fair and open, but that power is too concentrated in the Legislature. They have many dissatisfactions about service in the Legislature, but think it is generally a good place to be; yet many would like to leave. They are most unhappy about the lack of respect and understanding among the public. And they are nearly unanimous that some practices, such as abuse of the conference process, should be changed.

Reform of the Legislature is largely in their own hands. It will not come easily — many of the changes needed would strengthen the Legislature as an institution at the expense of individual members' short-term advantages and goals. Leaders will somehow have to take a longer view, and install rules and enforce discipline that most members want, even though such action may disadvantage certain powerful members.

Likewise, indicated changes in staffing would broaden and deepen the supply of information, making the Legislature more effective overall; but it would weaken the power of the few who now possess the facts they need. Moving more toward full-time service, while benefiting the Legislature as a whole in its professionalism, does not meet the desires of many present members.

While all of these initiatives will have to come from the Legislature, it is not likely they will happen without strong media and public pressure and support, a commodity the legislators now find in tragically short supply.

10

The Future of the State Legislature

This study began with a discussion of the basic functions of a legislature, expressed in political theory and developed through the centuries-long struggle to establish representative government. In describing the evolution of the Minnesota Legislature over the last generation and its patterns of leadership and behavior, we have reflected, in passing, on implications for those basic functions. It is now time to take stock of the Legislature as an institution, to assess how well the Legislature fulfills its functions, and to identify things that might be done to strengthen it. The objective is to stimulate debate and action so that the Legislature might realize more of its potential as the central instrument of democratic governance as it comes to grips with the information age.

The Minnesota Legislature faces four crises that arise from its history and current practices. These are crises of competence, legitimacy, leadership, and accountability. Their resolution will not determine whether the state has a "good" legislature, but whether it is good enough for the tasks in policy and process that it must undertake during the next generation. In many respects, the Minnesota Legislature ranks high in comparison with the legislatures of other states. But in a state where "all of the children are above average," it seems reasonable to expect more than a high level of mediocrity.

A Competent Legislature

The policy agenda before the Legislature is complex. The studies of decision making and budgeting suggest that current systems for deliberation and choice, fiscal decisions, legitimation, and accountability are not as highly developed as would be desirable.

Developing an Institutional Intelligence Capacity

Institutional competence involves the operation of an intelligence capacity that can identify important state problems, provide analyses that illuminate reasonable options for addressing them, and provide means of evaluating how well policies enacted by the Legislature have been administered and applied. A competent legislature needs structural and political systems that can organize information and analysis to serve political values in ways that are acceptable to the publics affected by policy.

In the current Legislature, the primary formal instruments of institutional intelligence are the committees, the professional staff, and the caucuses. These are supplemented, of course, by the media, executive agencies, interest groups, and the networks of constituent and other political contacts, gossip, and anecdotes of apocryphal power. The legislative world of each house is divided into over 20 compartments roughly corresponding to committee jurisdiction. The Appropriations and Finance committees tend to have the widest scope, but even they and the Tax committees are compelled by the budget cycle to limit their horizons. The need for comity with other committees also restricts the comprehensiveness of their policy interests. As in the Superfund case, some bills move from committee to committee, so that they can be examined closely by those who are most specialized in their substantive, administrative, fiscal, or legal dimensions. Only a small cadre of leaders in each house even tries to have a broad view of either the issues before the Legislaure or the process through which they are decided.

As a general practice, the Legislature is reactive, dashing about to grease squeaky wheels. While waiting for needs to become politically salient before acting can be justified as conducive to the legitimation of policy, failure to develop and use any "advance early warning" system to identify emerging problems and issues and fashion approaches to them produces an air of perpetual crisis and impending catastrophe in the Legislature. The biennial fiscal crisis can be anticipated; it just seems not to be.

On a few occasions in recent years, there has been a modest attempt to provide legislators with the "big picture" of state trends and problems. In 1981, the Commission on Minnesota's Future, in collaboration with the leadership, presented an information program before the start of the regular legislative session that included a digest of major demographic, economic, and fiscal issues, trends, and forecasts. While generally well received by members, such a comprehensive briefing on the condition and prospects of the state has been only sporadically repeated. The governor's State of the State address offers the chief executive's perspective, but is inevitably attuned to the political exigencies of the session. Periodic reports by the state demographer provide helpful information on population trends. The recent establishment of the position of state economist, and the issuance, since 1985, of an annual economic report to the governor, provide the single, most comprehensive survey and analysis of state problems. This report, however, has received little legislative notice and is not the subject of careful legislative examination for its policy implications.

In short, the Legislature provides itself with no continuing, systematic way of keeping its members up-to-date and informed of significant developments that could have a pervasive or long-term effect on the efficacy of policy. The expansion of legislative staff in the 1970s gave the Legislature a number of well-trained and highly motivated staff members. But in light of the magnitude and difficulty of the problems the Legislature confronts, its future-oriented and context-setting analytical capacity remains minimal. Because of the speed with which events can move in an information age, and the extent to which local and state problems are inextricably linked to national and international developments and policies, the lack of such a capacity sends the Legislature like a drunk through an alley. It may get to the other end, but not without a lot of stumbling and spilling of garbage.

Providing the kind of intelligence capacity suggested by this discussion requires more than some new staff assigned to worry about trends. One approach that has proved successful in areas such as environmental policy is the establishment of a permanent legislative commission. In addition to legislative leaders and other key members representing both the majority and minority parties, such a Legislative Commission on Minnesota's Future could include several public members drawn from business, labor, higher education, agriculture, and other sectors of community and economic life. Staffed with permanent legislative employees and supplemented by consultants and scholars from the state's universities and colleges, the commission could be charged with making a biennial report to the Legislature on the conditions and needs of the state. If the report were made well before the beginning of the first session of the biennium, there would be time for the appropriate committees to hold informational hearings, for members and committees to develop legislation, and for the newly elected Legislature to be briefed by the commission on its findings. These reports would undoubtedly attract substantial public and media attention, thereby helping educate both the Legislature and the public through discussion and debate. The work of the commission would, therefore, provide not only a piece of crucially needed intelligence for the Legislature; it would help provide the electorate with a yardstick against which to measure the effectiveness of public policy.

A Commission on Minnesota's Future would help alleviate the absence of a capacity for macroanalysis in the Legislature. There will remain a need to strengthen microanalysis: the ability to understand particular problems and to fashion specific policy responses. The deficiencies in analytical capability are widely recognized by leaders and members at large, as shown in the survey of those who have recently served in the Legislature. In too many cases, public policy is informed largely by partisan positions, taken without substantial analysis or mastery of readily available technical information. Little use was made, for example, of the tax commission studies in enactment of the 1985 tax bill. Almost no analysis was done of the claims and counterclaims concerning Superfund. In her study of state policy for the economic development of the Iron Range, Margaret Dewar (1986) found strong resistance in the Legislature—especially from those whose constituencies were directly affected—to economic analysis that might question the assumptions on which the policy was based. Many of the difficulties experienced in implementation of the legislation were easily avoidable, had analysis been permitted during the development of the legislation, and later, in the evaluation of proposed development projects (Dewar, 1986).

The object of analysis is not to replace partisanship or other forms of political responsiveness, but to inform it, for on important matters, people are likely to differ even if they agree on the facts and understand fully the bases for different professional judgments about them. But if they can know and disagree intelligently, the values that distinguish the views of parties and interest groups are likely to be better served, and so will the broader public. The task of analysis is not to resolve issues (although it can help) but to illuminate them.

It is often asserted that the Legislature does not need a strong independent analytical capacity because it can get its information from the executive agencies, the private sector, or the University of Minnesota. This assertion misapprehends the role and importance of the Legislature in our scheme of governance as well as the nature of the political processes that make it work effectively in the public interest. First of all, the cost of independent legislative analytical capacity is minuscule to the extent that it duplicates work done by others.

The basic reason for independent capacity is to insure its authenticity to the users. In a legislature the coin of the realm is trust. Because a legislature is constitutionally separate from the executive branch, and because it has a constitutional responsibility to oversee administration—to be suspicious of it—a legislature should never fully depend on the executive branch. This institutionalized mistrust is heightened by partisan differences that almost guarantee that the members of the Legislature who affiliate with a different party than the governor will be concerned that they are getting "cooked" information from the administration. Although they may be dead wrong, they will still not trust such information. They are more likely to trust an independent legislative staff that has developed a tradition of candor and competence. They are even more likely to trust staff who are employed to serve their party.

This suggests a need for analytical capability that is professionally competent as well as loyal to the Legislature as an institution and divisions of staff that are loyal to the caucuses. The Minnesota legislative staff structure recognizes these basic needs. Its problem is primarily one of depth and breadth. Caucus staff, for instance, are highly competent in management of the legislative process, understanding of procedures, and political operation of the caucus. The central staff agencies, such as the House Research Department and the Offices of Senate Counsel and Research, the Revisor of Statutes, and the Legislative Auditor, contain a number of talented policy analysts and attorneys. But these staff units lack the personnel to cover the range of policy problems that confront a session of the Legislature or to work with the leadership to prepare the agendas for committees. Most of the standing committees of the Legislature still lack permanent professional staff support.

The Importance of a Competent Minority

One of the most serious problems of the Minnesota Legislature is the incompetence of the minority on committees in performing its central function of effective opposition, both in criticism of the policy proposals of the majority or the administration, and in the development of alternative programs. To discharge seriously that responsibility, the minority on each standing committee needs staff assigned to it. This presumes, of course, that there is also a strong committee staff. An added value of regular staff assigned to the minority as well as the majority is the stability it provides when party control of the house switches. The former minority staff can move readily into majority staff positions, and vice versa. This allows the new majority to function immediately with staff support that is both informed on the issues and cognizant of the institutional history of the committee.

In some cases, the existence of majority and minority staffs on committees can exacerbate conflict. That should not be of concern if the conflict goes to the heart of the problems and issues the committee is trying to resolve. When staffs agree on the material facts and on viable options for dealing with problems, that can make possible consensus or agreement without unnecessary partisan wrangling. The important point is that staff must be sufficient in number and quality to allow for careful professional analysis of problems and policies. This implies more than mere ability to respond to questions raised by members, or to conduct quick computer runs on formula changes. Both the majority and minority on a committee need first-rate professionals who can help them understand problems, frame issues, and analyze alternatives. This kind of staff support does not diminish but enhances the role and power of members. It contributes directly to the quality of deliberation by the Legislature and to the soundness of policy choices, both by improving the substantive content of debate and by sharpening the debate itself so that the prevailing side is challenged publicly to defend its position even though it may have the votes to pass anything it wishes.

Strengthening the Legislative Budget Process

Taxes and appropriations take up more time than any other issues in a legislative session. They are, year in and year out, the most important things the Legislature does. They usually present the most difficult problems to resolve, and they inevitably tend to be among the last things done, usually in the crush of adjournment after hurried and complicated compromises and extraneous additions in conference.

A Joint Budget Committee

If a bicameral system is retained, a joint budget committee should be created. The members of such a joint committee should include the party leaders and ranking minority members of the financial committees of each house. Its principal function would be analysis of the governor's budget and presentation of a resolution to both houses, during the first month of a session, that sets levels of expenditures and taxes for the coming fiscal year. This would force early resolution of issues that now wait for last-minute consultations among the leadership, the governor, and conferees. It also would remove some of the leverage that the leadership has in the final days of the session, when it can use its ability to control the money conferences to exact support for measures some members might not otherwise favor.

An Office of Legislative Fiscal Analysis

Nowhere is the need for increased analytical capacity for the Legislature clearer than in the budget process. It seems conceivable that a bicameral staff, working under the direction of the joint budget committee and modeled on the Congressional Budget Office, could be a major asset to the budget system in Minnesota. Such an office of legislative fiscal analysis could perform several tasks of great utility to the legislative process, and to the entire state fiscal policy system.

A legislative fiscal staff could, as in some other states, participate with the Departments of Revenue and Finance in the development of the quarterly revenue and spending forecasts, and verify them. It could design and test alternative scenarios of particular interest to the majority and minority on the joint budget committee and the financial committees in each house. This independent analytical capacity would provide the leadership and these committees with the capacity to ask and find answers to penetrating questions. The process should not only increase the confidence of members in coping with budget issues, but it should also sharpen the work of the administration in budgeting by forcing it to make harder justifications of its budget proposals. In addition, it would provide a continuing educational mechanism for members of the committees, thereby increasing their individual capacities to work on important financial issues.

A Governor's Budget Bill

Going beyond staffing to the budget process itself, Minnesota's Legislature should borrow from its neighbor, Wisconsin, and provide for a governor's budget bill, which would be automatically introduced by the presiding officers of each house. A requirement for a budget bill should strengthen the role of the governor in the management of the administration. It also would force the governor to commit early in the session to specific spending and taxing targets and to back them with concrete proposals. From the point of view of the Legislature, this would make it possible to focus attention from the outset of the session on the specific budget proposals of the administration. The principal task of the Legislature would become one of evaluating those proposals and modifying them to the extent it deems desirable. This would allow faster development and framing of the fiscal issues before a session and should generally expedite the budget process by setting budget targets for both revenues and expenditures early in the session.

An Annual Budget Cycle

Adoption of an annual, as opposed to biennial, budget cycle would also strengthen the fiscal capacity of the Legislature. Almost as important, it would improve the appearance of competence. A two-year budget cycle requires forecasts of revenues and expenditures that extend the state of the art of fiscal soothsaying beyond its competence. The result is an almost inevitable fiscal and political crisis in the second year of each biennium. In an economy as volatile as that now enjoyed by Minnesota and the nation, assumptions on which budgets must be based are barely good enough for one, let alone two, years in advance. This change would represent more work for both administrators and legislators, but it is done in over 25 other states without the need to turn the legislature into a full-time activity. It probably would require that the second session of a biennium be longer, but the use of a joint budget committee and the establishment of an office of legislative fiscal analysis could help shorten the first session. On balance, there seems no need to increase the total number of legislative days used in a biennium.

A Six-Year Capital Program

Finally, the Legislature should require the adoption of a regular capital programming and budget cycle. If established on a six-year cycle, covering three biennia, the state capital program could be updated in the second year of each biennium and a two-year capital budget adopted. This would provide a better mid-range planning tool for the construction and replacement of state infrastructure, and a better process for resolving the many political issues that impinge on legislative public works decisions. If combined with a joint commission or capital budget subcommittee on the joint budget committee, the Legislature would be equipped to demand of the governor and to review effectively a capital investment program for state facilities.

Tighter control of the public purse is not only good public business in an era of economic uncertainty; a strengthened competence in budgeting can contribute to a better informed deliberative process and to greater confidence in and public acceptance of the fiscal decisions the Legislature makes. The real and apparent competence of the Legislature is instrumental in legitimating policy because it is more likely to be both sound and fair.

Improving the Deliberative Process

A competent legislature has not only the capacity for undertaking and using policy analysis, it has an institutional capacity to take wise action. Wisdom in policy involves the ability to make policy fit the circumstances and culture of the state. Developing such policy requires the Legislature not only to have a strong intelligence capacity, but to perform a sensitive educational and political function at the same time.

Interim Studies and Commissions to Supplement Hearings

Traditionally, the public hearing has been the forum in which the Legislature tests policy proposals for their sensibility and fitness. In practice, the public hearing has become primarily a means of giving public notice that the Legislature is considering a particular policy or idea. It then allows interests to vent their endorsement or displeasure and alerts lobbyists to focus their immediate attention on the members of the committee.

The hearing still serves a useful purpose in educating legislators and the public about issues that are emerging or "off center." The great issues, however, are only slightly affected by the hearing process. For them, it is a ritual, an opportunity for a display of political strength. The issues themselves are decided by the caucus and the leadership. That both the House and Senate tax bills in 1985 were "announced" to the committees by their chairs is a significant example of the declining role of the committees—even powerful ones like the Tax committees.

For complicated issues, the format of the hearing is rarely helpful. Witnesses have a few minutes, often five or less, to state their positions. This leads to simplification of issues, and efforts to be dramatic and quotable. The format does not encourage deliberation so much as posturing. The need of the committee to consider many, perhaps hundreds, of bills further limits discussion during work sessions on legislation. The formality of the amendment process and the deadlines for reporting bills to the floor tend further to limit thoughtful deliberation.

The formal committee hearing probably cannot be dispensed with because of the notice function it provides and the opportunity for some who have not previously been heard to make their views known. For many of the most complicated problems, however, hearings need to be supplemented with other approaches to policy development. Some committees already use seminars and information sessions, where witnesses with special knowledge are invited for longer presentations of give-and-take sessions with the committee.

There is also a history of effective use of interim commissions and committees by the Legislature. Whether permanent bodies, such as the Legislative Commission on Minnesota's Resources, or interim study groups, they have served the Legislature well, both in their ability to analyze and understand the problems assigned them and in their ability to test ideas for their workability and public acceptability. When problems seem to require deeper or more persistent attention than a standing committee can provide, the interim study commission or committee can be an effective device. Two elements are advisable, however: strong staff support, and the addition of public members when there is a need to consider not only the internal workability of policies, but their acceptability and impact on important sectors of the state.

The use of interim study committees and permanent commissions to prepare information and bills for committee action in the regular session does not diminish the authority of the committees. Rather, it adds a dimension to the deliberative process that provides for both deeper and broader consideration of major issues.

Prefiling and Prehearing of Bills

Finally, a small change in legislative procedure could help unjam committee calendars and reduce congestion of the calendars of both houses. A number of legislatures now allow both the prefiling and prehearing of bills. Some set deadlines, well before the beginning of a regular session, for filing of local bills and reporting them from committee. Committees can then hear such bills in meetings during the interim between sessions, and the bills can be brought to the floor for action during the first two weeks of a session, when little else is happening. This clears the calendar for more important, statewide measures and helps the Legislature focus its attention on them.

Interim hearings by committees have been resisted in Minnesota, in part due to a concern that they might be the first steps on the slippery slope to a full-time legislature. Instead, the leadership has occasionally scheduled a midsummer minisession, at which all committees could meet over the course of a few days. The minisession has the advantage of bringing all members together for an updating on issues, but it tends to force business on committees that have little, and not allow committees to follow their own sense of timing on matters they need to consider.

Whatever device is used to allow committees to meet, the more important factor is to allow them to act even though the Legislature is not formally in session.

Current rules requiring public notice of committee meetings and open sessions are a sufficient safeguard against clandestine committee action of which those interested are unaware, especially when balanced against the need for more effective use of legislative time once the Legislature convenes for its regular session.

Making Legitimate Policy

The legitimation crisis of the Minnesota Legislature arises from practices that invite challenges to policy primarily on grounds that it was not fairly made. The three practices that seriously undermine the legitimacy of the Legislature's work and processes are the abuse of the conference process, the emasculation of the minority, and the growing disrespect of many members, and even leaders, for procedure and decorum. Thus far, the Legislature has escaped charges of corruption or of excessive influence from special-interest groups.

Taking out the Garbage

The most serious problem for the legitimacy of public policy produced by the Legislature is the abuse of the conference process by the garbage bill syndrome. As discussed in Chapter 6, there is only one sure cure for the problem: unicameralism.

Enforce the Single-Subject Rule

Court enforcement of the single-subject rule could ameliorate the problem. If irrelevant provisions were regularly struck down by the courts, an effective deterrent to garbage bills would probably develop. The history of Minnesota jurisprudence is not encouraging on this score, but if bicameralism is retained, an effort should be made to persuade the Minnesota Supreme Court to take the constitutional single-subject rule more seriously.

Written Conference Reports

The only other remedy within the bicameral system is tighter rules against nongermane provisions and requirements for printed conference reports, and their enforcement by the leadership. The long-term odds on self-policing do not appear bright, in light of recent history. In spite of the tendency of leaders to wink at their own rules whenever they "need" to add an extraneous provision to a conference report, it would be highly desirable to require that all conference bills be accompanied by a written report identifying the source of each provision. Under such a rule, the members voting on the conference bill would at least have constructive knowledge of what was in the bill and where it originated.

Recess for Conferences

Finally, it would be useful to allow the Legislature, on its own motion, to recess for up to 30 days, but allow the conference committees to continue to work, if the additional time is needed to conclude a session in an orderly manner. While such a provision does not in itself cure the problem of conference abuse, it makes it possible for the Legislature to conduct its concluding business in less disarray than has recently been the case.

Recognition of the Role of the Minority

The Senate minority is respected for the contributions of its individual members. The House minority is the Rodney Dangerfield of Minnesota politics. It "don't get no respect." The result of the diminishment of the minority is a reciprocal disregard by the minority toward much of the work of the Legislature.

In the House, especially, the political status of the minority as outcasts from the process leads to guerrilla tactics and perfunctory challenges to the speaker. These in turn produce rulings by speakers that are, or seem to be, arbitrary, capricious, and prejudicial to the minority. Majority tactics in committee and on the floor that ignore minority members, fail to make any constructive use of their talents, and deprive the minority of voice in staffing, facilities, committee processes, and conferences undermine the legitimacy of the entire legislative process. In addition, they have triggered an unhealthy level of resentment that is eroding the House as an institution. Each change in control seems to ratchet the level of acrimony a notch higher as the new majority seeks retribution for the real and imagined slights of its former tormentor.

The Right to Staff and to Control Minority Appointments

Respect for the minority should entail providing the minority members of each committee with enough staff support to enable them to oppose effectively majority measures and to develop their own programs. It would also involve recognition of the right of the minority leader to name the minority members of committees and at least one member of each conference. The argument that allowing the minority leader to name committee members would disturb geographic and ideological balance does not wash. The leadership of the majority caucus surely has the right to try to balance committees to its satisfaction, so far as placing majority members is concerned, but no right to dictate to the minority how it shall be represented on committees. In a system that respects the minority, some comity between the leaders is likely to develop that will deal adequately with the committee balance problem. On the other hand, it may be integral to the strategy of the minority to try to unbalance a committee by placing on it members who will challenge established ways of doing business. The majority retains always the margin of votes it needs to enact its program. It should not also run its opposition. The approach suggested here is also more likely to produce an alternative minority program that speaks to the substantive issues before the Legislature, rather than concentrating minority energies, as now happens, on planning for the next election and revenge.

These recommendations recognize the critical role that a minority party plays in democracy, and the importance of preparing it for the assumption of power. They also recognize that irresponsible and disruptive behavior by legislators contributes to public disillusionment with the Legislature and diminishing public respect for the policies the Legislature enacts.

The Importance of Decorum

This brings us to the third factor that undermines the legitimacy of the Legislature's work: disrespect for its own rules and decorum. This, by all accounts, is a fairly recent phenomenon, and is confined largely to the House of Representatives. Beginning with the equally divided House in 1979, the combination of a belligerent and defiant DFL leadership and a large crop of green IR freshmen who watched their tenuous control slip away in the Pavlak affair, challenges to the speaker have been followed by demonstrations of arbitrary power. Decorum and courtesy have suffered, and some recent speakers have themselves not insisted on behavior, dress, and language appropriate to a lawmaking body. The attempt of Speaker Robert Vanasek in 1988 to improve the decorum of the House by insisting on coats and ties and other improvements in manners, was met with such strong opposition from members that he had to lower his expectations and relax enforcement to the traditional level of informality. It is not formality of appearance and procedure, however, that is at the heart of the matter, but fairness and civility.

A *Speaker for the House, Not Just the Majority*

Part of the problem, perhaps the key part of it, lies in the office of the speaker, which combines the party leadership with the responsibility to the whole House to preside fairly. While there are many examples, in both Minnesota history and in other states and the U.S. House of Representatives, to suggest that one person can handle both jobs well, the recent history of the speakership in Minnesota puts that premise in question for this state. In contrast, the presidency of the Senate, which does not entail the necessity also to lead the party, seems to have been better able to preserve order and decorum. The British House of Commons, which allows an even livelier level of debate than is often seen in Minnesota, offers another example. There the speaker, once elected (usually from the majority party, though not always), resigns from active participation in the parliamentary party, and assumes the task of impartially presiding over the House of Commons, bound to rule against the majority if the rules command it.

The House of Representatives should consider separation of the speakership from the leadership of the majority party. The majority leader does not need, and should not be able to use, the chair as an instrument of raw power. Such use damages the authority of the House and undermines respect for the chair and for the rules. That respect for fair procedure is at the heart of democratic processes and fundamental to the legitimation of public policy.

Separation of the function of presiding over the House from its political leadership will not make the speaker an unimportant figure, but attract to the office members of both parties who have a reputation for fairness and a talent for presiding. While the speaker would still make appointments, that function would become ministerial rather than discretionary; the speaker would appoint the nominees of the party leaders to committees and conferences. The speaker, like the president of the Senate, would still be elected and removable by the majority. The majority would still prevail on any issue it chose and on which it could muster its members. But the speaker's first loyalty, once elected, would be to the institution and to ensuring that the House obeys its own rules. Such a system has a greater chance of dealing straightforwardly with challenges to nongermane amendments, for example, than one in which the presiding officer is virtually obliged to overrule such challenges because they would undo deals to which he or she was a party. A caucus would still be expected to vote with its leader on procedural issues, but leaders would be less inclined to rely on procedural legerdemain to achieve their objectives. In some respects, this would be a harder system to operate, and a harder one to manipulate. It is one that is more likely to command and insist on respect based on fairness. And if it so operates, it will do much to restore the House as a legitimate maker of policy because it will be harder for any minority party to claim that it was fouled.

Improving Legislative Leadership

Minnesota has enjoyed a remarkable set of legislative leaders during the last 25 years. The overall quality of the membership has been quite high. The Legislature has not been a dumping ground for party hacks who would be embarrassments to the ticket in more visible positions. In earlier times, election to the Legislature was seen in some districts as a reward for those who had served their communities well in other capacities. More recently, a higher number have less prior public or civic experience, but are more likely than those elected a generation ago to come to the Legislature with an action agenda in mind. There has been some erosion in the number of members with long experience in the Legislature, but the Legislature that convened in 1987 was almost as experienced, on the average, as the one that took office in 1963.

Fostering Legislative Careers

In many respects, the challenge for the next generation is to foster legislative careers for effective legislators in both parties. The idea of a career is important. Much of this study illustrates the importance of experience in the Legislature. In the first place it takes time to learn how the Legislature itself works — the rules, procedures, rituals, and customs of the place. Effective legislators not only know what these are, they have become thoroughly assimilated into the culture of the Legislature. The have learned that effectiveness in the Legislature is more than knowledge of issues and programs, although it can take several years to become familiar with the nuances of policy. They understand that "touch" is also important. One must be aware of how particular personalities intersect with policies, and what one must do to move a member, a committee, an agency, or the governor in a certain direction. An experienced member also develops a sense of public opinion's ebb and flow on issues, essential to the timing of action so that the force of public sentiment can be used to propel a matter to the top of an agenda or to slow down action. We would not expect a new employee, albeit a very bright one, instantly to know how to run a major corporation, and we should not expect inexperienced legislators to grasp all of the essentials of state policy and act effectively in two years, or even four.

Building legislative experience is hard. It may conflict with other important values in a democratic system. The need for the system to be representative demands frequent elections and periodic redistricting of seats to ensure that political power in the state is distributed in proportion to population. While short terms of office and reapportionment are fundamental to the legitimacy of democratic government, both place strains on the ability of members to pursue legislative careers. We also harbor a deep cultural bias against official sinecures, tending to think of those long in office as somehow flawed people who have been unable or unwilling to pursue a normal career. They frequently are derided as "feeding at the public trough," or as people who "couldn't get an honest job." We have not valued the career politician even when we have reluctantly recognized that our most effective leaders have been people whose central experience has been in politics, even though they may bring to political office knowledge gained in other professions or occupations. The most effective speakers and other leaders in the legislature have, with few exceptions, been people whose lives have been devoted primarily to public service.

Four-Year Terms for All Legislators

Development of career legislators is less a problem in the Senate than in the House. Turnover is lower and careers are longer. Moreover, a substantial number of senators already have several years of legislative experience in the House when they are initially elected to the Senate. In 1987, for example, 25 senators (38 percent) had served previously in the House of Representatives. One factor that appears to contribute to high House turnover and shorter tenure is the two-year election cycle. Although actual turnover in the off-year election is low, the frequency of elections reduces the willingness of members to continue in office, as evidenced by the large percentage who serve less than three terms, leaving just as they begin to be able to play effective roles in the House.

Legislative careers would be encouraged if all members were elected for four-year terms. Only two other states, Maryland and Mississippi, now elect both houses of their legislatures and the governor once every four years. Such a suggestion goes against the tradition of distinguishing between the houses by having the larger house be elected more frequently. But it is hard to find the value served by the tradition. Only once in the last 24 years has the midterm election changed control of the Minnesota House. In most off-year elections, turnover is lower than in gubernatorial years.

If the aim of midterm elections is to take a referendum on the extent to which the Legislature is aligned with the wishes of the people, a mandate for change is likely to be at least partially frustrated, since the Senate's membership will be unaffected by the election and the governor remains in office. The result, as in 1985–86, is more interhouse conflict in the Legislature and increased likelihood of stalemate between the houses of the Legislature and between the legislative and executive branches of government. Turnout in off-year elections is usually lower, so the election measures less than it might. The two-year cycle also heightens party conflict in the House by making every session a time for each caucus to position itself for the next election. Finding a sound basis for policy becomes secondary to development of campaign themes.

Finally, the two-year election cycle gives new members no time to learn the ropes and begin to achieve something of value to their constituents before they must justify their performance. Ironically, a system designed to make the Legislature more accountable to the people tends to make it less responsible and gives members of the House less for which to be held accountable.

Four-year terms for members of the House as well as for Senators would simplify the election system for state government and costs would be reduced. By making legislative terms coincide with gubernatorial terms, the chances of the same party controlling both branches of government would be enhanced. While some might prefer a divided government, and it would not be impossible to have a different party controlling each branch or even each house, there are advantages to having the majority party clearly responsible for the whole operation of government for a four-year period. There is then no escaping of responsibility for performance by blaming failures on the other parts of the government.

One disadvantage of four-year terms for members of the Legislature is that once every 20 years, a new legislative reapportionment measure would not take effect until the 4th year after the census, instead of the second year. So long as reapportionment is regular, however, this delay in adjusting the distribution of seats is insignificant, when measured against the problem existing before the one-person, one-vote decision, when decades passed without any reapportionment at all. The aim of the decision was to achieve regular adjustments in apportionment, and that would still be achieved every 8 and 12 years, respectively. In the future, a move to a census every 5th year could correct the "lag" problem. It would also be possible to make adjustments, if policy considerations recommend it, by updating the census by survey techniques. It is technically feasible to adjust district lines every 4 years, although that does not seem necessary.

Reapportionment itself is a value that tends to conflict with the value of extensive legislative experience to the degree that it changes the districts of experienced members to an extent of making it more difficult for them to be reelected. Most committee chairs and other leaders, for instance, are from districts that are not competitive, in that margins of victory for the incumbents exceed 55 percent and voters in those districts rarely switch parties from election to election. Thus, members are able to serve a long time if they wish to do so. One argument frequently made is that more districts should be drawn that are competitive so that each party would have to field its strongest candidates and so that the most important statewide or local issues would have to be discussed. If most districts were competitive, the argument goes, the election would more accurately reflect statewide sentiment. While most Minnesota legislative districts are not competitive, the Legislature tends, on the whole, to reflect fairly closely the statewide distribution of the vote. Given the distribution of partisan voters in the state, it is in fact almost impossible to produce a set of compact, contiguous districts that would also be competitive, unless the state were to adopt a scheme of large, multimember districts.

On balance, then, four-year terms for members of the House of Representatives would seem desirable for Minnesota. The advantages of the change outweigh the disadvantages. It should encourage longer tenure by more members of the House, producing a more experienced body of legislators, more capable of dealing with the Senate and with the significant policy problems and issues the state is likely to confront.

Is the Citizen-Legislator Obsolete?

A four-year term would probably encourage more members to serve longer. Clearly it would reduce the number who now leave after only one two-year term. But it does not fully address the problem of transforming members into leaders.

Becoming a legislative leader involves having not only the talent and interest, but the opportunity, to gain increasing levels of experience. This usually comes from serving as vice-chair, then chair of committees, through service on confer-

ences, assignment of leadership roles in the caucus, and opportunities to participate in national and international meetings of legislators. One of the problems
identified in this study is that as members take on leadership responsibilities,
more of their time is required, and there are a disquieting number of examples of
able and promising members who find that they cannot maintain simultaneously
private and public leadership careers. Most opt for the private career because it
pays better and offers more time for family. Full commitment to a private career
is basically incompatible with a position of leadership in the Legislature.

If the Legislature were crawling with talented members who were able and
willing to take on major leadership responsibilities, this situation would be of
little concern. However, there are relatively few individuals with the vision,
drive, and policy skills that a Legislature needs. It is time to rethink some con-
cepts of legislative service, when following them deprives the public of some of
its ablest officials.

Salary Recognition for Leadership

The concept of the citizen-legislator is even older than the idea of the citizen-
soldier. We have, since the birth of the Republic, treasured the idea that public
service should be a job that good citizens undertake as part-time community service, or as a short period of full-time work. Substantial people, however, are supposed to have a "real" occupation or profession apart from their public life. Accordingly, public official salaries have been set low, to avoid attracting people
who "are in it for the money." The idea has been abandoned now for members
of Congress and for some other public elected officials at state and local levels,
but salaries are for the most part substantially lower than for private positions of
comparable responsibility—a condition that extends to federal service as well.

State legislators remain one of the bastions of part-time public service. And
the evidence of this study suggests that for most members, part time is enough.
But there is also strong evidence that those who take on leadership responsibilities must devote much more time to legislative duties than the average member.
One way of coming to terms with this dilemma, without abandoning the idea of
a citizen-legislature, is simply to recognize the difference in the work load of
leaders. The party leaders are, for all practical purposes, full-time state officials.
Their work year may not be as regular as that of a business executive, but it is
nonetheless full, if not overflowing. If we expect the most talented members of
the Legislature to aspire to these positions and then to remain in them so long as
they enjoy the support of their colleagues, we ought to recognize them for what
they are. Leaders should receive reasonable levels of compensation as full-time
public servants.

A second tier of leaders, chairs of major committees, presiding officers, and
assistant floor leaders also have additional responsibilities deserving of compen-

sation. Although most of them are not employed full time at legislative work, many of them devote well over half of a normal work year to public service. They may be able, unlike the party leaders, to maintain a second job, but the point is that their private occupations are second jobs, not first ones.

The bulk of the members still regard legislative service as a second job, occupying them fully only during the regular and special sessions. This gradation of work load suggests that it would make sense to recognize the differences in effort expended by leaders and compensate them accordingly. This could be done by establishing a legislative salary commission, which would undertake a periodic survey of leadership positions and determine appropriate salaries for each position.

There will be several objections to this proposal. One is that it discriminates among members of the Legislature, and that the present system allows for the differences by providing per diem allowances for the members who spend more time on legislative business. The per diem allowance, of course, does not discriminate as to levels of responsibility. And it clearly does not provide a very good replacement for compensation lost by members who have reached points in their careers where they are sought for comparable responsibilities in other occupations.

Another objection is that if leadership positions are compensated as such they will attract hacks who need the money. While there may be some danger that the positions will interest underqualified aspirants, it seems a slight one. Even members who sought election to the Legislature because they needed the income (there appear to be only a few) seem to understand that the risks of incompetent leadership are too great to hand it over to mere power seekers, much less money seekers.

The aim of such an approach is at least to make it possible for some of the ablest members to think seriously about having a legislative career. Of the leaders studied here, none since the mid-seventies have been able to maintain a private career and fulfill their leadership responsibilities. Even leaders such as Holmquist, Dirlam, Rosenmeier, and Duxbury, who began their careers in another era, were, by the time they reached leadership positions, devoting substantial amounts of their time to the Legislature. Beginning with Sabo, every speaker has served virtually full time, if not a considerable amount of overtime. In the Senate, Coleman and Moe were fully occupied leading that chamber, although they listed other occupations.

The time may come when the entire Legislature should operate on a full-time basis. That time seems well into the future. For the time being there is virtually no support in the legislature itself for year-round operation. There is, however, a growing recognition that something is wrong when some of the most talented members withdraw even though they have shown real zest for leadership and face no serious electoral competition. While the financial rewards of legislative leadership cannot be expected to match those available in industry or the professions, they should at least make it possible for leaders to enjoy a respectable income.

Making the Legislature More Accountable

The Minnesota Legislature is reasonably well apportioned; party strength in the state is roughly reflected in both chambers, although probably slightly distorted to favor the DFL in the Senate. The legislative process is remarkably open to ideas and interests, and the members work hard at being responsive to their constituents and to organized interests seeking legislative help. There is no hint of scandal or of kowtowing to a political machine or to a major interest group. Minnesota's small racial minorities are not proportionately represented, but the Legislature has been solicitous of interests of concern to racial groups. Women are also not present in proportion to their numbers in the population, but in recent years they have begun to play important roles in the leadership of the Legislature. Although it is still male-dominated, the leadership has been sensitive to feminist issues. Minnesota, for instance, was the first state to enact comparable-worth legislation that requires the state and local governments to pay women employees on a basis equitable with men.

While the Legislature is not perfect in performing its function of representation, there do not appear to be any glaring problems that undermine its credibility as there were before the reapportionment revolution. The most serious problems of the Legislature revolve around accountability, the function that is the concomitant of representation.

The crises in competence, legitimation, and leadership can all be surmounted without fundamental structural change, with the possible exception of the problems with conference committees. It will be difficult to address issues of accountability, however, without considering fundamental changes in the structure of the Legislature.

The accountability crisis involves public expectations of its Legislature. We have assumed that Minnesotans expect their Legislature to meet rather than trail the challenges to state government that will be presented during the next generation. As a state with a tradition of public participation and involvement, a history of public innovation, and a communitarian political culture, Minnesota's citizens can be expected to judge the work of their Legislature against high standards of performance for both its processes and its policies.

The preconditions for an accountable institution of governance are that it must be possible to fix responsibility for the actions it takes; it must be possible to register public sentiment clearly and simply; and it must, therefore, be visible; and its actions and operations must be widely understandable and understood.

In the Minnesota Legislature, the dependence on the conference to make the critical decisions on important matters has institutionalized the blurring and evasion, rather than the fixing, of responsibility. Neither house must take the blame or credit for what the Legislature does. They both are responsible; hence, neither of them are responsible. Even when the same party controls both houses, representatives may evade responsibility by shifting it to the Senate, and senators may point to how they were frustrated by the House. The system encourages actions that neither house would take if it had to live politically with the consequences. The most disturbing aspect of these "but for" excuses is that they often are true. But for the House and its refusal to give up Representative Stanius's exclusive agreements amendment, the Legislature would have passed the Senate bill providing for prepaid health plans, and have saved the state $5 million. But for the Senate's unwillingness to accept the amendment, the bill failed. Both are responsible, but neither can be held to account.

When a conference report is stuffed with garbage, some of it blatant special-interest legislation, the whole Legislature is responsible, in a sense, for both houses have probably overwhelmingly approved it. Yet, can members really and fairly be held to account for a garbage bill they had to accept, without possibility of amendment, in order to get all of the good content of the conference bill? Most legislators would argue that they should not be held responsible unless they were actually members of the conference. While there are logical flaws in this argument, it is not implausible.

Minnesota's tradition of strong caucus control of each house does provide a base for holding the political parties, through individual candidates in legislative elections, accountable for the actions of the Legislature. That works reasonably well when both houses are controlled by the same party. It is much harder for voters to sort out responsibility when, as in the 1985–86 session and earlier times, different caucuses control each house. On the whole, however, the strong role of the parties is an advantage to the electorate because, in Minnesota, the party affiliation of members is significant, and it does make a difference in what the Legislature does.

The inescapable fact is that bicameralism frustrates legislative accountability. Theoretically, that frustration is supposedly offset by the advantages two houses provide in deliberation. But those advantages are largely ephemeral. While in Minnesota the houses are different in their approach to policy, the system does not promote careful consideration of bills. To the contrary, the system is often counterproductive of deliberation due to the need to rush legislation through one house so it can have enough time to be considered in the other. Moreover the rise of conference committees as the real powers in handling the major issues has stripped both houses of much meaning in their deliberative functions, and of their power to choose among policy options. If conferences were restricted to their historic functions of reconciling differences between the houses rather than investing them with the power to act de novo on some matters, then the houses could reassert their decision-making authority.

Time for a Unicameral Legislature

Given the history and imbedded practices detailed in this study, tinkering with the rules seems unlikely to suffice. More basic change is needed not only to correct the problems that have been documented, but to give the Legislature a new start and to raise the level of public-and self-expectations of it. Minnesota should amend its constitution to provide for a unicameral legislature.

A unicameral legislature can be more competent at less cost. In a one-house system, it would be possible to make the staffing improvements advocated in this study at far less cost than in a bicameral system. Many staff could be consolidated. It would be possible to provide adequate staffing for the minority. Legislators could be paid better with less embarrassment to them and less strain on the budget if only one house existed. The larger legislative role of each member should justify better compensation.

A unicameral legislature should be more accountable. Switching to a single house would drastically simplify the legislative process, both for members of the Legislature and for the general public. Duplicate bills, hearings, and debate would not be needed. The time now spent presenting the same testimony twice could be used more fruitfully in debate and deliberation.

The processes of amendment and voting should be more straightforward. The opportunity would be eliminated for amendments designed principally as negotiating ploys or as efforts to appease some interest group with the confidence that the other house would kill them. Members would have to accept full responsibility for their actions. They could not write slipshod language into a bill on the assumption that the other house or a conference would clean it up. The full contents of a bill would be subject to debate and amendment, in contrast with the current situation where conference reports are not subject to amendment, forcing members to vote for measures that have not been subjected to the scrutiny of full deliberation by committees and one or both houses.

The argument that the second house is needed to check the excesses and mistakes of the first will not stand careful examination. More abuses occur because of the second house than are prevented by it. It is true that the second house sometimes catches errors in bills it receives from the first, but the second house produces the necessity of conferences, which habitually report provisions that have had no scrutiny in either house. Technical errors could easily be corrected in a single house by the simple device of requiring that all bills be reviewed by the revisor of statutes or a committee on enrollment and engrossment before being placed on the calendar for final passage. This review could correct spelling, punctuation, and grammar, but not change the meaning of the bill. Inconsistencies in language and conflicts with other laws could be brought to the attention of the Legislature and it could then decide whether to reopen the bill to amendment or even return it to committee for additional hearings or other work. Such a technical review would be far more likely to catch genuine errors of legal significance than a second house's legislative committee.

Errors in judgment may also be tempered by requiring that bills be laid over for a reasonable period of time between the second reading, when they are open to amendment, and the final reading, when they are finally passed. The Nebraska Legislature, for example, subjects a bill to four readings, rather than the traditional three in most state legislatures. And it is possible for a majority to return the bill to second reader (amendment stage) or to committee, even if it is on the calendar for final action.

Canadian provincial legislatures, which are all unicameral bodies, subject a bill, after its first reading, to a general debate by the entire body before it is referred to committee for detailed work. This debate on the "principle" of the bill is designed to take the sense of the house on whether it is likely to favor such legislation at all and to identify problems and issues that the house would like the committee to address during its hearings and work sessions on the bill. This step allows the leadership and the committees to gauge the temper of the house and identify political and substantive problems the committee will have to address.

The point is that a unicameral legislature makes it possible for the house to take enough time in the first place in its deliberations that it is not necessary to maintain a second house as an error detector. The secret of good legislation is to do it right the first time, rather than poorly twice. A bicameral legislature chews twice, but often does not take time to digest.

A legislature whose members are more visible to the public, as the sole representatives from their districts, and as the single set of lawmakers covered by the media when in session, would be virtually forced to act with a higher degree of public responsibility. None of the members would have the shield of anonymity or the luxury of diffusing responsibility for their acts, the acts of their party, or for those of the Legislature as a whole. They alone would have to accept the political consequences of their decisions. Electoral attention would not be divided between a senator and a representative.

Local and statewide media would find the Legislature easier to cover and explain to readers and viewers. When a bill passed, it would be passed. It would not be necessary to try to cover activities in two places at the same time. There would be no conference committees, and consequently, no need for private meetings to decide on the final form of a conference report. It would not be necessary to fashion compromises that have more to do with face saving and power than with policy.

A single-house legislature does not operate without checks. The governor retains the power to veto legislation. It seems likely that in a unicameral system, governors would become more attentive to the legislative process than has been the norm in Minnesota. This would have the salutary effect of sharpening the governor's legislative program and developing closer working relationships between the executive and legislative branches of government. Minnesotans should expect their governors to produce more detailed programs for legislative review and to exercise a greater leadership role than has been common. Only a few governors have been effective in developing a legislative agenda. These include the greatest governors in the state's history: Floyd B. Olson, Harold Stassen, Luther Youngdahl, Orville Freeman, and Wendell Anderson. They earned the respect of the Legislature by their careful attention to policy needs and their interest in policy details.

The notion that another house is needed to maintain the system of checks and balances in state government has a very weak foundation. The concept of checks and balances is designed to prevent one of the three branches of government from abusing its power. In the modern era, the most serious problems of governmental overreaching tend to come not from the legislative branch, but from the executive. The trend in almost all states has been for the legislature to cede power, or lose it by attrition, to the executive. Part of the original attraction of bicameralism was that in an era where legislative power was feared — after all it was Parliament, not the king, which imposed the intolerable acts on the colonies — two houses would operate to frustrate each other. In the last century, especially, executive power and the quasi-legislative power of administrative agencies have become a far greater concern than legislative abuse or stupidity, which after all can be vetoed by the governor.

One advantage of a single house is that it could improve the balance between the legislative and the executive branches, marginally strengthening the Legislature by increasing its political prestige, visibility, competence, and capacity for administrative oversight. The latter is concededly performed poorly in the bicameral system. In many respects it is not taken very seriously at all. In the best of circumstances, oversight is divided between the houses, and a committee in one house may take a harsh view of an agency's operation, while its counterpart in the other house champions the same agency. Again, the division of responsibility tends to mean that no one is responsible, and a vital function of the legislative branch tends not to be performed. Reports by the legislative auditor are lightly reviewed, if at all, by the committees of each house. The Legislature tends to oversee the administration on the principle of exception: If it hears nothing bad, it assumes things are going all right. Some review occurs in the appropriations process, but it tends to be triggered by complaints rather than systematic analysis of agency operations or evaluations of policy implementation.

There is no guarantee that a unicameral legislature would do a better job than a bicameral system in conducting administrative oversight. There is, however, no reason to suspect it would do any worse. There is at least the advantage in unicameralism that public attention and scrutiny are more focused and there is no way for members to argue that they thought someone else was doing the job.

One of the frequent arguments against unicameralism is that it would strengthen the power of lobbyists, since they would have to influence only a single house, whereas they now must convince two. That is, of course, only if they wish to get a new piece of legislation enacted. Most of the time, the aim of lobbyists is not to get legislation enacted, but to prevent its enactment. The bicameral system is better designed for that purpose because the opponent gets two chances at stopping it rather than one. Bicameralism, especially as practiced in Minnesota, is also a lobbyist's friend because it is possible to avoid having to convince either house if a few members of the conference committee can be persuaded to slip a provision into a conference report, or insist on its deletion if it passed only one house. In some cases, it may be necessary to convince only a single member who will decline to sign the report if the provision is not inserted or deleted.

There is only one inherent reason to believe that the power of lobbyists would be less in a unicameral legislature than in a bicameral system. Unicameralism promotes a more open process in which it is easier for members, the press, and the public to see and understand what is going on. Ultimately the power of lobbyists should depend on the plausibility of what they have to offer and the political strength of their cause among the state's groups and constituencies. A unicameral legislature, which is capable of conducting a more open process of deliberation and decision, of taking the time needed to expose issues to careful scrutiny, and of supporting and concentrating staff resources on the matters before it, should do at least as good a job, if not a better one, as a bicameral system that lacks the time, resources, and processes needed for proper deliberation.

While there are many arguments for unicameralism on its comparative merits with bicameralism, there is one overarching argument that recommends it. That is the need to establish a new vision of the Legislature of the future. It may well be possible to deal with all of the issues of legislative reform that have been discussed above through changes in rules and other incremental steps. The chances are that these changes, if made at all, will come slowly over many years. The changes will be imperceptible to most of the public. It is equally likely that reforms will be offset by countervailing trends, such as continued use of conferences to produce garbage bills. Many legislators, frustrated by years of trying to reform or redirect administrative institutions, advocate major institutional changes in established organizations, such as the school system or the regulatory processes, to create new standards of performance. It is time to apply that approach at home.

A decision by the voters of Minnesota that they want a unicameral Legislature would be a dramatic break from the past. It would establish a new basis for legislative behavior and produce a higher level of public expectation for the Legislature. It would be easier for the leadership of the Legislature to set high standards of debate and decorum, to provide a graduated system of compensation that rewards leadership ability and career commitment to the Legislature, and makes possible the development of an outstanding professional staff serving the Legislature as an institution and both of the political parties. It should create an environment conductive to creative and satisfying work, allowing members and their constituents to take greater pride in their Legislature and its role in government. And it would also be a signal that the public expects the Legislature to take seriously its deliberative and oversight functions and that the minority party is expected to perform its functions of opposition and development of alternative programs.

Reduce the Size of the Legislature

A change to unicameralism is also a time to make other useful changes in the Legislature. There have been, from time to time, calls for changes in the size of the Legislature. Virginia Gray's (1985) study of the 99 U.S. state legislative bodies suggests that size, in itself, makes little difference in how a legislature functions with respect to work load productivity or in the costs of government. Size does affect access to the legislature, and it may affect political behavior and constituent relationships. Basically, there may be reasons to change the size of the Legislature, but the often-cited ones of efficiency and cost are not ones for which there is much, if any supporting evidence.

Adoption of unicameralism would, of course, require an examination of the size issue. Grau and Olsen (1986) studied three alternative sizes for a unicameral legislature in Minnesota: 67, 135, and 201 members. A 67-member legislature corresponds to the size of the current Senate. One hundred thirty-five members exceeds by one the current House membership, thereby avoiding a repetition of the party tie experienced in the 1979 session. A legislature of 201 members equals the combined membership of the current House and Senate.

Using either 67 or 135 members would have considerable advantages. Even a 201-member unicameral legislature would produce marginal economies by consolidation of staff and other services or facilities. Legislatures of 67 or 135 would make the adjustment the simplest. There would be, however, some advantage in selecting a legislature with a membership of 99, halfway between the size of the existing House and Senate.

The reason for selecting a different size is to emphasize the change, to signal that the new one-house legislature is not simply a reincarnation of one of the two old chambers, but an entirely new body, that is expected to behave in a different way. Its presiding officer should be called the president to distinguish the post from that of the speaker of the old House and to indicate that it should function more like the president of the senate functions. A body of 99 members would allow for more people to do the work than are available in the Senate, but would not be so large as to make some members superfluous, as happens in the House.

The idea that every member is going to have an important role to play in the legislative process should help attract able candidates and put party organizations on notice that they cannot afford the luxury of nominating duds to any legislative seats. The fact that all members can expect important assignments and will be involved in significant work, whether they are in the majority or the minority, should provide a more stimulating environment and encourage able members to seek longer careers. A 99-member legislature would produce a district population of slightly over 40,000, halfway between the size of current House and Senate districts. This would allow for reasonably priced campaigns, and avoid districts as large in geographic area as some of the rural senatorial districts that now exist.

Conclusion

In the years immediately preceding and following the Second World War, the national government expanded its powers and activities. For more than a generation, state government atrophied. It performed routine functions, but did not function as the engine and innovator of the Republic. Since the early sixties, however, there has been a renaissance in state government, and state legislatures have again become institutions that must rise to the challenges of the economic, technological, and demographic transformations that have changed the nation and its politics.

In the generation to come, many of the most difficult issues of education, health, criminal justice, environment, economic development, and social welfare policies will be worked out in the experimental laboratories of the states. This will occur in part because federal resources will be in shorter supply than in the past, regardless of which political party controls the national government. It will also occur because there is no national consensus on which policies to pursue, and there is a need to develop workable models at the state level before nationwide applications are made. More than at any time since the establishment of the federal system, state legislatures need to be capable of taking and responding to leadership on a broad agenda of public business, redefining the relationship between the public and private sectors in American governance, and devising ways of managing a democracy and an economy that is based in scientific knowledge and technology.

This task is too important and too complex to expect that the institutional inertia of legislative tradition and practice will somehow muddle through to do what has to be done. Legislatures are too important to be left to chance. Minnesota has the civic capacity to transform its Legislature into an instrument of governance that is worthy of being called "The Tribune of the People."

References

Adams, J. C. 1970. *The Quest for Democratic Law: The Role of Parliament in the Legislative Process*. New York: T.Y. Crowell.

American Assembly. 1966. *State Legislatures in American Politics*. New York: The American Assembly.

Backstrom, Charles. 1986. *The Legislature as a Place to Work: How Minnesota Legislators View Their Jobs*. Minneapolis: Hubert H. Humphrey Institute of Public Affairs.

Baker v. Carr. 1962. 369 U.S. 368.

Bandemer v. Davis. 1986. 478 U.S. 109.

Bernstein v. Commissioner of Public Safety. 1984 351 N.W. 2d 24 (Minn. App.).

Besseltee, Joseph M. 1979. Deliberation in Congress. Paper delivered at American Political Science Convention.

Buchanan, James, and Gordon Tullock. 1962. *The Calculus of Consent*. Ann Arbor: University of Michigan Press.

Burke, Edmund. [1774] 1857. Address to the Electors of Bristol. In *The Works of Edmund Burke*, vol. 1, 219–222. New York: Harper.

Burns, John. 1971. *The Sometime Governments: A Critical Study of the 50 American Legislatures*. New York: Bantam.

Cavanaugh, Thomas E. 1982. The Calculus of Representation: A Congressional Perspective, *Western Political Quarterly*: 20–129.

Citizens Conference on State Legislatures. 1976. *State Legislatures: An Evaluation of Their Effectiveness*. New York: Praeger.

Clapp, Charles L. 1963. *The Congressman: His Work As He Sees It*. Washington, D.C.: The Brookings Institution.

Cooper, Joseph. 1986. Assessing Legislative Performance: A Reply to the Critics of Congress, *Congress and the Presidency*, 13 (1): 21–40.

Council of State Governments. 1968. *Legislative Modernization: A Report of the Committee on Modernization*. Chicago: Council of State Governments.

Dailey, Debra. 1985. Health Care Cost Containment and the Minnesota Legislature, 74th Session. Unpublished paper. Minneapolis: Hubert H. Humphrey Institute of Public Affairs.

Davidson, Roger H. 1969. *The Role of the Congressman*. New York: Pegasus.

Dewar, Margaret. 1986. Development Analysis Confronts Politics: Industrial Policy on Minnesota's Iron Range, *Journal of the American Planners Association* 52 (3):290–98.

Dunn, Millard H. 1958. No Law Shall Embrace More Than One Subject, *Minnesota Law Review* 42:389–95.

Fenno, Richard. 1966. *The Power of the Purse: Appropriations Politics in Congress*. Boston: Little, Brown & Co.

_____. 1978. *Home Style: House Members in Their Districts*. Boston: Little, Brown & Co.

Fisher, Roger, and William Ury. 1983. *Getting to Yes: Negotiating Agreement without Giving In*. New York: Penguin Books.

Frickey, Philip P. 1986. *The Constitutionality of the Legislative Veto in Minnesota*. Minneapolis: Hubert H. Humphrey Institute of Public Affairs.

Friedrich, Carl. 1950. *Constitutional Government and Democracy*. Boston: Ginn & Co.

The Gallup Report. 1985. Report No. 239 (August).

Grau, Craig, and Dale Olsen. 1986. *The Unicameral Option*. Minneapolis: Hubert H. Humphrey Institute of Public Affairs.

Gray Virginia. 1985. *Does Legislative Size Make a Difference?* Minneapolis: Hubert H. Humphrey Institute of Public Affairs.

Griffith, Ernest. 1965. *The American System of Government*. New York: Praeger.

Gross, D. A. 1980. House-Senate Conference Committees: A Comparative State Perspective, *American Journal of Political Science* 24:768–78.

_____. 1982. Bicameralism and the Theory of Voting, *Western Political Quarterly* 35:511–26.

Hatfield, RaDene. 1985. The Making of Tax Policy in the 1985 Minnesota House of Representatives. Minneapolis: Hubert H. Humphrey Institute of Public Affairs.

Huitt, Ralph. 1964. What Can We Do About Congress? *Milwaukee Journal*, Dec. 13, 1.

Huntington, Samuel P. 1968. *Political Order in Changing Societies*. New Haven: Yale University Press.

Immigration and Naturalization Service v. Chada. 1983. 103 S.Ct. 2764.

Jefferson, Thomas. [1816] 1943. Letter to Samuel Kercheval. In *The Compete Jefferson*, ed. Saul Padover. New York: Duell, Sloan, & Pierce.

Jernberg, James E. 1988. Minnesota—Searching for Stability. Minneapolis: Hubert H. Humphrey Institute of Public Affairs. Working paper.

Johnson v. Harrison. 1891. 47 Minn. 575, 50 N.W. 923.

Keefe, William J., and Morris S. Ogul. 1964. *The American Legislative Process: Congress and the States*. Englewood Cliffs, N.J.: Prentice-Hall.

Kennedy, John F. 1957. *Profiles in Courage*. New York: Pocket Books.

Key, V. O. 1961. *Public Opinion and American Democracy*. New York: Alfred A. Knopf.

Kingdon, John. 1981. *Congressmen's Voting Decisions*, 2d ed. New York: Harper & Row.

Kozak, David. 1984. *Contexts of Congressional Decision Behavior*. Lanham, Md.: University Press of America.

Locke, John. [1688] 1947. *Two Treatises of Government*. New York: Hafner ed.

Loewenberg, Gerhard, and Samuel C. Patterson. 1979. *Comparing Legislatures*. Boston: Little, Brown & Co.

Longley, Lawrence. 1986. Bicameral Politics in the American States, *Newsletter of the American Political Science Association* 9 (2 April–May):60–64.

Luce, Robert. 1924. *Legislative Assemblies*. Boston: Houghton Mifflin Co.

Madison, James. [1789] 1941. Nos. 49, 51, 71, 73. In Alexander Hamilton, John Jay, and James Madison, *The Federalist*. New York: Modern Library.

Mather, Jeanie, and Gloria Abney. 1981. The Role of the Conference Committee in State Legislatures. Paper prepared for delivery at the 1981 meeting of the Southern Political Science Association, Memphis, Tenn., Nov. 24.

Mayhew, David R. 1974. *Congress: The Electoral Connection*. New Haven: Yale University Press.

McCormack, Patrick J. 1985. *The Third House: The Role of Conference Committees in the Minnesota Legislature*. Minneapolis: Hubert H. Humphrey Institute of Public Affairs.

McNabb v. United States. 1943. 318 U.S. 332. Opinion for the Court by Felix Frankfurter.

Mezey, Michael L. 1986. The Futile Quest for Congressional Power. *Congress and the Presidency*, 13 (1):1–20.

Mill, John Stuart. [1859] 1951. *Utilitarianism, Liberty, and Representative Government*. New York: E. P. Dutton & Co.

Minnesota Department of Commerce. 1984. Environmental Impairment Insurance and the Insurability of Minnesota Risks under the Minnesota Environmental Response and Liability Act. Report to the Minnesota Legislature, December.

Minnesota ex rel. Mattson v. Kiedrowski. 1986. 391 N.W. 2d 777 (Minn.).

Montesquieu, Baron de. [1748] 1949. *The Spirit of the Laws*. New York: Hafner ed.

Nelson, Barbara. 1984. *Making an Issue of Child Abuse*. Chicago: University of Chicago Press.

Olson, Mancur. 1971. *The Logic of Collective Action: Public Goods and the Theory of Groups*. Cambridge: Harvard University Press.

Page, Benjamin I. 1978. Cooling the Legislative Tea. In *American Politics and Public Policy*, eds. Walter Dean Burnham and Martha Wagner Weinberg. Cambridge: MIT Press.

Parkinson, C. Northcote. 1957. *Parkinson's Law*. Cambridge, Mass.: Riverside Press.

Patterson, Samuel C. 1972. Party Opposition in the Legislature: The Ecology of Legislative Institutionalization, *Polity* 4:345–66.

Pitkin, Hanna. 1967. *The Concept of Representation*. Berkeley: University of California Press.

Pole, J. R. 1966. *Political Representation in England and the Origins of the American Republic*. New York: St. Martin.

Polsby, Nelson W. 1984. *Political Innovation in America: The Politics of Policy Initiation*. New Haven: Yale University Press.

Reynolds v. Sims. 1964. 377 U.S. 533.

Rittel, Horst, and Melvin Weber. 1973. Dilemmas in a General Theory of Planning, *Policy Sciences* 4: 155–69.

Roche, Jim. 1985. Superfund Revision: A Legislative Case Study. Minneapolis: Hubert H. Humphrey Institute of Public Affairs. Unpublished paper.

Roden, Lisa. 1986. ''Long-Term and Cyclical Change in the Minnesota Economy.'' In *Minnesota Tax Study Commission Final Report*, 3–22. St. Paul, Minn.: Butterworth Legal Pubs.

Rosenthal, Alan. 1974. *Legislative Performance in the States*. New York: Free Press.

_____. 1981. *Legislative Life: People, Process, and Performance*. New York: Harper & Row Pubs.

Sandburg, Amy. 1985. Tax Policy in the Minnesota 1985 Legislative Session: The Senate Perspective. Hubert H. Humphrey Institute of Public Affairs. Unpublished paper.

Smith, T. V. 1940. *The Legislative Way of Life*. Chicago: University of Chicago Press.

Strom, Gerald S., and Barry S. Rundquist. 1977. A Revised Theory of Winning in House-Senate Conferences. *American Political Science Review* 71: 448–53.

Thornburg v. Gingles. 1986. 478 U.S. 109.

Tocqueville, Alexis de. [1835] 1945. *Democracy in America*. New York: Vintage Books ed.

Train v. City of New York. 1975. 420 U.S. 35.

42 U.S.C. §9601 et seq. 1980. Comprehensive Environmental Response, Compensation and Liability Act (Superfund).

Vogler, David J. 1970. Patterns of One-House Dominance in Congressional Committees. *Midwest Journal of Political Science* 14: 303–20.

_____. 1971. *The Third House: Conference Committees in the United States Congress*. Evanston, Ill.: Northwestern University Press.

_____. 1974. *The Politics of Congress*. Boston: Allyn & Bacon.

Wahlke, John. 1970. Policy Determinants and Legislative Decisions. In *Political Decision Making*, ed. S. Sidney Ulmer. New York: Van Nostrand.

Wass v. Anderson. 1977. 312 Minn. 394.

Wildavsky, Aaron. 1988. *The New Politics of the Budgetary Process*. Glenview, Ill.: Scott, Foresman.

Wilson, Woodrow. [1885] 1956. *Congressional Government*. New York: Meridian Books ed.

Interview Subjects

Irv Anderson*
Robert O. Ashbach*
AnnDrea Benson
Linda Berglin
John Brandl*
Richard Braun
Steven Cross
Jack Davies*
Edward Dirkswager
Aubrey Dirlam*
William Dosland*
Lloyd Duxbury*
Willis Eken*
Ray Faricy*
Linda Feist
Richard W. Fitzsimons*
Patrick Flahaven
Mary Forsythe*
Edward J. Gearty*
Joseph Graba*
Paul Hess
John Himle*
Stanley Holmquist*
Jerome Hughes*
Karen James
David Jennings*
Douglas Johnson*
Phyllis Kahn*
Jerry Knickerbocker*
Connie Levi*

Gene Merriam*
Roger Moe*
Ken Nelson*
James R. Nobles
Fred Norton*
Alec G. Olson*
C. Tom Osthoff*
James Peterson
George Pillsbury*
John Post
John Redmond
Gordon Rosenmeier*
Martin Sabo*
Henry Savekoul*
Jerry Schoenfield*
William Schreiber*
Rodney Searle*
Glen Sherwood*
Harry Sieben*
Ronald Sieloff*
Wayne Simoneau*
Warren Spannaus
Allan H. Spear*
John Tomlinson*
Tom Triplett
Gordon Voss*
Charles R. Weaver*
Ann Wynia*

*Served in the Legislature

Index

272

Superfund (Minnesota Environmental Response and Liability Act—MERLA): business attack, 163–64; health issue, 165–66; Merriam-Sviggum bill, 164–66; 1983 act, 160–62; task force, 158, 164; victims compensation fund, 166–68, 169
Superfund Act, U.S., 160
Supreme Court: Minnesota, 113, 142, 145, 149, 249; South Dakota, 149; U.S., 3, 12, 29, 36, 37
Sundown laws, 32
Sviggum, Steve, 164–66, 168

Taylor, Glen, 181
Tax Committee, 71–73, 76, 93, 95, 110, 112, 114, 119, 167, 174, 175, 176–81, 218, 220
Tax conference, 126, 133, 136–38, 141, 181, 182
Tax cut, 136, 157, 158, 160, 172–74, 178–85, 194, 202, 210, 212
Thornburg v. Gingles, 13
Tocqueville, Alexis de, 3
Tomlinson, John, 176
Train v. City of New York, 29

Triplett, Tom, 164, 168
Tullock, Gordon, 19

Unicameral legislature, xv, 8, 149, 150, 237, 249, 260–64

Vanasek, Robert, 86, 87, 251
Vogler, David, J., 130
Voss, Gordon, 72

Wahlke, John, 97
Wass v. Anderson, 142
Ways and Means Committee, 82, 210, 222
Weaver, Charles, 67
Weber, Melvin, 154
Wildavsky, Aaron, 201, 203
Willet, Gerald, 111, 118
Wilson, Woodrow, 19, 23
Wood Ticks, 76
Wright, Donald, 103, 104, 108
Wynia, Ann, 67

Youngdahl, Luther, 262

Zwach, John, 108

Royce Hanson is dean and professor of political economy in the School of Social Sciences, University of Texas at Dallas. From 1983 until mid-1987, he was the associate dean and a professor in the Hubert H. Humphrey Institute of Public Affairs at the University of Minnesota. Hanson earned his Ph.D. in government and public administration and his J.D. at The American University and taught there for many years. During the 1970's he served as chairman of the Montgomery County Planning Board and in the early 1980's was senior staff officer and project director for the Committee on National Urban Policy, National Research Council. Hanson's books include *The Political Thicket: Reapportionment and Constitutional Democracy* (1966), *New Communities: Laboratories for Democracy* (1971), and *The Evolution of National Urban Policy, 1970-1980* (1982). His articles have appeared in *The Annals of the American Academy of Polictical and Social Sciences*, the *Journal of the American Planning Association, Future*, and the *Georgetown Law Journal*.

Charles Backstrom has been a faculty member at the University of Minnesota's department of political science since 1959. He received his doctorate in political science from the University of Wisconsin at Madison. Backstrom is co-author, with Gerald Hursh-César, of *Survey Research* (second edition, 1981) and has contributed articles to *Constitutional Commentary, Minnesota Law Review, Publius, American Political Quarterly* and *New England Journal of Human Services*.

Patrick J. McCormack is on the staff of the Minnesota Senate Office of Counsel and Research. He has master's degrees in sociology from the University of Notre Dame and in public affairs from the Hubert H. Humphrey Institute at the University of Minnesota. While at the Humphrey Institute, McCormack received the Lloyd M. Short Award for excellence in writing.